Improving What is Learned at University

What is learned in universities today? Is it what students expect to learn? Is it what universities say they learn? How far do the answers to questions such as these differ according to what, where and how one studies?

As higher education has expanded, it has diversified both in terms of its institutional forms and the characteristics of its students. However, what we do not know is the extent to which it has also diversified in terms of 'what is learned'. In this book the authors explore this question through the voices of higher education students, using empirical data from students taking 15 different courses at different universities across three subject areas – bioscience, business studies and sociology. The study concentrates on the students' experiences, lives, hopes and aspirations while at university through data from interviews and questionnaires, and this is collated and assessed alongside the perspectives of their teachers and official data from the universities they attend.

Through this study the authors provide insights into 'what is really learned at university' and how much it differs between individual students and the universities they attend. Throughout, notions of 'best' or 'top' universities are challenged and both diversities and commonalities of being a student are demonstrated. Posing important questions for higher education institutions about the experiences of their students and the consequences for graduates and society, this book is compelling reading for all those involved in higher education, providing conclusions that do not always follow conventional lines of thought about diversity and difference in UK higher education.

John Brennan is Professor of Higher Education Research and Director of the Centre for Higher Education Research and Information at the UK Open University. **Robert Edmunds** is a Research Student in Systems Engineering and Human Factors at Cranfield University in the UK. **Muir Houston** is Lecturer in Adult and Continuing Education in the Faculty of Education at the University of Glasgow, UK. **David Jary** is Visiting Professor in the Centre for Higher Education Research and Information at the UK Open University. **Yann Lebeau** is Lecturer in Educational Research in the School of Education and Lifelong Learning at the University of East Anglia, UK. **Michael Osborne** is Professor of Adult Education in the Faculty of Education at the University of Glasgow, is Professor of Student Learning and Assessment Technology at the UK Open University.

Improving Learning TLRP

Series Editor: Andrew Pollard, Director of the ESRC Teaching and Learning Programme

The Improving Learning series showcases findings from projects within ESRC's Teaching and Learning Research Programme (TLRP) – the UK's largest ever co-ordinated educational research initiative. Each book is explicitly designed to support 'evidence-informed' decisions in educational practice and policy-making. In particular, they combine rigorous social and educational science with high awareness of the significance of the issues being researched.

Improving Learning How to Learn: Classrooms, schools and networks
Mary James, Robert McCormick, Paul Black, Patrick Carmichael, Mary-Jane Drummond, Alison Fox, John MacBeath, Bethan Marshall, David Pedder, Richard Procter, Sue Swaffield, Joanna Swann and Dylan Wiliam

Improving Learning Through Consulting Pupils
Jean Rudduck and Donald McIntyre

Improving Learning, Skills and Inclusion: The impact of policy on post-compulsory education
Frank Coffield, Sheila Edward, Ian Finlay, Ann Hodgson, Ken Spours and Richard Steer

Improving Classroom Learning with ICT
Rosamund Sutherland

Improving Learning in College: Rethinking literacies across the curriculum
Roz Ivanic, Richard Edwards, David Barton, Marilyn Martin-Jones, Zoe Fowler, Buddug Hughes, Greg Mannion, Kate Miller, Candice Satchwell and June Smith

Improving Learning in Later Life
Alexandra Withnall

Improving Inter-professional Collaborations: Multi-agency working for children's wellbeing
Anne Edwards, Harry Daniels, Tony Gallagher, Jane Leadbetter and Paul Warmington

Improving Mathematics at Work: The need for techno-mathematical literacies (forthcoming)
Celia Hoyles, Richard Noss, Phillip Kent and Arthur Bakker

Improving Research Through User Engagement (forthcoming)
Mark Rickinson, Anne Edwards and Judy Sebba

Improving What is Learned at University

An exploration of the social
and organisational diversity
of university education

John Brennan, Robert Edmunds,
Muir Houston, David Jary,
Yann Lebeau, Michael Osborne
and John T.E. Richardson

Routledge
Taylor & Francis Group

LONDON AND NEW YORK

First published 2010
by Routledge
2 Park Square, Milton Park, Abingdon, Oxon OX14 4RN

Simultaneously published in the USA and Canada
by Routledge
270 Madison Avenue, New York, NY 10016

Routledge is an imprint of the Taylor & Francis Group, an informa business

© 2010 John Brennan, Robert Edmunds, Muir Houston, David Jary,
Yann Lebeau, Michael Osborne and John T.E. Richardson

Typeset in Charter ITC and Stone Sans by
Florence Production Ltd, Stoodleigh, Devon
Printed and bound in Great Britain by
CPI Antony Rowe, Chippenham, Wiltshire

British Library Cataloguing in Publication Data
A catalogue record for this book is available from the British Library

Library of Congress Cataloging-in-Publication Data
Improving what is learned at university: an exploration of the
social and organisational diversity of university education/
John Brennan . . . [et al.].
      p. cm. – (Improving learning series)
   1. Education, Higher – Social aspects – Great Britain – Case
studies.   2. College students – Great Britain – Social
conditions – Case studies.   I. Brennan, John, 1947–.
LC191.98.G7l67 2010
   306.43'2 – dc22   2009024724

ISBN10: 0–415–48015–9 (hbk)
ISBN10: 0–415–48016–7 (pbk)
ISBN10: 0–203–86323–2 (ebk)

ISBN13: 978–0–415–48015–4 (hbk)
ISBN13: 978–0–415–48016–1 (pbk)
ISBN13: 978–0–203–86323–7 (ebk)

Contents

Illustrations

Figures

Tables

Acknowledgements

The authors wish to acknowledge the many contributions that have made this book possible. The first to be mentioned must be the hundreds of undergraduate students who took part in our interviews and focus groups and completed our questionnaires. Second, we should also mention the staff of the universities who took part in the project, including the many teaching staff who were interviewed as well as the academic and administrative staff who assisted us in the organisation of the fieldwork. Third, the project benefited throughout its duration from the advice of the members of its steering group, chaired by Bahram Bekhradnia and comprising Liz Beaty, Chris Duke, Laurence Howells, Mike Prosser, Peter Scott, Peter Williams and Michael Young. Fourth, the project also benefited from its two international advisers: Francois Dubet of the Université Victor Segalen Bourdeaux 2 in France and Patrick Terenzini of Pennsylvania State University in the United States. Fifth, as part of the larger Teaching and Learning Research Programme (TLRP) funded by the Economic and Social Research Council, the project benefited from the activities and advice of the TLRP team led by Andrew Pollard and, in particular, at different times during the project by its assistant directors, Kathryn Ecclestone and Miriam David. Sixth, the preparation of this book would not have been possible without the invaluable assistance of Kavita Patel. And seventh and finally, the entire project benefited enormously from the support of Tarla Shah, the project manager, and Deana Parker, the project assistant.

John Brennan, on behalf of the authors
June, 2009

Part I

Chapter 1

Commonalities and diversities of UK universities

Introduction

As in most developed countries, higher education in the UK has expanded massively over recent decades. From under 10 per cent of the relevant age group going on to higher education at the end of the 1960s, by the first decade of the twenty-first century over 40 per cent were attending university. Over the same time period, the number of universities in the UK more than quadrupled and individual institutions grew in size substantially.

This expansion has in part reflected national policies based on assumptions of economic need for highly educated manpower and in part has been in response to a growing demand from young people and their parents, especially from more socially advantaged backgrounds, for the credentials and other forms of cultural capital necessary to achieve or maintain advantaged social positions. In this respect, expansion of higher education has been both a major route to social mobility and the means by which those already advantaged groups in society reproduce and legitimise their advantages.

One of the earliest sociological studies of graduates in the UK carried the sub-title, 'the sociology of an elite' (Kelsall *et al.*, 1972). Such a term would hardly be applied to graduates today. While all the evidence indicates that graduates as a whole are quite a privileged group in the labour market, they are also to be found in jobs that would never previously have required high level qualifications. And in political and cultural terms, it would be difficult to make any special claims for the role or status of graduates in general, although elite groupings within the graduate population can, of course, quite easily be recognised.

Expansion of higher education has, in the words of the American sociologist Martin Trow (1973), involved a move from elite forms to 'mass' and 'universal' forms. But Trow also pointed out that the three forms of higher education could, and were likely to, exist simultaneously within individual higher education systems. Thus, the elite, mass and universal concepts can be applied both at the system level and in respect of sub-groups of institutions and students within those systems. So although UK higher education is generally regarded as a mass going on for universal system, within it can be identified 'elite' parts with something of a hierarchical ordering of the remainder.

Differentiation is generally regarded as a defining feature of expanded systems of higher education. This may be perceived as being largely hierarchical – some parts of higher education perceived to be 'better' than others – or as being largely functional – based on vocational/academic distinctions or range of subjects. Teichler (2007) has made the distinction between 'vertical' and 'horizontal' forms of higher education differentiation and, along with others, places the UK firmly within the former.

All of this should remind us of very basic distinctions that can be made about the functions of any form of education as being primarily about 'socialisation' or 'selection'. The former would place the emphasis on knowledge and learning, and on personal enlightenment and social development. The latter would place the emphasis on educational credentials as a 'positional good' with a central role to play in the stratification of societies and in providing the means for mobility and reproduction within those societies. The former may sometimes appear to be emphasising 'education for its own sake' but arguably it is also about the 'public good' and about contributing to the achievement of social characteristics such as equity and social cohesion. The latter is typically about 'doing better than others', about achieving more and more highly-rated credentials from prestigious institutions and obtaining the social capital available within them.

Of course, most forms of formal education are about both selection and socialisation. Some pupils and students do better in their examinations than others. Even where selection and hierarchy are predominant, most students learn something. Places at a particular university may be sought after because the institution is highly rated, attended mainly by students from 'top schools' and 'good families', providing clear pathways after graduation to wealth, status and power! But the university's students may also learn a lot while they are there. Arguably they may learn more or different things than their peers attending less prestigious institutions. Or they may not!

One of the aims of the ESRC 'SOMUL' project[1] on which this book is based was to explore 'what is learned' within an increasingly differentiated higher education system populated by increasingly diverse groupings of students. As already noted, higher education in the UK is differentiated particularly in vertical terms. From the point of view of individual students, their families and their schools, this can put a premium on getting into a 'top place'. From the point of view of (certain) employers, this will put a premium on recruiting 'top students' from 'top universities'. But can students expect to learn more or different things from attending some higher education institutions rather than others? Can employers expect to obtain more able and productive workers by recruiting the graduates from some institutions rather than others? Assumptions that they will and that they can are deeply embedded in major parts of UK society, including the most powerful and privileged parts.

In posing the question, 'What is learned at university', the SOMUL project was interested in the ways and extent to which differences in the institutional forms of higher education and in the kinds of students who attended them were matched by differences in the outcomes of learning from those institutions. How much does it really matter where one studies? And if some institutions seem to do better than others, are there lessons that can be learned and applied more generally across our universities, irrespective of where they stand in contemporary hierarchies, league tables and the like? The project's central concerns with the 'social and organisational mediation of learning' assumed that differences can and do matter, but differences in terms of how studies are organised or of the aspirations and lifestyles of the students, rather than in relation to simple hierarchies of institutional prestige. But the project was also interested in the *commonalities* that existed across all forms and settings of higher education: commonalities derived from the subject content and disciplinary norms of courses in particular fields; commonalities derived from longstanding traditions of what higher education – or more particularly a university education – represents in the UK, or more accurately in its constituent nations; and commonalities derived from the regulatory apparatus applied by various state agencies to ensure common standards and comparable experiences irrespective of where learning actually took place.

In setting the scene for an exploration of what is shared and what differs across the diverse settings of higher education in the UK, this opening chapter will explore some of the main dimensions against which both commonality and difference may be found. This will involve some consideration of how higher education is organised both nationally and institutionally as well as consideration of the backgrounds, lives and aspirations of its students. Although the focus will be on the UK, reference will also be made to experiences and conceptualisations from other parts of the world.

It will be necessary in later chapters to consider whether particular differences actually 'matter' and why, and to consider whether certain differences when found in combination may serve to benefit some students rather than others. It will also be important to ask whether there are 'best practices' to be identified that would be of benefit to all students irrespective of where they study. Or, within an increasingly diverse system, does practice need to be tailored to the particular and distinctive needs of different types of student? Above all, is the increasing diversity of higher education a reflection of an increasing diversity within the larger society? Or might it indeed be a cause, or at least a legitimiser, of larger diversities?

First, however, it is necessary to flesh out some conceptions of 'learning' that can be applied to the experiences and outcomes of a university education. Clearly, whole books can and have been written on this subject. The intention here is simply to map some possible dimensions of learning, to consider the different kinds of answer that might be found to our central question of 'what is learned at university'.

What is taught and what is learned

The most obvious answer to the question of 'what is learned at university' is, depending on the chosen course, a 'lot of history, or chemistry, or economics' or whatever the chosen curriculum sets before the student. And, of course, this is a perfectly valid answer and one which we shall explore in this volume through a focus on three contrasting subject areas. Subjects, we would argue, are a source of commonality that cuts across the diversities of institutional settings and student circumstances. In some senses, the economics student (or chemistry or history or whatever) at university A has more in common with another economics student at universities X, Y and Z (whatever the characteristics of those institutions) than he or she has with a biology student at university A. Degree courses in particular subjects involve the transmission of a body of knowledge largely unique to that subject, a 'way of knowing' particular to the subject and, most likely, sets of values and attitudes that go along with membership of that subject community. Writers such as Henkel (2000) and Becher and Trowler (2001) have written about subject-defined 'academic identity' and an undergraduate education is generally the first step in acquiring such an identity.

An answer in terms of subject knowledge would certainly be the likely answer that most academics would give to the question of 'what is learned' at university. For it is the subject that provides them with an important part of their own identities. It is what they are in business to transmit when they teach. This is what they want the students to learn. This is what the university prospectus says the students will learn. But is it the whole story? Or even the most important part?

In later chapters of this book, we will consider how far subject knowledge and identity does indeed provide a common experience across different universities. We shall note that subject communities differ in the degree of consensus about the content of the curriculum and how it is organised. And many students study several subjects simultaneously. Graduate employment in the UK reveals only a loose link between subject studied and job acquired. For the moment, we just want to acknowledge the importance of subject content to any appreciation of what is learned while suggesting that it is far from being the whole story.

A different emphasis and potential answer to the question of 'what is learned' sees subjects as the vehicle rather than the content of learning. A university education, from this perspective, is about the acquisition of high level cognitive processes, of 'learning how to learn', of 'doing things' with knowledge and of gaining competences and skills derived from this knowledge. This is the reason why many graduate employers are not particularly concerned about what particular subject a graduate has studied. It is not the subject knowledge that is important but the abilities and skills to manipulate and exploit knowledge. This seems to be particularly the case in the UK labour market (in contrast to other European countries) where graduates are valued by employers less for their subject expertise and more for their general abilities and competences. However, this does not mean that all graduates are regarded as the same. There will be differences between individual graduates and differences perceived to be related to the subjects studied, the institutions attended and various characteristics of the student experience. In referring to 'perceived' differences, we are suggesting a possible contrast between the abilities

and skills actually possessed by individual graduates and the perceptions of significant stakeholders, especially employers. There are a
number of established instruments for the measurement of various
cognitive abilities and competences and these have been used
extensively during the SOMUL project and the results will be reported
on in later chapters, especially Chapter 6. Here, we might just note
that while subject learning tends to cut across institutional hierarchies,
perceptions of more general cognitive learning attainments generally
follow them, with assumptions that the 'best' graduates are to be
found in the 'top' universities.

Another and rather different answer to the 'what is learned' question places the emphasis not on knowledge but on personal confidence,
identity and aspiration. It is the personal achievement of getting into
university and gaining a degree which is the source of fundamental change in the individual. It is to do with how the individual
student sees him- or herself and with how he or she sees him- or herself
in relation to others. From the perspective of identity, going to university may be about shedding existing identities and acquiring new
ones. At least that may be the experience for some students. For other
students, it may be about confirming and reinforcing an existing
identity (as a 'high achiever', as a 'leader', as a 'success'). And for still
other students, it is about acquiring an ability to juggle multiple
identities as being simultaneously a 'student', a 'parent', a 'worker'.

The acquisition of confidence and aspiration, of course, rather
assumes that these qualities were not already possessed by the student
before he or she entered higher education. And in this respect, student
diversity in terms of social and educational backgrounds may be
important. The student who has known nothing but educational
success since the first few months at prep school may be full of
confidence on arrival at university and have little more to gain while
at university which, for such students, takes more the form of 'status
confirmation', in the words of Brown and Scase (1994). Conversely,
the student who left school without qualifications at age 16 and
who 10 or 15 years later manages to get into university after years
spent in evening classes in further education colleges is likely to have
a much greater sense of achievement and boost to confidence from
gaining a university place. Whether the responsibility for it lies with
the university or elsewhere, the student with confidence and ambition
has been equipped to do more things with his or her life, almost
irrespective of the knowledge, competencies and skills possessed.

Another sphere of learning, or 'impact' to follow the terminology used by many American researchers (see Feldman and Newcomb, 1969; Pascerella and Terenzini, 1991 and 2005), lies in the effects of going to university on the attitudes and values of the individual, whether making him or her more tolerant, more political, more environmentally aware, more internationally-minded or in developing a sense of civic responsibility, of engaged citizenship.

It follows, of course, that many of these more diverse outcomes of a university education may have less to do with what goes on within classrooms and more to do with the people you meet, the things you do with them, the things they say and so on. The residential tradition of university education, in England and the United States at least, has placed much emphasis on the extra-curricular world that the student enters, on the opportunities and activities available and the personal change and development that can derive from them. However, while this tradition continues – and is well-represented in the universities covered in the SOMUL project – it is by no means the only or even the dominant pattern of student life today. The classroom may be common to all. Everything else – whether rugby pitch, concert hall, gym, bar, coffee shop – reflects the great diversity of student life today and of the institutions they attend.

In this book we are regarding university learning as multifaceted and containing potentially all of the different elements mentioned above, albeit in different combinations in different places. In particular, we shall be giving a voice to student perceptions of what they have learned and of its importance to their present and future lives.

Institutional differences and hierarchies within UK higher education

We have already noted the high degree of institutional stratification that exists within UK higher education. While the technologies of rankings and league tables bring a touch of 'science' to these hierarchies, it is also worth remembering that the single most salient factor in determining institutional status is usually history. The older the university the better it is deemed to be! As with the brewers of bottled beers, universities can rarely resist drawing attention to their relative antiquity. If you've been around that long, you must be good! And, of course, there is a logic to this. The older institutions developed as part of 'elite' systems of higher education and their identities and self-images are a reflection of that history. Elite systems and institutions were privileged parts of society and were relatively small so that they could be resourced at levels impossible in larger mass systems.

It should also be remembered that the English residential tradition of higher education – of young people going away (or 'up') to university – has been conducive to stratification and hierarchy of institutions. In countries where students traditionally study at their local or regional institution, there is less potential for the development of institutional hierarchies based on differential demand and the willingness of the 'best' (or the richest) students to travel to the other end of the country in order to attend the 'best' (or most prestigious) universities.

As well as finding historical and cultural reasons for the steep hierarchies of status and prestige in UK higher education, there are also functional reasons. It is going to be much more difficult for a 'mass' system of higher education to perform functions of elite reproduction and legitimation if the system is not differentiated in terms of prestige and if differentiated outcomes in terms of access to wealth, status and power are not accorded to the graduates of different institutions.

In UK higher education, therefore, the history, culture and wealth of different higher education institutions combine with the social and educational backgrounds, aspirations, qualifications and resources of different students to produce, in Teichler's terms (2007), a strongly 'vertically' differentiated higher education system.

But hierarchies are not the only kinds of differences to be found in UK higher education. Universities differ in terms of their size and location, in terms of their architectures and organisation, and such differences bring with them different experiences for the students who attend them. The SOMUL project's concept of 'organisational mediation' will be explored in later chapters. But one of the underlying assumptions of the project is that much student learning – in its broadest senses – is a social experience and differences in who one learns with, in whether one learns in solitude or with others, may be conducive to differences in what is learned (and in what is valued in what is learned).

Yet, for all the attention that is given to diversity and hierarchy in discussions about higher education in the UK, there are also pressures and mechanisms to ensure a degree of standardisation and commonalities. There is a national qualifications structure and quality assurance arrangements to ensure at least common minimum standards. The Quality Assurance Agency for Higher Education possesses an elaborate apparatus for the audit and assessment of the education provided in UK universities and colleges that seeks to ensure that a range of common standards and processes are in place in all institutions, irrespective of their status and hierarchical position. All universities are expected to have effective procedures for ensuring the quality and standards of their courses and the work undertaken by their students. Benchmarks are set for what is to be learned in particular subject fields. And external examiners (from different institutions) look directly at the work produced by an institution's students to ensure that it is comparable to the work achieved on similar courses elsewhere.

It must, however, also be noted that of late quality assurance in higher education has become as much about demonstrating difference as it has been about demonstrating commonality (Brennan and Singh, 2009). Whether they be in terms of the research prowess of their staff, the satisfaction levels of their students or the employment rates of their graduates, data produced in the cause of accountability and quality assurance are increasingly used to produce rankings and league tables of hierarchical difference between individual institutions.

We have already noted the commonalities in the experiences of students provided by the study of a particular subject. Subjects are in fact a source of both commonality and difference. They provide boundaries between the learning experiences of different students. But there is not an infinite variety to these experiences. Some subjects lead directly to entry to specific professional careers. Others seek to provide students with a 'tool-kit' of knowledge and skills that is applicable to a range of careers in a particular area of employment. And yet other subjects leave options wide open, having no explicit link to any profession or particular employment field. Thus, the subject mix of an institution is another important source of difference. Technological universities and vocational schools are different places from universities with large arts and social science faculties.

An alternative to the hierarchical emphasis of much institutional differentiation is an emphasis on distinctive institutional 'missions'. From this approach, institutions are not to be judged hierarchically against a common set of criteria. Thus, we can find 'widening participation' universities as well as 'research universities'. We can find regionally-focused universities as well as real or aspirant 'world-class' universities. We can find universities who proclaim their close links with employers and others that emphasise their 'collegial' experience or campus life.

To some extent, different kinds of university may attract students who are looking for different kinds of things. The positive way of looking at this is to emphasise the large amount of choice that is available in UK higher education and the potential that exists for matching the various forms of institutional differentiation with the various forms of student diversity. There is also considerable potential for mis-match, of course. In practice, within limits set by qualifications, wealth, time, background and aspiration, students generally attempt to 'get to the best place that they can'. Whether they are well advised to do so is a key question to which we should return.

Student experiences in mass higher education

The many differences that exist in the institutional settings of higher education in the UK are themselves important sources of differences in the experiences of students. But differences in the latter are also a product of wider social differences, in the backgrounds of students, in their current lifestyles and in their aspirations for the future.

As we have noted, the traditional experience of university in the UK was a residential one, of leaving home and immersing oneself in university life with one's peers full-time for three years or more. This kind of experience still exists but is nothing like as dominant as it once was. Many students live at or close by their homes. They are still subject to the influences of family and friends. They may have part-time jobs and/or domestic responsibilities. They have *less* time available to spend as students, less time to be physically present at the university, less time to socialise with other students, less time to sample new experiences – whether in the fields of sport, art or politics or in the fields of drugs, drink or sex.

The phenomenon of 'part-time' students on full-time degree courses is an increasingly common one. Even among the 'traditional' school-leaver students living far from home, many take part-time jobs while at university, whether to avoid the build-up of debt or to finance a particular lifestyle. With the introduction of student fees, going to university increasingly represents a significant financial investment, either for the student him- or herself or for the student's parents.

The increasing cost of higher education is closely related to another phenomenon, the widening of participation in higher education to include groups traditionally under-represented. There is some dispute about how much participation in higher education has really widened in terms of social class over the last decade or so but it remains true that certain social groups remain significantly under-represented in higher education. On the other hand, there is more diversity in terms of the age profile of students, with higher education occurring at different stages in the life-course for different students. Some students attend the same universities as a parent or sibling while others are 'first generation', among their nuclear and extended families and among their 'street' and neighbourhood.

Diversity in the backgrounds and lifestyles of students maps onto the differentiation of higher education institutions to a considerable extent. Many students find themselves spending their lives as students in the company of other students pretty much like themselves, in terms of their age, their social and educational backgrounds, their ethnicity, their interests and their activities inside and outside higher education. In some universities, greater diversity is to be found in all of these things. Whether diversity is something to be enjoyed or resisted is partly a matter of individual preferences and partly about the social and organisational conditions under which different kinds of people are kept apart or brought together.

Another way of looking at the experience of higher education is in relation to the orientations and aspirations that individual students bring to it. One increasingly hears claims made about the growing 'instrumentality' of students, whether in terms of the importance of qualifications and graduate jobs or in terms of the effort afforded to the meeting of course requirements, especially in terms of assessment demands. Such instrumentalities may be contrasted with orientations of 'interest in my subject', 'having fun', 'making new friends' of previous generations of students but, as we shall see, which may also be found among today's students.

One of the key questions that the SOMUL project asked was the extent to which the experience of being a student differed in different places and whether such differences appeared to be related to differences in what was learned. As we have already noted, a consideration of differences between people and institutions needs to be set within a consideration of what they share in common. Students spend large amounts of time in lectures and classes, laboratories and libraries. They spend a lot of time reading and writing. Within the same subject fields, they spend a lot of time reading and writing the same things. As we explore in future chapters the various diversities of today's higher education, we should not forget the many commonalities that also exist.

The aims of this book

There is a substantial literature on student learning in higher education (Perry, 1970; Marton, 1976 and 1984; Säljö, 1979; Marton and Booth, 1997). Most of it focuses on 'how' students learn, on the relationships between study methods, approaches to learning and eventual learning outcomes. While such matters are not ignored in this book, the rather different question of 'what' is learned is to the fore. This partly reflects commonly-held assumptions that there are institutional and other differences in learning outcomes and in the qualities of graduates, that some know more or different things from others. But it also addresses questions of what 'needs' to be learned by students who will be facing societies in which employment and career trajectories will be taking new and complex directions, in which sources of knowledge and learning will become ever more diffuse, and in which issues of social cohesion and citizenship may become as, if not more, important than the economy and its skills requirements.

In exploring 'what is learned' in these changing contexts, we shall be giving 'voice' to the experiences and views of many students in different kinds of university about what they wanted and what they found and achieved during their time spent in higher education. While there will be much diversity in the views, circumstances and experiences of the students as well as in the university settings in which they have been studying, we shall also be reporting some important commonalities in their experiences and views. These may not always accord with the views of their teachers or with the priorities of policy makers and they may suggest that rather 'more', or at least rather different, things are being learned than are sometimes recognised. 'Improving' what is learned may be partly about granting greater recognition to a wider range of outcomes of learning that are already occurring as well as identifying ways in which universities can achieve greater harmonisation between the experiences on offer and the experiences being sought by students within an expanded and differentiated higher education system.

In the next chapter, we describe the background and objectives of the SOMUL project in more detail, outlining the conceptual framework and approaches used in the project and reflected in the analyses contained in the subsequent chapters of this book. Chapter 3 looks at differences between universities using the project's concept of organisational mediation. It examines diversity and differentiation in UK higher education and its implications for the experiences of students and the outcomes of their learning. It also introduces the 15 case studies that form the empirical heart of the project and the rest of this book. Chapter 4 explores the characteristics of the three different subjects that were used in the study and describes the curriculum and academic staff orientations that were found in the different universities that took part in the project. Chapter 5 looks at the diversity of students, their backgrounds, lifestyles and forms of engagement and integration. A mixture of diversity and commonality will be revealed, suggesting that students are approaching university learning in a variety of styles and levels of engagement and with different degrees of integration, most of which have viability. The rest of the book attempts to look more explicitly at 'what is learned' and its implications for those who teach and those who manage and fund today's universities. Chapter 6 adopts a quantitative approach to the questions of learning outcomes, presenting the results of measures of students' concepts (or mental models) of learning, their approaches to studying, their personal and educational development, their broader views of personal change and the extent to which these change over the time spent at university. Chapter 7, using a mixture of quantitative and more qualitative data on students' experiences, looks more explicitly at how students believe that they have changed, in terms of 'identity', both professional and personal, and in terms of their plans and aspirations, the friendships and contacts they have acquired, and the significance attached to these as well as to the achievement of getting a degree. Both Chapters 6 and 7 will draw out the similarities and the differences found in the outcomes of learning identified in the project's different subjects, universities and cases. Chapter 8 attempts to summarise the main findings of the project and, in particular, the extent to which, and the conditions under which, differences in the student experience lead to differences in the outcomes of higher education. Chapters 9 and 10 look at the implications of all of this for both universities and society as a whole. Chapter 9 will consider the implications for a whole range of teaching and learning issues within universities, relevant irrespective of the subject being taught and reflecting both the commonalities and the diversities between different kinds of university. Chapter 10 examines the project's implications for the role played by higher education in today's 'knowledge society', a role with economic, social, political and cultural dimensions.

Can we 'improve' what is learned at university? Is there a need to do so? On the whole, the rest of this book replies to both questions in the affirmative while, we hope, remembering at the same time to give proper recognition to the very considerable achievements in learning and personal development that are already taking place in our universities.

Note

1   'What is learned at university. The social and organisational mediation of university learning (SOMUL)'. A project funded by the Economic and Social Research Council (ESRC) as part of its Teaching and Learning Research Programme (TLRP).

Chapter 2

The social and organisational mediation of university learning

Introduction

The expansion and diversification of higher education described in Chapter 1 raises questions about the comparability of the experiences, learning and credentials available across a complex and differentiated higher education system. We have been asking 'what is learned at university?' at a time when higher education in the UK comprises many different kinds of universities, different kinds of courses, and students from different backgrounds (both educational and social) studying in very different circumstances and at different stages in their lives. This is what we meant by 'social and organisational mediation' in the project's title. How is learning affected by the way courses are organised, by the places in which it is taking place, by the people one is learning alongside, by the reasons people have for studying and by the other things that are going on in their lives while they are studying?

Not so long ago, the British model of higher education could be equated with 'going away to university', or 'going up' for those who had gained entry to the most elite of the institutions. It was a residential experience as celebrated in many novels and described in the academic literature (e.g. Halsey and Trow, 1971). It was as much to do with personal development and character formation as it was to do with mastery of a particular subject or the acquisition of particular skills. It was experienced at a particular point in the life-course by people from largely similar backgrounds who had recently completed a largely similar educational preparation within a quite selective secondary education system. As we have already indicated in Chapter 1, this traditional model may not have completely disappeared, but it exists alongside a variety of other contemporary models of the student experience, sometimes to be found alongside each other within a single university but sometimes defining the central feature or distinctive 'mission' of the particular university. And many students (and their parents and school teachers) exhibit signs of desperation to attain access to a higher education of the 'superior' traditional model. But is it necessarily so superior? Is it necessarily so different? These are some of the questions we will be posing in the following pages.

We shall be looking at how universities differ in the ways in which they attempt to organise the learning experiences of their students. We shall be looking at how students differ in their backgrounds, their circumstances and their aspirations. We shall be looking at how these sources of difference interact and combine to produce distinctive experiences and achievements for students.

We shall be taking quite broad conceptions of learning. We shall be interested in whether students believe they are learning the things that their teachers say they are meant to be learning – both in rela- tion to the substance of course content and more general aspects of cognitive development. But we are not assuming that 'what is learned' can simply be equated with what is taught. We are also interested in how university affects students' attitudes and values, their ambitions and plans, their sense of who they are and who they want to become, in both professional and personal terms.

In this chapter, we discuss some of the previous research on student learning that has influenced our thinking and the overall con- ceptualisation of the project. We shall pose some research questions and describe how we attempted to answer them during the four years of the SOMUL project.

Researching student learning

While there is a distinctive research literature in the United States on 'the impact of college' (e.g. Pascarella and Terenzini, 2005), the UK and European literatures are more fragmented. We can identify largely psychologically based theories of learning in higher education, some studies of academic and disciplinary cultures and identities, and sociologically-based studies of the effects of higher education on students; the latter taking account of factors such as student culture and the 'whole college' experience. The project attempted to draw on and integrate these different traditions of research.

Taking the first of these, an active research field has been estab- lished, building on the work of people such as Perry (1970), Marton (1976, 1984) and Säljo (1979), that has explored processes and outcomes of student learning in a wide range of contexts (Richardson, 2000). Different conceptions and levels of learning have been identified, elaborating on earlier distinctions between 'deep' and 'surface' processing (Marton, 1976).

In the SOMUL study, such theories of learning have had a status both as intervening variables (i.e. as learning processes that might be related to the achievement of particular learning outcomes) and as potential learning outcomes themselves. With regard to the latter, the literature over the last 25 years shows an ongoing concern with promoting student development. The assumption is that students manifest increasingly sophisticated levels of development as they proceed through higher education, and that their development from one level to another arises as the result of both planned and fortuitous encounters during their experiences of study.

These models accord with the kinds of conceptions of learning typically used by academics when considering the achievements and failings of their students. Concepts such as critical thinking and complexity (e.g. Barnett, 1997) are employed to indicate the intellectual goals of an undergraduate education and the assumption is that it is the experience of formal education (i.e. what happens in and around university classrooms) that drives student development (e.g. Pascarella and Terenzini, 1991, 2005). In this literature, learning outcomes are regarded essentially as cognitive. There has been considerable progress in developing research instruments to measure student learning in these terms and the project was able to make use of several tried and tested tools to address student learning in this sense.

The second identifiable research tradition places its focus on the subject being studied in higher education. As we have already noted, perhaps the most commonsense and straightforward answer to the question of 'what is learned at university?' would be 'knowledge of physics, chemistry, geography, history, English literature' or whatever is promised by the title of the course being undertaken. Another of the traditional features of British higher education has been the specialised 'single honours' degree where learning is bounded by quite powerful subject-defined boundaries. From this perspective, learning at university becomes a socialisation process into the ways of thinking and knowing of a particular academic subject. Moreover, a lot of the people you spend time with at university – both teachers and students – are also likely to be members of the same subject or disciplinary 'tribe' (Becher and Trowler, 2001).

Within the academic community, student learning is still frequently conceptualised in terms of particular subjects or disciplines (a point reflected in the subject benchmarks issued by the Quality Assurance Agency for Higher Education[1] and in the subject centres of the Higher Education Academy[2]) and notwithstanding the growth in recent years of multi- and interdisciplinary courses. Relevant to this conception of student learning is a significant body of literature that examines academic disciplines as distinctive epistemological and social communities (Geertz, 1983; Becher, 1989; Maassen, 1996; Henkel, 2000; Becher and Trowler, 2001). However, these studies have focused mainly upon academic staff for whom academic disciplines are variously considered to be 'ways of life' (Maassen, 1996) or sources of 'languages, conceptual structures, histories, tradition, myths, values, practices and achieved goods' (Kogan, 2000). Basil Bernstein referred to the importance of 'subject loyalty' and to the capacities of academic subjects to create 'new realities', at least for the privileged few who gain access to the 'ultimate mystery' of the subject (Bernstein, 1975).

For teachers, academic identities are intimately linked to professional identities. For students, embarking to a greater or lesser degree on a process of academic and professional socialisation, the existence of distinctive disciplinary cultures is an important part of their experience – even when taking multi-disciplinary courses. Becher and Trowler (2001) note that the development of that academic identity and commitment often begins as an undergraduate. But what of students who do not see themselves as would-be academics? How, if at all, do these students' identities relate to disciplinary cultures and academic identities? What of students whose studies encompass several disciplines? Do these students compartmentalise or integrate their learning?

The strength of the disciplinary academic culture experienced by undergraduates is, in part, influenced by the form of curriculum organisation through which it is transmitted. Here the work of Bernstein is relevant. In a classic 1975 paper, he introduced his concepts of classification and framing and his theory of educational knowledge codes by distinguishing between educational curricula that stand in 'open' or 'closed' relationships to each other. He goes on to consider how educational curricula relate to 'commonsense knowledge' or 'everyday community knowledge' and suggests how different types of classification may impact differently on different types of student (Bernstein, 1975). We return to the relevance of Bernstein's work for the SOMUL project below and in Chapters 3 and 4.

While learning undoubtedly takes place in a context of a subject or subjects, it must also be recalled that a feature of the UK higher education tradition is that 'what you have studied' seems to count for rather less than it does in many other countries when it comes to getting a job after higher education. The match between course of study and graduate job is much looser in the UK than it is in most other European countries (Brennan and Tang, 2008). And this reflects the findings of another research tradition of student learning, the strongly-influenced US 'college effects' literature. Even the most cursory acquaintance with American campus movies will be sufficient to remind one that going to university is about having fun, playing sports, falling in love, making new friends and generally 'growing up'. Such things are not entirely unknown on UK university campuses. From this perspective, 'where' you study may be as or even more important than 'what' you study.

Popular in the United States from the late 1960s onwards, sociologically-based studies of the effects of higher education on students have drawn attention to the importance of student culture and the 'whole college' experience. This work includes the 'interactionist' studies of Howard Becker and colleagues (1961, 1968) as well as more quantitative studies carried out by researchers such as Feldman and Newcomb (1969). Alongside this work, one might also refer to the various contributions of Pierre Bourdieu (1988, 1996), which have linked the experience of attending higher education to broader social processes of elite reproduction and change. A number of substantial reviews of the US literature in this field exist (e.g. Feldman and Newcomb, 1969; Pascarella and Terenzini 1991, 2005).

Although there is considerable diversity of approach in this part of the literature, what these studies tend to share is a refusal necessarily to equate what is learned in higher education with what is taught. This is frequently linked to an interest in the role of higher education institutions in 'shaping' personal identities and group cultures (Becker et al., 1968; Dubet, 1994). More generally, it extends our notion of learning outcomes to areas such as attitudes, values, confidence, personal autonomy, self-esteem and moral development (Pascarella and Terenzini, 1991, 2005).

Another general feature of this body of work is the suggestion that student learning is in part determined by students' contacts with their teachers and their peers outside formal educational settings and by their extra-curricular activities (including work experience and other part-time employment) more generally (e.g. Terenzini et al., 1996).

This is the point developed by the classic studies of student life by Becker and his colleagues (Becker *et al.*, 1961, 1968) and which in many ways foreshadowed more recent constructivist approaches emphasising 'the role of individual agency in identity and cultural construction' and 'communities of practice' (Becher and Trowler, 2001). For Becker and his colleagues, an overall disjuncture between faculty objectives and student strategic behaviour in the pursuit of 'the grade' exerts a major influence on what is learned.

While the 'college impact' studies – especially in the US – have tended to focus on campus settings and on the lives of students within the university's 'walls', the same approach can be taken to researching student lives that are more fragmented, more often 'off' campus than on, where patterns of interaction move between several cultures and where the student must acquire and live plural identities. For many of today's formally full-time students, study is essentially a part-time activity, and 'being a student' is but one identity among many.

Our project has attempted to draw on these different traditions of research into students but to do so selectively and, wherever possible, to integrate different perspectives. Key concepts are the social construction of learning outcomes, disciplinary cultures, levels of learning and student identity. These have been explored empirically through an investigation of student learning largely from the perspectives of the students themselves within particular subjects and distinctive social and organisational contexts.

The organisational mediation of learning

Of the diversities of UK higher education described in the first chapter of this book, we noted the growing differentiation of higher education in terms of its institutional forms and the ways in which the work of the members of these institutions – staff and students – was organised. A large part of the SOMUL project has been concerned with the ways in which different organisational factors affect (or 'mediate') the student experience.

Initially, the project's conception of organisational mediation was defined solely in curriculum terms:

> the ways in which curriculum knowledge is organised, including the influence of modularity, extended student choice and different modes of study – together providing the 'principles of curriculum organisation'.

Our interest in the organisation of the curriculum was strongly influenced by the work of Bernstein (1975) whose concepts of 'classification' and 'framing' were suggestive of what might be learned and not learned in particular learning contexts and of the controls over the selection and sequencing of that learning. Following Bernstein, curriculum boundaries are drawn differently in different places and are relatively 'open' or 'closed'. Learning opportunities and expectations also vary in their explicitness to students – 'visible' and 'invisible' pedagogies in Bernstein's terms. And what may be 'visible' to one student might be 'invisible' to another student from a different social or educational background.

Curriculum organisation thus has a strong social element. It can determine who will study alongside whom, whether learning is an individual or a collective experience, the nature of the student's interaction with academic and other university staff, and whether student leisure and friendship patterns are shaped within the study programme or are largely outside it. However, what became apparent as the project progressed was that there existed a further set of organisational factors that also affected these patterns of social interaction within universities.

Thus, we became interested in how students and staff were organised (the relative powers and responsibilities of courses, departments, faculties and central service units within universities) and in how space and time were organised. All of these factors set constraints and opportunities for patterns of interaction and for what could be learned. These factors are elaborated on further in Chapter 3.

As we shall see in later chapters, central to the lives of many students and to what they value about their time at university are the friendships they make, the people they spend their time with and learn from. These are strongly affected by the organisational factors considered above. But they are also affected by the students themselves, by what they bring with them to higher education and by the kind of world that they construct for themselves while at university. These are the factors which the project attempted to explore under the notion of 'social mediation'.

The social mediation of learning

Social mediation is partly personalised – students bring with them backgrounds, expectations and lives outside of the university that 'personalise' the experience of study. The new arrival at university living in the university hall of residence who is fresh from eight years of boarding school education brings a very different set of personal baggage from the new arrival living at home who must balance paid work and domestic responsibilities and has had a ten-year 'gap' from any experience of formal education. But social mediation is also partly a collective thing – students create collective values, expectations and lifestyles (which we might call 'student culture') that potentially affect all students within the educational setting (albeit in different ways).

Our initial conceptualisation of social mediation refers to:

> the life situations of the students on a particular programme of study – individually and collectively – and including the social and educational backgrounds of the students as well as features of the student culture within the particular institution or programme – together providing the 'social context of study'.

This draws attention to three forms of social difference. First, there are differences that are *imported* into higher education and that arise from the social and educational backgrounds of the students and which determine their initial competences, expectations and ambitions in higher education (the student 'habitus' in Bourdieu's terms (Bourdieu and Passeron, 1990)). Second, there are differences in the student experience during higher education that are *externally generated* and which determine student lifestyle choices and necessities (where to live, whether to take a part-time job, domestic commitments, etc.). Third, there are differences in the student experience that are *internally generated* within the university and which determine both the level and nature of the student's engagement with his or her studies and the level and nature of the student's engagement with other aspects of university life, for example, clubs, sport, drink, etc. Crucially, all three forms of social difference are interrelated.

As with the features of organisational mediation, these social factors both set limits to and provide opportunities for learning. They may form the basis for distinctive student sub-cultures – with their own learning implications – or they may simply point to the different values, orientations and motives for study between individual students. Academic staff are well aware of the different orientations to study to be found among those present in their lecture theatres and classrooms. And there is a long tradition of research into these different student orientations.

Table 2.1 The Clark-Trow typology of student orientations

1 Academic
Primary importance of knowledge and ideas.

2 Collegiate
Wider university activities and experience at least as important as academic engagement.

3 Vocational
Gaining a career-related credential is uppermost.
An instrumentalist orientation.

4 Non-conformist
While wider college experience and intellectual engagements may be stimulating, but formal college activities and experience are subordinated to other goals.

In a seminal US study, *Making the Grade,* Becker *et al.* (1961) found the vast majority of Kansas students to be instrumental in their studies. Apart from an 'emphasis on grades', these students also prioritised the social experience of higher education above the academic, demonstrating that it is not just recently that students have failed to fulfil the more academic expectations of academic staff. The significant study by Marris (1964) from the same era supports a similar conclusion for the UK.

The leading US sociologists of higher education, Burton Clark and Martin Trow (1966), formulated an influential four-fold typology of student orientations (see Table 2.1). Employing this typology in her study, *Students in a Class Society,* the UK sociologist Joan Abbott (1971: 45) concluded that we can 'expect to find a preponderance of students belonging to one or two of these sub-cultures in different institutions depending on social class composition, residential organisation, physical layout of the campus, history and traditions, and so on'.

A more recent typology employed in the SOMUL project is an adapted version of an eight-fold typology constructed by the French sociologist Dubet (1994) (see Figure 2.1). Dubet's typology of student orientations in a mass higher education system is based on a combination of three elementary dimensions:

- The nature of the personal project, i.e. a clear life plan in relation to higher education.
- The degree of integration in the life of the university.
- Engagement with a subject, as a kind of intellectual vocation.

	Vocation (Engagement) +		Vocation (Engagement) −	
Project +	1	2	3	4
Project −	5	6	7	8
	+	−	+	−
	Integration		Integration	

Figure 2.1 Dubet's typology of student orientations

According to Dubet, the combination of the three dimensions captures differences in subjective orientations to higher education among students while also reflecting the broader influences of higher education – our 'mediating' factors. Dubet emphasises the fluidity, the change over time of student positions, especially in the intermediate positions 2–7, making his typology a useful basis for the analysis of change. We return to this typology in Chapter 5.

We thus have a number of models in which a range of organisational and social mediating factors interact with each other to both provide opportunities for and limitations to the learning experiences and achievements available to students in particular learning contexts (courses, programmes, institutions) and which at the same time help influence the orientations of individual students towards these learning opportunities.

Many diversities

Another way of thinking about these various organisational and social mediating factors is as representing a series of 'diversities': of students' backgrounds and lives before entering higher education, of the experience of higher education itself (with both group and individual dimensions), of the organisational and social contexts to that experience (including the characteristics of the particular higher education institution attended by the student). These different types of diversity are summarised in Figure 2.2.

Imported diversities related to the class, gender, ethnic composition and previous education of the student population determine the degree of heterogeneity of the student groups in question. Such diversities have been the subject of a number of research studies of 'widening participation' in recent years (e.g. Reay *et al.*, 2005; David, 2009;

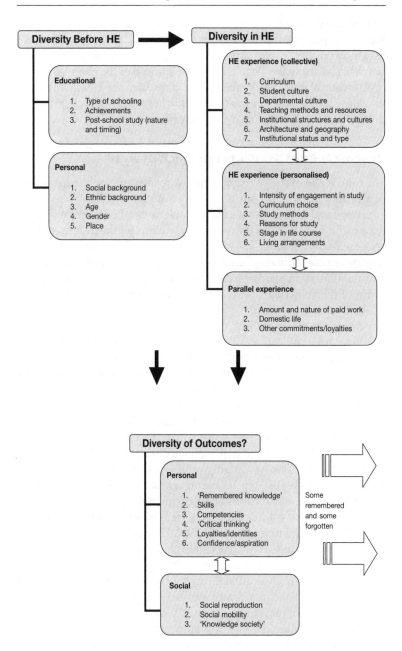

Figure 2.2 What is learned at university

Gorard, 2008). In turn, these differences impact upon experiences and forms of engagement which students make at university and which are balanced through choice and necessity against other internal institutional and disciplinary demands as well as those of the external world.

The central question for the project concerned the extent and ways in which these diversities related to a further type of diversity, i.e. the diversity of outcomes of study at university.

Research questions and project design

The central aim of the project was therefore to examine the experiences of students in different social and organisational contexts in higher education and to see whether and to what extent differences in experience could be related to differences in 'what is learned'. A case study approach was adopted, investigating the experiences of students on particular programmes of study using a mixture of both quantitative and qualitative methods of data collection. Recognising the significance of the subject of study, the cases were limited to three subject fields, with five contrasting cases selected in each. The subjects were biosciences, business studies and sociology.

These three subjects were selected for a mixture of theoretical and practical reasons. They took account of academic/vocational and science/non-science dimensions and of previous research indicating that students studying these subjects differed in terms of their study goals and attitudes (Pascarella and Terenzini, 1991, 2005; Brennan et al., 1993). The subjects represented three of the four types identified by Becher and Trowler (2001) drawing on the work of Biglan (1973) using hard/soft and pure/applied distinctions. We intentionally avoided the inclusion of a highly professional field of study – or the 'occupational specialist' type of Brennan and McGeevor's 1988 study – because professional socialisation and identity construction on such programmes were considered to require a more explicit employment focus than was the intention of the SOMUL study. However, students from a broader range of subjects and subject types were examined by means of a survey towards the end of the project.

Five contrasting institutional cases were selected for each subject from different universities. Cases were selected to represent the different social and organisational contexts described above. Particular attention was paid to the mix of students taking the course and to the way the curriculum had been organised, reflecting an 'open' and 'closed' distinction. The cases are described in more detail in Chapter 3.

Table 2.2 Summary of project design

Three conceptions of learning outcomes	Three ways in which learning is mediated	Three subject fields
• as cognitive development • as academic and professional identity • as personal identity and conception of self	• by formal educational curricula and assessment • by the organisational context of study • by the social context of study	• bioscience • business studies • sociology

The overall design of the study is summarised in Table 2.2. In addition to the three subjects that provided the 15 case studies for the project, students from a wider range of subjects were investigated by means of a questionnaire administered in their final year of study.

Over a period of three years, researchers paid regular visits to the 15 cases, interviewing students and staff, organising focus groups, administering questionnaires and collecting relevant course and institutional documents. The research focused on two cohorts of students in each case, an 'entering' cohort followed up from their first year to the beginning of the third year, and an 'exiting' cohort followed up from the beginning of the final year into the year after graduation. Fuller details of the case studies and of the research instruments used can be found in the methodological appendix.

The project identified seven initial research questions, reflecting both the policy and institutional contexts of UK higher education at the time of the study and issues raised by the previous research literature and the project's overall conceptualisation. The questions were:

1   What are the various conceptions of student learning that underpin subject benchmark statements, associated programme specifications and methods of student assessment?
2   What is their relationship to conceptions of student learning held by students and graduates and to the changes effected in them?
3   How do student identities and conceptions of self impact on or are otherwise related to formal learning outcomes?
4   How and to what extent are student identities and conceptions of self formed by the interactions of disciplinary cultures and student experiences, both inside and outside higher education?

5   How and to what extent are student learning outcomes mediated by social and organisational factors?

6   To what extent and under what circumstances are student identities and other learning outcomes maintained after leaving higher education?

7   How might 'official' conceptions of learning outcomes (formal assessments of learning, programmes specifications, benchmark statements) be adapted to take greater account of research into student learning and be used to shape and improve learning experiences and outcomes?

Throughout, the project has sought to juxtapose student voices (there is never a single voice) with the voices of their teachers, their universities and the makers of national higher education policy.

The next three chapters look at the contexts and experiences of student learning from different perspectives – the characteristics of the universities the students attended, the subjects they were studying, and the lives and orientations of the students themselves. We then turn to the question of 'what was learned?', first in relation to the cognitive aspects of learning and then in relation to what the students learned about themselves.

Notes

1   The Quality Assurance Agency for Higher Education is the national body in the UK with oversight of quality and standards in UK higher education institutions.

2   The Higher Education Academy is another UK national body, financed by government and universities, established to support the enhancement of quality and the development of effective teaching and learning practices in UK higher education.

Part II

Chapter 3

The universities
Cultures, organisations and reputations

Differentiation and diversity

As we have already noted, expanded systems of higher education are generally differentiated ones, in terms of their functions, their institutions and their programmes, and the populations they serve. Scott has described the evolution of UK higher education systems from pre-binary, through binary and unitary to market systems (Scott, 2004). Such system evolution is accompanied by system differentiation and, as Teichler has pointed out, differentiation may be realised through 'types' of higher education institutions, 'curricular approaches', 'levels' of programmes and degrees, 'length' of programmes and varied 'reputation' and prestige among formally equal institutions and programmes (Teichler, 2004). Trow's well-known distinction between elite, mass and universal systems (Trow, 1974 and 2005), though often regarded as a model of system evolution was in fact a model of system differentiation as it was perfectly possible for elite, mass and universal systems to exist simultaneously in Trow's conceptualisation.

We referred in Chapter 1 to a recent distinction made by Teichler between 'horizontal' and 'vertical' forms of differentiation, the former emphasising functional differences (programme types, subjects covered, links with industry) and the latter reputational and prestige differences ('top-ranking', 'world class' and the like) (Teichler, 2007). These concepts are useful in highlighting some of the distinctive features of the UK higher education system.

UK higher education fits many of the features of Teichler's 'vertical' form of differentiation with strong reputational distinctions between institutions. Unlike most continental European systems of higher education, it is relatively more important 'where' you study than 'what' you study (Brennan, 2008). The UK higher education system has become increasingly vertically differentiated with different sets of institutions informally playing distinctive roles (see Osborne, 2005). At two extremes of a spectrum an elite, as represented by the Russell Group of universities, are increasingly focusing a mission led by research and internationalisation while others, largely from the former polytechnic sector, see their market as being local and regional with teaching at the fore. Yet this functional division cannot hide the hierarchical division in which participation in the elite end of higher education is regarded as bestowing all sorts of advantages, both in the student experience and in life opportunities following graduation. However, there is a real question of how well reputational differences between institutions relate to real differences in the experiences of their students.

The system differentiation of UK higher education can be linked to increasing diversity within the student population. The rhetoric of widening participation in higher education for groups disadvantaged by virtue of their socio-economic background, race, gender and a range of other personal and situational characteristics, has been a prominent driver for national policy within the UK during recent decades (David, 2009). A range of 'carrots and sticks' has been introduced into the system of funding for higher education (see Thomas *et al.*, 2005; Gorard *et al.*, 2006). The carrots have been in the form of development funding at national and regional level (Action on Access,[1] Lifelong Learning Partnerships[2]) and at institutional level premium funding for achieving targets in the recruitment of traditionally non-participant groups.

However, despite these initiatives the most advantaged 20 per cent of young people are up to six times more likely to enter higher education than the most disadvantaged 20 per cent (see Higher Education Funding Council for England (HEFCE), 2004, p. 97, section 3.26 and HEFCE, 2005). In fact in some places regional inequalities are increasing: young people living in London are now 50 per cent more likely to go to university than those living in the North East. In certain elite institutions and disciplines (e.g. medicine), the disparities in access between socio-economic groups are much greater than in others (see Thomas *et al.*, 2005). An important consideration for the SOMUL project is the implications of widening participation for the diversity of the student populations within different institutions and courses. Later on in this chapter, we distinguish between higher education settings marked by high and low diversity among their student populations.

Disparities in diversity have social and organisational components. Widening participation within current UK educational policy has been promulgated as a challenge for both individuals and institutions. Diversity, as Archer (2007) argues, 'is elided with "choice" (in the context of institutions) and is closely linked with and used to signify "equality" or "social justice" (in the context of students)'. However, as she further suggests, in reality the ability to exercise choice depends on the possession of economic, social and cultural capital, disproportionately held by higher socio-economic groups (see also Reay *et al.*, 2005). Choice is thus dependent on what is available and what is allowed, and has a significant organisational component.

Policies that have sought to achieve a more diverse student population are challenged in two ways, both linked to a reduction in the public funding of university education. On the one hand, universities have to juggle with multiple missions, some antithetical to diversity and, on the other, students have to balance the costs and benefits of participating in a system that requires considerable personal upfront investment and perceived risk of debt.

The rest of this chapter considers the SOMUL project's notions of institutional diversity in relation to the experiences available to learners rather than to external and historical factors of status and prestige. But it ultimately raises questions about whether different forms of student experience are being made available to different groups in society, whether defined in terms of social class, ethnicity, age and gender or in terms of aspirations, previous education or life circumstances more generally.

Developing the concept of organisational mediation of learning

We set out the project's initial conceptualisation of organisational mediation in Chapter 2. It drew upon Bernstein's (1975) concepts of the *classification* and *framing* of knowledge within educational curricula and on related notions of 'boundary' and 'control'.

As the project proceeded we examined other conceptualisations of organisational mediation. Nespor (1994), drawing upon a range of literatures from psychological anthropology (e.g. Lave, 1988), social studies of science (e.g. Latour, 1987) and geography (e.g. Massey, 1993; Gregory, 1994), has explored the extent to which students become enrolled in an actor-network that connects them to a disciplinary network. Here the potential factors at work at the level of the discipline are the degree of spatial localisation; patterning of time; narrowing/broadening of interests; standardisation of curriculum; and allowable identities and interests. Analysis across these dimensions can provide insight into how students move into (become enmeshed in) fields of practice and ways of producing activities, spaces, and times. For Nespor, social life (and the life of students) in an actor-network is both space-forming and space contingent.

There are also important organisational factors that go beyond and are not directly related to curricular matters. These include 'whole institutional' factors including relatively clear-cut ones such as status, size, location and rather more complex ones such as institutional culture or 'habitus'. For example, quality assurance mechanisms, widening participation imperatives and the Research Assessment Exercise are three major stressors on UK higher education institutions. Each is part of the wider organisational context in which university departments operate, and the strength of the central management of institutions will determine the extent to which teaching and learning is prioritised in relation to other imperatives, and the way in which it should be organised to accommodate a diverse student body.

These factors from the external environment operate locally upon institutions though they may differ in their impact between basic units within the same institution. Factors related to the basic unit's relationship to its wider subject 'field' *and* to its relationships (both horizontal and vertical) within its home institution may also be important. While a certain amount of discipline-specific insulation may exist (in part because of the strength of external ties in the field), wider institutional concerns and higher level external constraints will undoubtedly impinge on practice.

For example, Bourgeois *et al.* (1999: 41) in the context of adult access and participation, identify four areas of conflict: between 'multiple and ambiguous roles and missions'; between the 'social necessity of those missions and the need to achieve the "system" goals'; among the academics who . . . look more like a fragmented collection of quasi-autonomous clusters, tribes and territories; and between professionals doing their job in the classrooms and laboratories on the one hand and an administration and 'top management' on the other.

The project has attempted to take account of these features of the institutional contexts within which the student experience occurs although we have always considered that organisational differences are only of direct interest to the project if they can be shown to mediate the processes and outcomes of student learning.

It is also important not to view organisational mediation as being completely distinct from social mediation, and we make this point throughout this book. Organisational mediation itself has a strong social element. The way curricula are organised can determine who will study alongside whom, whether learning is a collective or an individual experience, the nature of student interaction with academic staff, and whether student leisure and friendship patterns are shaped 'within' the study programme or are largely outside it.

The way in which the curriculum is organised within individual institutions is of particular importance to certain groups of students. For example, some students have a need for flexibility – in terms of when courses are taught or what can be combined with what – and these are frequently the students with the greatest constraints in their personal lives (for example, from their families and the need to work). While some institutions show considerable flexibility in time, place and mode of study, many still offer a traditional curriculum structure with very little flexibility.

Dimensions of diversity

Organisational mediation within the SOMUL project was operational-ised through data concerning the principles of curriculum organ-isation, the organisation of space and time, the wider institutional context and the perceptions of staff and students. As with social medi-ations we have operationalised organisational mediations through variables concerned with diversity. More specifically, the project has characterised organisational diversity in a number of forms as follows:

- **Structural diversity**: open/closed programmes; degree of temporal and spatial flexibility or choice available; core and pre-requisites; how staff and students are organised within basic units (faculties, departments, etc.).

- **Cultural diversity**: culture, mission, size; proportions of residential/commuting students.

- **Environmental diversity**: ownership of space; quality of space; surroundings.

- **Reputational diversity**: informal classification label; Teaching Quality Assessment scores; Research Assessment Exercise scores; research income; National Student Survey data.

The main focus of our analyses has been 'structural' diversity but the other diversities are also part of the context for each case that we discuss, and we selected our case studies to represent as far as possible these different dimensions of diversity. We wanted to distinguish between 'closed' and 'open' curricular experiences. The former are characterised by the traditional single honours degree where students spend three or four years mainly in the company of students and academic staff within the same subject community. Such curricular models tend to consist of a tightly defined common core from which there is little possibility of deviation, and narrowly prescribed pre-requisites for progression. The more 'open' curricular experiences are represented by the flexible multiple choice modular degrees where students can, in principle, experience a much wider range of contacts and forms of knowledge.

Forms of organisational diversity are inevitably informed by cultural, environmental and reputational diversities and these all have social as well as organisational dimensions. The culture, mission and scale of institutions may impact upon the way in which the curriculum is organised and provide the impetus for the range of student experiences. Some case sites can be viewed as organised for a 'residential' experience, catering for the 'traditional' undergraduate student who leaves home to study, often with accommodation made available on campus. Other universities with fewer bed spaces on campus are more strongly 'commuting' institutions with proportionally greater numbers of local students living at home. These differences in residential status may impact on aspects of social and academic integration (Patiniotis and Holdsworth, 2005; Holdsworth, 2006). We selected our case studies to reflect both residential and commuting models and to obtain differences in the sizes of the student populations and whether they were generally 'selecting' or 'recruiting' institutions or a mixture of both. In relation to reputational diversity, cases were selected to reflect differences in scores in the relevant unit of assessment in the Research Assessment Exercise of 2001 and Teaching Quality Assessments; external funding in the form of research income; and their position in externally generated league tables. Environmental diversity was not a feature of our selection of cases; rather we observed in our visits to sites the forms that their built and natural environment took, and the extent and the nature of the 'allowable' spaces for students. Other relevant features were those of the larger geographical setting, the attractions and accessibility of the local city or town in which the university was situated. It was acknowledged within several of the participating institutions that their attractiveness to students had as much (if not more) to do with the features of the adjacent town or city as it had to do with the features or reputation of the university itself.

In the rest of this chapter, we discuss how our conceptions of social and organisational mediation have evolved as we came to know the 15 case study sites more intimately over the course of the project. Our emphasis has been not only on the ways in which the organisational and social features of higher education institutions shape the experiences of the students who attend them but also on the ways in which students themselves, individually and collectively, construct and make sense of the experience of being in higher education.

Implications for the student experience

Following Bernstein, the project's initial conceptualisation sought to make distinctions between the 'open' and 'closed' curricular experience. In practice, however, this model proved to be much too limiting.

First, we found that despite a theoretical openness in many modular degree programmes, the actual choices made by students (and encouraged by staff) were in many places quite constrained and conservative ones, and an approximation of the relatively 'closed' educational setting often pertained even where structures were theoretically open. Second, was the realisation that curriculum structures were not the only organisational factors that mediated the student learning experience. As discussed above, how students and staff were organised (faculties, departments, etc.), the institutional architecture (*where* students were taught and otherwise spent their time), where students lived and the facilities and attractiveness of the campus in relation to other local amenities all had implications for how students spent their time and who they spent it with. Third were the characteristics of the subjects themselves. These are discussed in more detail in Chapter 4 but here we can note the interdisciplinary and thematic nature of business studies, the rapidly changing disciplinary contours of the biosciences and, in contrast, the relatively strong disciplinary features of sociology. And finally, there were the social factors referred to in Chapter 2, and including the widening participation factors discussed above, the diversity of the students on a particular course and the patterns to their lives as students – away from home for the first time versus home-based, full-time students balancing study with employment and domestic responsibilities, etc.

While recognising that in all higher education settings there are considerable differences between the lives of individual students, it was also clear that the social and organisational mediating factors discussed above combined to shape the collective experiences of students. It was the effect of these differences on the learning outcomes of the students that was to be the prime object of the study. As a starting point for the analysis of these differences and as a way of synthesising many of the organisational and social factors discussed above, we distinguished between our 15 cases in terms of two main dimensions: (i) the extent to which the student experience was a shared or an individualised one; and (ii) the extent of the diversity of the student population taking the particular course (see Figure 3.1).

This is a model of the potentially different student experiences arising out of our concepts of social and organisational mediation and capable of enabling us to begin to make some sort of sense of the empirical diversity and complexity in our cases (and within higher education more generally). In other words, it attempts to link the

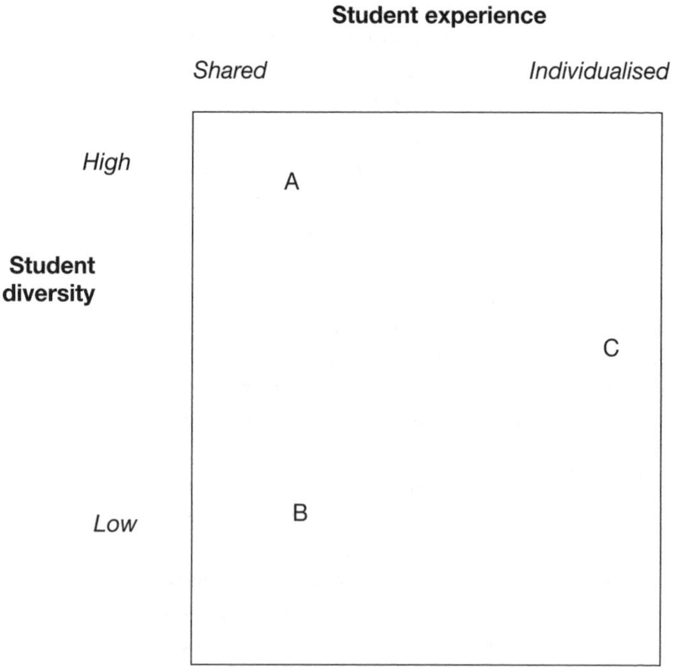

Student experience

Shared   *Individualised*

High   A

**Student
diversity**

                                                              C

Low   B

Figure 3.1 Three types of contexts for student learning

empirical complexity of the real world with the conceptual basis of our project.

In a type A context, a diverse group of students come together to share a largely common experience during their time at university. This provides opportunities for 'learning from difference' and might be linked to the promotion of greater 'social integration and cohesion'. In a sense, it exemplifies the 'promise' of widening participation but set within the conventional setting of a shared and largely 'collegial' experience of study.

In a type B context – the so-called 'traditional' context of higher education in the UK – broadly similar kinds of students come together to share a largely common experience. This might imply the 'maintenance of existing differences', of 'reinforcement of existing identities', the promotion of 'status confirmation and legitimisation'. It reflects the residential tradition of UK higher education and is most commonly associated with its elite forms.

Finally, in a type C context, students have only limited contact with other students, thus the diversity of the group is not particularly significant. These are the students who typically have demanding outside commitments, whether domestic or employment-related. Their time for study is limited and even more so is their time for other aspects of university life. For such students, university may be more about 'living with difference', about 'maintaining and constructing multiple identities' – at university, at home, at work. We have described the experiences of these students as individualised rather than shared, where university is not a place for the acquisition of new friendships, where time on campus is limited, where university is about study and credentials rather than the larger socialisation claims made traditionally for the university experience.

It is of course possible for individual students to have, say, a type C experience in a type B setting. But in relation to the dominant experience in each of the 15 case study universities, there appeared to be three examples of type A, eight examples of type B and four examples of type C.

The 15 cases investigated during the study can be located within this typology as shown in Table 3.1.

Of the eight type B university settings, the shared student experience in two of them was largely confined to the subject – at Weighton and Wistow. In other words, students spent time with other students on a range of academic and non-academic activities but these were largely restricted to other students taking the same course. In the other type

Table 3.1 Typology of 15 cases investigated during the study

Type A	Type B	Type C
Langtoft (biosciences)	Warthill (biosciences)	Ulleskelf (biosciences)
Fenton (sociology)	Fridaythorpe (biosciences)	Bugthorpe (business studies)
Wilton (sociology)	Givendale (biosciences)	Bramham (business studies)
	Husthwaite (business studies)	Bilton (sociology)
	Wistow (business studies)	
	Weighton (business studies)	
	Tockerington (sociology)	
	Holme (sociology)	

B universities, the student experience was shaped much more widely and was based on relationships established through involvement in university societies, sports, living arrangements (e.g. friendships established in halls of residence) and so on.

That as many as eight of the 15 cases reflect the traditional features of UK higher education – relatively low diversity of intakes and reasonably high level of shared experience – should perhaps come as no surprise. Nor is it so much of a surprise that seven of the eight were pre-92 universities. In fact, of the other seven cases, only one – a type A sociology course – was at a pre-92 university. Thus, it has to be acknowledged that reputational and selection factors will inevitably interact with the features of the student experience which are the main focus here.

The 15 case studies[3]

Type A cases

There were one bioscience and two sociology cases approximating to type A characteristics. All of the type A cases were in 'post-92' universities reflecting the leading role that these institutions have played in widening participation in UK higher education. They had relatively diverse intakes of students for many of whom the student experience was a shared one, whether with other students taking the same course or with new friends made at university, perhaps living in the same hall of residence during the first year. However, in one and possibly two of the type A cases, there were significant numbers of students living a type C experience, based locally with family and paid work commitments, which minimised both time and opportunities for spending time with other students.

Langtoft was the type A case in biosciences. The university is situated in a large regenerated multi-cultural city. It is a large multi-campus post-92 university with an ethnically and socially diverse student intake and a wide age range. There is little by way of space that is identifiably biosciences at Langtoft with only a section of one corridor under the department's ownership, although this may be changing as part of restructuring/refurbishment. The department sees itself as responding very much to local needs. There is considerable emphasis within the university on student support and skills acquisition, both at departmental level and through a central help facility. The degree programmes on offer have changed during the life of the project, and have tended to move towards a common core leading to a range of named degrees. This programme is more open than other bioscience cases in terms of inputs to and from other related subject areas. There is little expectation of progression to postgraduate study. There is also little engagement of students with the students union or in clubs and societies. City nightlife is a big draw and features as an element in students' choice of Langtoft. However, there may be some element of 'two worlds' at Langtoft, as in Fenton and Ulleskelf (see below), and similar effects on engagement/interaction.

The two sociology type A cases were **Fenton** and **Wilton**. Fenton was an inner-city post-92 'recruiting' university. Recruitment was diverse and predominantly local. Sociology lacked both institutional 'space' and independence within the structure of the university. It formed a small part of a largely vocational school of health and social sciences. Course structures tended to be 'open' with students taking quite a wide variety of individual course modules. The student composition of these individual modules also varied considerably. Students thus found themselves in the company of different groups of students according to the particular module they were studying. The inner-city location meant that student life frequently crossed the city/university boundaries and the large number of local students meant that the university campus was not especially active at evenings and during weekends. One senior member of the university described the campus as comprising 'parallel universities': one university was made up of young students living away from home for the first time; the other university was made up of a more mixed age range of students, mainly living at home, often with significant domestic and paid work commitments. It appeared to be students from the first of these parallel universities who were the more likely to be found on campus, more likely to be involved in student societies and sports, more likely to be active members of the Students Union and more likely to be members of course and other committees within the university. Arguably, the second of the parallel universities provided more of a type C experience for its students.

The final type A case was provided by the University of Wilton. This was also a post-92 'recruiting' university but this one was located in a small working-class town some distance away from the nearest city with its night life and facilities. In other words, Wilton was a bit remote. There was not a lot to do off campus but not all that much to do on it either. Many students commuted daily from other towns and villages in the region. They were a quite diverse group with a particularly high proportion of older female students. Organisationally, Wilton seemed to share much in common with Fenton. The sociologists were part of a school of humanities and social sciences. While the sociology staff were located along a common set of corridors, teaching took place elsewhere in multi-purpose teaching accommodation in a different part of the campus. Students handed in their assignments to the larger faculty office. Teaching groups were quite mixed with many students studying sociology as part of a broader-based non-specialist degree. Again, there were type C elements of this experience for some students at Wilton. However, quite a number of the students shared rented accommodation with other students, often studying similar courses, and for such students the student experience was a shared one, informally among university friends rather than having much to do with the facilities and activities on campus.

Type B cases

There were eight examples of type B cases, three each in biosciences and business studies, and two in sociology. Here, the residential traditions of UK higher education (at least the English variant) were in evidence. University life and the friends made there were the most important aspect of the student experience for many of the students. Subject-related factors varied in importance between the cases, in part reflecting the reputation of the subject department concerned. Most students were straight from school, sometimes after a gap year, and many were living away from home for the first time.

Warthill is a prestigious 'old' university situated in an attractive county town and containing all the classic features of a 'type B' student experience within the biosciences. A common core curriculum for biosciences operates at the main campus, yet although this might indicate a subject-based shared student experience, this is off-set by student allegiance to one of the colleges of the university. The role that the college system plays is of great importance at Warthill. Even within what is largely an elite intake of students (as measured by social class profile) colleges are further differentiated in terms of social status. By contrast, a strategy for widening participation places some students at a new campus several miles away in a somewhat depressed industrial conurbation. The college system still operates nominally at the outlying site, but is not as important to the culture and ethos as at the main Warthill campus. The same staff teach at both sites, however, and there is a recognition from these staff that approaches to teaching styles differ slightly between the two campuses.

The school of biosciences is part of the science faculty and has a recognised and owned space in the university with some room for socialising among students and staff, although students are restricted at certain times. Staff members are referred to by title; indeed, one professor remarked that he allowed the students to call him by his first name on fieldwork but they were reminded that he was Professor X when they returned to university. Although there is an active Student Union, very few cafés or snack bars are found in central teaching buildings as colleges play this role. This contrasts with all other case sites in the project. On the university's other campus, delivering a professionally accredited degree, there is no choice or option available in the programme. It is a small modern campus but facilities are somewhat restricted.

For those on the main university site, identity is strongly formed at the level of the college. Social capital is acquired there, which is exploited following graduation through formal and non-formal college alumni networks. On the basis of the 'Warthill effect', a number of students expect to enter high paying jobs, often in the 'city' and quite unconnected to their bioscience education.

Fridaythorpe is another of the type B bioscience case study universities. It is a large traditional pre-92 'civic' university with a strong research focus at both institutional and departmental level.

The curriculum has a common core with deferred choice after Stage 1 (which lasts until midway through year 2). There is considerable crossover and linkages between the individual named routes in Stage 2. The research-led nature of the department is reflected in the expectation that around a third of its graduates will go on to postgraduate research study.

Fridaythorpe has the greatest gender imbalance of the bioscience cases in favour of women. There is some evidence of students being 'failed' aspirants to medical degrees, who hope to take up the competitive option to transfer from their biosciences degree into medical school. This option is aided by the fact that many academic staff undertake some teaching for medical and dentistry degree programmes. Biosciences is part of the medical faculty at Friday-thorpe. The student intake is both from the region and the rest of the UK with some social diversity in terms of class.

The social scene in the city is often mentioned as a positive attraction for intending students. Student social life is partly organised around the department and accommodation arrangements also often play a large part in social networks. The department has 'owned' space within the medical faculty and there is shared student social space, all of which is accessed through the operation of a swipe card system.

Givendale is the third of the biosciences type B cases and is located within a prestigious pre-92 'civic' university. It was the strongest biosciences staff group in terms of research achievements and reputation. As with Fridaythorpe, there is a strong expectation from staff that around a third of the students will move on to research degrees. Notwithstanding the research strengths, all staff teach and no-one is allowed to 'buy out' their teaching duties. As in other cases, the department operates a deferred choice common core leading to a number of named degrees. Compared with other places, student choices are relatively controlled. At levels 2 and 3, 'team teaching' operates whereby specific lectures are taken by specific members of staff tied to research interests. There is a strong student community at both departmental and institutional levels with the Student Union regularly cited as a source of 'top' entertainment. There is some ethnic diversity among the bioscience students but little in terms of class or age or in terms of educational background.

The department has high visibility and defined 'owned' space, which includes its own lecture and seminar rooms that are not part of a central room booking system. There is also staff social space which has some student access. As with the two other bioscience type

B cases, local nightlife is considered a plus when choosing Givendale. As with Fridaythorpe, accommodation arrangements have a large impact on social networks. There is one form of shared student experience in terms of class contacts within the subject, and another experience through living arrangements, which tend to cross subject boundaries. Both are important to many students.

Turning to business studies, **Husthwaite** is a well-regarded pre-92 university with an attractive 'green fields' campus on the edge of a popular cathedral city. The campus is an active one with good facilities and a lot going on. There are not really any subject-specific spaces or facilities for business studies students to use. Indeed, their teaching appeared to take place all over the campus. The well-appointed university business school building is mainly the preserve of MBA and other postgraduate students. The school's 43 full-time staff are located in this building. The majority of undergraduate students live in halls of residence at least in the first year of study and friendship patterns are established at that time that last for the rest of the time at university.

The curriculum is a relatively 'closed' single honours degree with options limited to business subjects. There is an optional sandwich year for the four-year programme although all students are expected to participate in some kind of work placement. There is strong competition for places. Good A levels are required. Around 60 per cent of the students come from within a 75 mile radius of the university. Students are socially and educationally homogeneous, mainly school-leavers, mainly white middle-class and mainly having attended 'good schools'. There are also quite a large number of international students, taught alongside the home students but relatively isolated otherwise.

Wistow is attractively located in a popular tourist town. It is the only post-92 university case study in the project that had the characteristics of a type B institutional setting, i.e. little diversity in the student population (predominantly white middle-class) and plenty of student interaction providing a largely 'shared' experience. Many students were clearly attracted to Wistow because of the facilities and attractions of the town. A majority of them came from the region, although not necessarily locally. A high proportion lived on campus during the first year when, as at Husthwaite, friendship patterns were established. Shared rented accommodation in town was the norm for the later years. There was plenty going on at the campus and the student experience was potentially rich and varied, and certainly not limited to the subject group.

Business studies is clearly very important at Wistow with cohorts of around 250. The curriculum is modular in organisation with plenty of choice and including a part-time degree route. It recruits well and is regarded as one of the strongest undergraduate programmes in the university. Partly for this reason, it has quite a lot of autonomy. Curriculum boundaries (with non-business subjects) are fairly closed. Teaching is not shared with other groups of students although it is fairly dispersed around the university. There is little by way of 'business studies space' although most staff are located in a particular building and this is where work is generally handed in, notice boards are located, etc. Business studies is part of a large school (equivalent of a faculty) shared with law and finance.

Weighton is rather remote and quite small. It is a pre-92 university with most of the characteristics of a type B setting. Business studies students were socially and educationally homogeneous though, unlike the students at Husthwaite and Wistow, they were predominantly working class. They were also mainly from the region in which the university is situated. One of the consequences of this was that students tended to go home at weekends. Living accommodation was available on campus and in the nearby small towns. Students reported that they spent time with their 'house mates' rather than their 'class mates'. The university had good facilities on its modern campus although, beyond the familiar corridor and notice boards, there was little by way of meeting places or spaces specifically reserved for business studies.

Compared with the other business studies cases, the Weighton case was relatively small and we noted quite informal and intimate relations between students and staff, especially administrative staff. There were 14 business studies staff. Our focus was on the business and computing degree programme although students placed their emphasis on the business aspects of the degree. Full-time, sandwich and part-time routes were available.

The first of the two type B sociology cases was at **Tockerington**, a high reputation pre-92 'selecting' university located in what would generally be regarded as an attractive and prosperous city. It occupies a single site suburban parkland location containing research, teaching and residential accommodation some distance from the city centre. The university has a national recruitment profile and, in the case of sociology, attracts students as much for the 'university brand' as for the subject itself. While Tockerington is a highly regarded research university, sociology itself is not a front-runner research department in terms of national research assessment scores and reputation. However, it is a long-established department with its own traditions. It occupies its own accommodation at the university providing some opportunities for interaction between sociology staff and students.

However, the attractions of the university campus as a whole draw students away from the narrow social confines of the subject they are studying. The distance from the city, though not great, is nevertheless enough to make the campus relatively self-sufficient in terms of the facilities and activities available to students. It is a place where a good time is to be had and, as at Warthill, where social capital can be acquired in the process.

The second of the type B sociology cases was **Holme**, a research-led 'sixties' 'selecting' pre-92 university. Again located on a campus on the edge of the city, but in the case of Holme neither the university 'brand' nor the attractiveness of the location were in the same league as places like Warthill and Tockerington. More than any of the other sociology cases, students came to Holme because of its reputation as a 'good place' to do sociology.

Holme sociology was a strong research department, one of the country's leading sociology groups in terms of the national research assessment, and possessed a large number of postgraduate students. However, commitment to undergraduate teaching was strong, both across the university and within sociology itself. Intakes were some-what more diverse than at other type B cases. Undergraduate recruit-ment was a mix of both national and more local recruitment and the department made focused provision for both local and mature students as well as its more national recruitment, which tended to be of fairly homogeneous school leavers. The department had its own clearly bounded accommodation and there was a strong subject identity shared by both staff and students.

Type C cases

Four of the cases provided examples of what we have described as type C university settings. The defining characteristic of the type C experience is that it is 'individualised'. Students retain active lives outside of university, often with part-time jobs and domestic respon-sibilities. These are the students who are sometimes called 'part-time' even though their courses are full-time. For them, study and the resultant qualification tend to be the most important things, sometimes the only thing, as busy outside lives and interests remove any possibility of a 'wider' university experience. And in some ways, these students are not looking for such an experience. They are often older with plenty of life experience. They may be living 'at home' but generally not at the parental home. That was left a long time ago. These students are 'mature' in many senses of the term, further along the life-course and looking for rather different things from the university experience than their younger counterparts. Most of the project's 15 cases would have a few type C students, but in four of them the type C experience predominated. Of the four, there was one case in bioscience, two in business studies and one case in sociology.

Ulleskelf is situated in a large generally prosperous conurbation containing several other large universities. The university is a former polytechnic occupying a substantial city centre campus. Overall, it is the bioscience case that most strongly reflects the type C characteristics. While there are some students who have moved away from home and are having a broad and collective university experience, there are many local commuting students, who are less engaged or integrated with student life outside of class. Students are diverse ethnically with a large number of international students from a variety of African countries and a large Asian component from the local area.

There is a strong emphasis at Ulleskelf on skills acquisition and on teaching and learning, with staff appearing to recognise that the characteristics of their intake require particular pedagogical approaches. A wide range of types of assessments are used to measure progress.

There is an identifiable space 'owned' by the department in the university and basic student social space providing at least the opportunities for subject-based social interaction. The department has been the subject of restructuring during the life of the project. There has also been an expansion of degree programmes and these now tend to be on the common core model utilised in other bioscience cases. One degree is professionally accredited, a characteristic that is welcomed by students, as are the placement opportunities.

Bugthorpe is a quite small, recently designated and locally oriented university on the edge of a large industrial and commercial conurbation. The town centre campus has only limited facilities and little space for socialising. The students union was under constant threat of closure. Students tended to be older than the average business studies students at other places and there were also some international students. Students tended to commute and engagement in university life was limited. There was also considerable student diversity. Around 30 per cent were from ethnic minorities, about

50 per cent were mature students and there was a wider social class range than was found in many of the other cases.

Class sizes were quite small and organised in school-like classrooms rather than lecture theatres. The curriculum had a strong core and was available in both full-time and part-time modes, though without the usual sandwich option. Teaching appeared to be quite didactic and there seemed to be little out-of-class interaction, either within the subject or more broadly. Students seemed to leave the campus when they were not actually being taught.

Bramham is a post-92 university on a large campus close by a large city. Its business studies courses are well-established and highly rated. The university had been a major polytechnic and had been at the forefront of the development of undergraduate business studies programmes from the 1970s onwards. Bramham also provided the project with its only discrete part-time study programme. As might be expected from such a programme, the students tended to be older, heterogeneous with busy lives – all the characteristics of a type C setting. The university as a whole, and business studies in particular, recruited predominantly from its region. And this of course was particularly so for the part-time students. Dependent on the intensity of study and the frequency of attendance, the course could take anything from two to nine years to complete. Students attended either four or eight hours per week, either afternoon/evening or two evenings. The curriculum was relatively 'closed' in terms of the amount of choice available. The course was provided by three separate schools within the university's large business and management faculty. There was some joint teaching with full-time undergraduates.

Bilton was the final case study in the project. It was, in the project's terms, a type C setting for sociology teaching but, unusually, located within a pre-92 university, in this case an inner-city technological and vocational 'recruiting' rather than a 'selecting' university. While previously an autonomous sociology department, sociology at Bilton was now part of a larger multi-subject school and its specialist sociology provision was under pressure from new courses such as criminology.

Bilton had both local and national recruitment. There was a more even gender balance than at the other sociology cases and a relatively high proportion of ethnic minority students. In social class terms, students tended to be preponderantly lower-middle class. Although Bilton sociology had some type A characteristics – its own 'space' on campus, a strong research culture giving some potential for a relatively strong subject identity – the student experience was more like type C. Many students commuted from home each day and many more came from the larger city region. The attractions of the nearby large city inevitably limited the development of the university's main campus as a social and recreational meeting place. Thus, much social life was off campus and unconnected with the university. Students had local friends with whom they socialised and many of them were mature students with domestic commitments, which left little time for anything beyond attending classes as far as life at university was concerned.

Conclusion: what kind of university?

We shall revisit the above cases many times in the following pages. The above brief descriptions cannot, of course, do justice to complex institutional environments and the varied lives that are lived in them. The typology of A, B and C settings represents a much simplified breakdown of institutional settings according to the project's main concerns with the social and organisational diversity of contemporary higher education. But the types disguise much inner-diversity within individual cases and we have referred in a number of places to the idea of 'parallel universities' where at least two of the types exist side by side.

Students end up studying at a particular university for all sorts of reasons, not least where they can find a place – hence the distinction between 'selecting' and 'recruiting' universities used several times above. The same institution will not provide the 'best' setting for all students irrespective of their circumstances and aspirations. As we shall see in Chapter 5, students engage in university study in different ways and some settings may be more suited to some forms of engagement than others.

Nevertheless, notions of student choice are given increasing importance by government in seeking to ensure responsiveness and value for money from the diverse universities which constitute the bulk of higher education in the UK. In order to inform student choice, government has made arrangements for information to be made available to help guide student decisions. Intending students can enter various websites, which provide information about the relative attractions of different universities. Only at the end of the project, a new higher education website – Unistats – became available. This contained information for each subject at each university on the demand for entry (in terms of levels of pre-university attainment scores – reflecting the selecting/recruiting distinction referred to above), on the results of the 'student satisfaction' scores obtained through a national survey of final-year students, and on the proportion of graduates who had obtained 'graduate jobs' six months after their graduation.

The Unistats data for the project's 15 case studies are set out in Table 3.2. As can be seen, there are subject differences as well as type differences. The former will now be discussed further in Chapter 4. The students in the project's case studies had chosen, for whatever reasons, to study courses in biosciences, business studies or sociology. What are the characteristics of these fields? What is the balance between subject characteristics, institutional characteristics and student characteristics in determining 'what is learned' at university? In Chapter 3, we have looked at some of the institutional characteristics.

Table 3.2 Unistats data

Institution	UCAS points requirement for entry to course	Graduate job after six months (%)	Student satisfaction with overall learning experience (%)
Type A			
Langtoft *bioscience*	240	65	69
Fenton *sociology*	230	40	92
Wilton *sociology*	220	20	88
Type B			
Warthill *bioscience*	420	76	87
Fridaythorpe *bioscience*	370	57	87
Givendale *bioscience*	420	51	95
Husthwaite *business studies*	290	73	88
Wistow *business studies*	270	78	75
Weighton *business studies*	270	42	84
Tockerington *sociology*	360	45	86
Holme *sociology*	330	40	88
Type C			
Ulleskelf *bioscience*	250	55	83
Bugthorpe *business studies*	160	30	78
Bramham *business studies*	270	42	84
Bilton *sociology*	260	74	76

In Chapter 5, we turn to the students. Next, in Chapter 4, we examine the three contrasting subject fields that provided the intellectual focus for the student experience in the 15 case studies.

Notes

1   Action on Access aims to promote inclusivity and diversity. It is the national co-ordination team for widening participation in higher education, funded by the Higher Education Funding Council for England and Northern Ireland's Department for Employment and Learning. The team provides advice, information and support to institutions of higher education and specific partnership (for example, Aimhigher) on their widening participation activities, strategies and plans.

2   Lifelong Learning Partnerships were set up across the UK in 1999 to promote provider collaboration across sectors (schools, further education, work-based learning and adult and community learning) in order to widen participation in learning post-16 and to increase attainment, improve standards and meet the skills challenge. Currently, there is a network of 104 such partnerships.

3   The universities have been anonymised using a set of names discovered by two members of the project team during a visit to York Minster (following a meeting at the York-based Higher Education Academy). Below each of the windows in the Chapter House at the Minster can be found a plaque naming a member of the Minster's College of Canons, each representing a parish in the York Diocese. As we were in need of names for 15 fictitious university towns, we decided to 'borrow' some from the York list. We should emphasise that none of the Yorkshire villages named here has as yet acquired a university. Their names have just been applied to the project's 15 university cases.

Chapter 4

The subjects
Tribes and territories*

Introduction

Higher education is partly about general education and generic skills but it is also about separate subjects organised into their own 'academic tribes and territories' (Becher and Trowler, 2001), and separate academic sub-cultures belonging to those subjects. Universities have been described as 'plural institutions' (Clark, 1983). Academic subjects are an important aspect of this plurality.

Based on a consideration of the literature on disciplinary identities, 'communities of practice', and changing forms of knowledge (Bernstein, 1975 and 2000; Gibbons *et al.*, 1994; Lave and Wenger, 1998; Henkel, 2000; Becher and Trowler, 2001; Becher and Parry, 2005), this chapter provides an account of curriculum patterns and academic staff orientations in the three contrasting subjects in the SOMUL study – biosciences, sociology and business studies. As earlier noted, these subjects were selected as broadly representative of 'science', 'social science' and vocationally oriented subjects, and 'pure' 'soft' and 'applied' forms of knowledge as identified by Becher (1989) in his Biglan-inspired study of disciplinarity (Figure 4.1).

The detailed accounts of the three disciplinary areas are based on an analysis of 'official documents' prepared as part of the qualifications infrastructure created by the UK Quality Assurance Agency for Higher Education (including subject overviews, subject benchmark statements, programme specifications, and academic reviews) combined with observations of departments and interviews with academic staff. The chapter will highlight similarities and differences between and within the three subjects in the project's 15 case studies. It will outline the

* We are grateful to Rob Jones for providing an initial analysis of the interviews with staff at the case study departments.

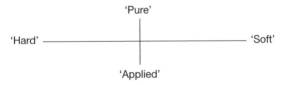

Figure 4.1 Forms of knowledge

implications for the curriculum and pedagogies and the student experience and learning outcomes associated with differences in disciplinary cultures. It will examine the different learning and teaching objectives and the different career trajectories (e.g. research versus teaching) of academic staff, including important institutional differences and differences between younger and older staff.

The implications, in response to student demand and market pressures, of a changing balance between general and subject specific elements in the educational experience provided by the three subject areas and within higher education more generally will also be examined. In sociology, for example, there are academic staff concerns that the integrity and coherence of sociology may be being undermined by a fragmentation of the discipline. This is sometimes seen as the outcome, in an increasingly 'massified' higher education system, of increasingly modularised and semesterised course structures and a variety of partial or 'standpoint' sociologies as well as student demand for more applied approaches, especially in newer institutions. However, in contrast with the fears of some of the academic staff we interviewed, we discovered a pattern of commonalities and more nuanced differences between and within subjects, with relatively limited evidence of dramatic change for the worse on the scale sometimes suggested.

Thus, the chapter will contribute to the further elaboration of the volume's overall portrayal of the character and outcomes of contemporary higher education in revealing neither a simple division of academic and applied subjects, nor a sharp polarisation of 'old' and 'new' universities.

Conceptualising disciplinarity

Bernstein's focus on 'pedagogy, control and identity' has been much used in educational research, though relatively little in research on higher education (Bernstein, 2000, provides an especially useful introduction as does Moore, 2004). Our thinking is informed but not ultimately driven by Bernstein's conceptual apparatus. For Bernstein, 'pedagogy' refers to 'varying sets of rules and principles and to devices that generate differing sorts of practices that produce different sorts of identities' (Solomons in Bernstein, 2000: 191).

Bernstein's best known contribution to the study of the organisational settings of education is his conception of curriculum codes defined in terms of two main dimensions: 'classification' and 'framing'. 'Classification' is about 'boundaries' and refers to the degree of separation/segregation of a 'subject' from other curriculum areas and from commonsense knowledge. 'Framing' is about 'control' and refers to the form of the structuring of the teaching relationship, e.g. whether it is strongly or weakly asserted from above and how far students have power to or are expected to frame the sequencing and selection of their own studies. These dimensions then enable an identification of two 'codes' (Bernstein, 1975 and 2000) as shown in Table 4.1.

Whereas a 'collection code' – in circumscribing a relatively closed discipline or 'subject' – involves strong classification and strong staff control of the framing of knowledge, an 'integration code' supports open boundaries, involves integration with other knowledge and applications. Bernstein's framework enables consideration of the kinds of differences and issues that appear central in a potentially more differentiated and more student-centred higher education. Bernstein's conceptions of educational knowledge codes were developed in relation to the organisation of the curriculum within secondary schools. We apply them here in part to the curriculum organisation within universities and in part to the internal characteristics of different academic subjects. At their heart are different rules about what may be put together and what must be kept apart, and differences in the power relations between teachers and the students in establishing and implementing these rules.

Although initially focused on research rather than teaching, a related slant on how knowledge is organised has been provided by

Table 4.1 Bernstein's conception of curriculum codes

	Classification	Framing
Collection code	Strong (+)	Strong (+)
Integration code	Weak (–)	Weak (–)

Gibbons *et al.* (1994). Here the distinction is between traditional disciplinary conceptions of knowledge (Mode 1) and the conception of Mode 2 knowledge, which focuses on forms and orientations to knowledge that emphasise applications and the integration of knowledge *across disciplinary boundaries* (see Table 4.2). Vocationally oriented departments and courses are also associated with such a perceived move away from traditional disciplinary boundaries towards more socially-accountable and reflexive programmes of study. Our selection of subjects and departments in SOMUL allowed us to explore such issues with business studies approximating the Mode 2 knowledge and the integrated code in Bernstein's terms, and the biosciences containing strong elements of Mode 2 knowledge but typically being organised with strong boundaries to other forms of knowledge, closer to the collection code. Sociology would typify Mode 1 knowledge although its organisation within educational curricula can take both collection and integrated forms.

A further aspect of disciplinarity is seen in the work of Nespor (1994 – noted in Chapter 3), for whom disciplinary power is about the production of *space-contingent* organisational social life at the expense of *space-forming* social practices. In his work, physics as well as management and sociology programmes were used to illustrate the processes that constitute and reproduce disciplines, in which students are drawn into discipline-specific patterns of temporal and spatial organisation of knowledge. The implication for what students learn arises from the ways in which disciplines capture students within particular material and social spaces and compress their time.

Becher and Kogan's (1992) approach to subject differences raises issues of a different order portraying the national as well as international cultures and structures of subjects as cross-cutting the forms of authority within the hierarchical organisational structures of

Table 4.2 Organisation of knowledge as conceived by Gibbons *et al.*

Mode 1 Knowledge
Traditional disciplinary knowledge

Mode 2 Knowledge
Emphasis on application and integration of knowledge – 'performativity'.

- Knowledge produced in the context of application
- Transdisciplinarity
- Heterogeneity and organisational diversity
- Social accountability and reflexivity

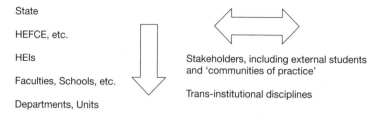

State

HEFCE, etc.

HEIs

Faculties, Schools, etc.

Departments, Units

Stakeholders, including external students
and 'communities of practice'

Trans-institutional disciplines

Figure 4.2 Forms of authority within higher education

higher education institutions. We can represent this as shown in Figure 4.2.

Thus subject-based departments in universities and their academic staff possess dual loyalties and frames of reference with their subject allegiances potentially in conflict with institutional as well as government goals. They may also conflict with students' needs and interests. Disciplinary goals include orientations to research and personal careers that transcend institutions and also reflect the prestige and socio-economic status of disciplines in the wider society. Where academics are associated with 'communities of practice' (Lave and Wenger, 1998) rather than disciplinary communities these too have the potential to be a further source of cross-cutting tensions.

What this literature on academic subjects indicates is the potential power of subject communities to subvert the influence of other forms of authority – whether these be derived from the management of individual universities, national policy bodies or the marketplace of students and the larger society.

The curriculum patterns for our three subjects can be hypothesised in relation to the above conceptualisations as outlined in Table 4.3. Thus, while offering 'scientific research' as a strongly performative vocational outcome, our representative 'science' discipline, biosciences, is nevertheless characterised by strong disciplinary controls. Sociology, our representative social science discipline, also with a relatively strong disciplinary shape but associated with fewer direct vocational outcomes, has nevertheless recently embraced new 'applied' areas such as 'Crime and Deviance'. Our representative 'vocational' subject business studies started life as a subject distinctive to the then polytechnics and is a clear case of the integration code, constructed as vocational 'performativity'. It has, however, subsequently shown a tendency to transmute into a distinctive 'new disciplinarity', especially in the post-92 universities.

Table 4.3 Curriculum differences between biosciences, sociology and business studies

Bernstein; Rustin (1981):
Collection code: strong classification
    and controlled frame
Gibbons et al.:
Mode 1 Knowledge:
Traditional disciplinary knowledge
	Bernstein; Rustin (1981):
	Integration code: weak classification
	    and more open frame
	Gibbons et al.:
	Mode 2 Knowledge:
	Application and integration of
	knowledge

1 Separate disciplines or as part of Joint Honours schemes, e.g. sociology; biosciences, at least in some forms.	**1** Integration across subject boundaries, e.g. business studies. Also modular pick-n-mix structures, with 'integration' dependent on student choice.
2 Strong academic control of curriculum/study. Emphasis on individual development/self-realisation but mostly relative to/internal to the subject. Sociology however closer than biosciences to integration type with more openness of framing.	**2a** Strongly integrating concept of the course, but with scope and/or requirement for individual/personal development. *or* **2b** Scope for student choice/ control of personal integrating themes, especially within 'purely modular' structures.
3 'Vocational' sources of integration external to the academy but largely controlled by the academy (as for biosciences). And also competing curriculum definitions or curriculum emphasis *within* collection subjects, including more applied, 'market led', courses arising from student framing (especially in 'recruiting institutions') e.g. 'crime and deviance' in sociology departments. However, tendencies to 'integration' are a source of tension, and possible transition, between codes/modes.	**3** Strong 'vocational' sources of integration external to the academy and dependent on new 'professional' ideologies. The push for a strongly integrated interdisciplinary curriculum may bear down heavily on students and academic staff, e.g. pressures on 'collection' academics in business studies (e.g. Macfarlane, 1997) or social work (Rustin, 1981) who may in turn press for broader external integration and more openness of student framing. Such a degree of integration raises the question: When does an integration code transmute into a collection code? A tendency to 'new disciplinary' is one reason for being sceptical about any simple contrast between collection and integration codes.

While there are clear differences between our three subject areas, there are also common features that will lead us to suggest that all three – and also in both pre- and post-92 universities – can be seen as involving a good deal of what can be described (using integration in Bernstein's sense) as 'subject mediated integration' alongside more traditional disciplinary control (Table 4.3).

Student characteristics, curriculum organisation and institutional context at our 15 sites and three subjects

Turning to an examination of our three subject areas, we first provide a summary of the benchmark statements for each subject area and then provide some details of the five cases in each one.

Biosciences

In biosciences the pattern of provision across our five cases is one of commonalities as well as differences. The 'typical standard' identified in the subject benchmarks for biosciences is given in Box 4.1, and reflects a general emphasis on an 'experimental approach'. Transferable skills emphasised include numerical and presentational skills. A related document *The Core Attributes of Biological Science Graduates* and a Subject Overview Report (Houston and Wood, 2005) commissioned by the SOMUL project also confirms that there is good agreement on the attributes – both subject-specific and generic skills – that would be expected of an honours graduate. Within this defining pattern for biosciences, however, significant differences also occur.

Biosciences encompasses a broad range of biology-related subjects sharing a common core, although applications and examples within each differ. Typically, year 1 and 2 courses have lectures and laboratory work in roughly equal proportion. In the final year much time is devoted to a research project, perhaps taking up one-third of the time. Around one-quarter of students take up the option of a sandwich year available on most courses.

As we have already noted in Chapter 3, three of the project's biosciences cases were in pre-92 universities (Warthill, Fridaythorpe and Givendale), all approximating the type B characteristics of student homogeneity and shared experiences discussed previously. Of the two cases in post-92 universities, one (Langtoft) approximated the type A

Box 4.1 Subject benchmarks – biosciences: typical standard (2007)

On graduating with an honours degree in biosciences, students should:

- be able to access and evaluate biosciences information from a variety of sources and to communicate the principles both orally and in writing (e.g. essays, laboratory reports) in a way that is well organised, topical and recognises the limits of current hypotheses
- have ability in a broad range of appropriate practical techniques and skills relevant to the biosciences. This will include the ability to place the work in context and to suggest lines of further investigation have a secure and accurate understanding of the explanation of biological phenomena at a variety of levels (from molecular to ecological systems) and be able to understand the relationship of evolutionary theory to their area of study
- be able to plan, execute and present an independent piece of work (e.g. a project), in which qualities such as time management, problem solving and independence are evident, as well interpretation and critical awareness of the quality of evidence
- be able to construct reasoned arguments to support their position on the ethical and social impact of advances in the biosciences
- be able to apply relevant advanced numerical skills (including statistical analysis, where appropriate) to biological data
- have well-developed strategies for updating, maintaining and enhancing their knowledge of the biosciences.

---

setting characteristics of high levels of student diversity and the other (Ulleskelf) approximated the type C characteristics of largely individualised student experiences.

With the exception of Langtoft, the curriculum was 'closed' at the level of the general subject field (i.e. in respect of knowledge areas beyond the biosciences) but relatively open within the subject. Students were typically faced with a common core plus a choice of options. Dependent on the particular combinations of options selected, students could end up with one of six different named degrees at Warthill, eight at Givendale, eleven at Fridaythorpe and four at Ulleskelf. At Langtoft, the curriculum was more open with options available from outside the biosciences. True to type, the three pre-92 cases would be considered to be 'research intensive' subject groups although there were differences in status and achievement, with Givendale the most prestigious in this respect.

In all three of the type B settings, students were generally residential, either living on campus in halls of residence or nearby in privately rented accommodation. Ulleskelf and Langtoft had a mix of residential and commuting students. Four of the cases were located in ex-industrial cities undergoing regeneration with city centres of varying degrees of attractiveness in terms of night life and social scene. The exception was Warthill where the university was located in a county heritage city.

As previously noted in Chapter 3, students in the three type B settings tended to be relatively homogenous in terms of their social and educational backgrounds. At Ulleskelf and Langtoft, students were socially relatively homogeneous but more diverse in terms of race and age. As far as gender was concerned, women tended to be in the majority on biosciences courses.

The relative attractiveness of the traditional type B settings and the prestige of pre-92 universities were reflected in the entry qualifications required of entering students, with minimum tariff points of 320 required at Warthill, Givendale and Fridaythorpe (representing what have sometimes been called 'selecting' institutions), 200 at Ulleskelf and between 120 and 160 at Langtoft (representing what have been called 'recruiting institutions').

One common strategy of 'recruiting' institutions is to blend and brand traditional subjects into more 'catchy' programmes in order to attract new students:

> Well yes, you label . . . a couple of years ago, put the word forensics on anything and they'd come rolling in, but really and truly our chemistry and forensics is chemistry with a forensic module, which is not quite what we thought about and anyway, we were already putting students from forensic science levels off the biological sciences degree, . . . but students wanted forensics, that's what caught their eye and we can certainly turn out students who will be employed there.
>
> (Ulleskelf lecturer)

However, an increase in the flexibility and market orientation of provision was evident in all five of our institutions. During our study there were changes at Warthill to the composition of the common core for first year and also some changes to the named degree routes available, although the number of options remained the same. At Langtoft, provision expanded and a new suite of programmes based around a common core had been introduced. This increased the options available to students to six choices of named degree, dependent upon the specific route chosen after the common core. As for other cases utilising a common core, there is a degree of commonality across the named routes. At Ulleskelf, a major reorganisation of faculties and departments was undertaken and it too has gone down the route of an expansion of the common core and an increase in the number of possible routes to named degrees.

A 'common core' would appear to be a feature of biosciences provision and has the advantage that it allows named degree routes to be viable with relatively low numbers of students. It is also popular with students who may not be sure either of their future career trajectory or of the content or focus of some of the named degree routes. It reflects the feasibility of the commonality of modules across degree routes and need not be construed as a sign of any major retreat from disciplinary controls.

Biosciences benchmarks and course structures and our own commissioned overview report all indicate that 'subject controls' in biosciences remain strong despite modular structures and pressures from students for popular course titles, which are apparently vocationally relevant. Thus, in Bernstein's terms, there is evidence in biosciences of both disciplinary control and wider disciplinary 'integration'. As well as an academic focus, a strong vocational element has always been a feature of biosciences courses and student motivations, with more opportunities for course related employment both inside and outside academia than is usually available to students in social science or arts subjects. The importance of placements and projects in biosciences provision is related to this. Thus, a Mode 2 orientation in biosciences provision can be seen as more integral and, arguably, gives rise to fewer tensions than exist in other subject fields.

Sociology

Again, a mixture of commonality and diversity can be found. Box 4.2 summarises the 'typical standards' identified by the subject benchmarks

Box 4.2 Subject benchmarks – sociology

'Typical standard' (2007 benchmarks, slightly modified from earlier formulation):

On graduating with an honours degree in sociology, students should be able to:

Subject knowledge and understanding

- describe and examine a range of key concepts and theoretical approaches within sociology and evaluate their application
- provide an analytical account of social diversity and inequality and their effects
- understand and evaluate the issues and problems involved in the use of comparison in sociology
- analyse the nature of social relationships between individuals, groups and social institutions
- examine the processes that underpin social change and social stability
- examine a range of research strategies and methods and assess the appropriateness of their use
- evaluate the relationship between sociological arguments and evidence in a range of contexts
- analyse ways in which sociology can be distinguished from other forms of understanding.

Cognitive abilities and skills

- assess the merits of completing explanations of human behaviour, social situations and events
- draw on evidence from a range of sources and demonstrate an ability to synthesise them
- draw on evidence to evaluate competing explanations
- evaluate competing explanations and to draw reasoned conclusions.

Discipline-specific skills

- construct appropriate sociologically informed questions
- summarise and explain the findings of empirical sociological research, including a critical assessment of the methodological frameworks used
- select and use appropriate research tools
- investigate sociologically informed explanations
- analyse the ethical implications of social research in a variety of applied research settings
- discuss sociological topics with appreciation of theory, evidence and relevance to current debates and to present the conclusions in a variety of appropriate sociological formats
- identify and comment on the value of sociological work with regard to social, public and civic policy issues.

for sociology. In the first instance, these are standards claimed specifically for sociology. A second set of more generic outcomes is also identified.

Sociology benchmarks emphasise that the subject is 'a reflexive discipline', embracing consideration of the nature of knowledge as well as student self-reflection as a member of the social world. A further aspect of sociological inquiry emphasised is its 'critical' element. Critical sociological inquiry is expected to enable students to evaluate the role of social institutions and to identify and reflect upon their own and others' assumptions. Emphasis is also placed on fostering the acquisition of skills that will equip students to assess competing sociological theories in terms of their logical coherence and in the light of empirical evidence of a quantitative or qualitative nature. Beyond this, the subject is presented as encouraging scepticism in its students, while simultaneously positing the need to recognise a firmly grounded and conceptually well-developed theoretical framework. Sociology students are also seen as having a number of options as to how to position themselves in relation to their chosen field of study. The sociology benchmark statements present the subject as both scientific and humanistic.

The further section of the sociology benchmarks addressing wider skills indicates that sociology students should develop both general and discipline-specific cognitive skills. This includes the ability to locate and acquire information pertinent to a given task together with the accumulation and retention of the most salient aspects of this information, and the ability to work independently and to work co-operatively in groups.

Attention to generic transferable skills is also evident in the programme specifications of our five cases. This is not to be seen as something that has simply arisen as a response to recent government and QAA pressures. This is evident from Albrow's (1986) Presidential Address to the British Sociological Association in which he advanced the case that sociology was well suited as the basis of a 'humane education', although it needed to review its first degree curriculum to ensure that it actually promotes the skills and capacities of which it is 'an inherently suitable bearer'.

Sociology provided two of the project's type A cases, both post-92 universities (Fenton and Wilton). There were two type B cases (Holme and Tockerington), both pre-92 and the type C case (Bilton) was also a pre-92 university.

While there were undoubted differences between departments, with those in post-92 universities rather likely to offer more obviously market-oriented courses, there also existed commonalities and overlaps between the sociological experience on offer at the different sites. This suggests the persistence, albeit with some change over time, of a shared sociology curriculum based in what has been called – as is echoed in a number of our interviews with students – 'the sociological imagination', and is reflected in the sociology benchmark statements. At both Holme and Tockerington, the sociology curriculum was relatively 'closed' in Bernstein's terms with a mix of compulsory core courses and options, all within the subject. At Holme there were also some 'joint honours' courses with other subjects, and at Tockerington sociology shared a department with applied social studies. At the other three sociology cases, the curricula were more 'open' with students able to combine sociology courses with courses in other subject areas where they were taught alongside students from a wide range of subject fields. In Bilton, there was a particularly popular sociology and criminology option. However, despite a theoretical openness in these programmes, actual student choices often followed quite traditional disciplinary lines, evidence arguably of the strength of subject identities and their authority to subvert the possibilities provided at institutional levels.

While Holme and Tockerington were both pre-92 universities and approximated the type B characteristics of the project's typology of learning settings, there were in fact some interesting differences between them. Sociology at Holme was research-led with a strong international research reputation with students recruited both locally and nationally. Students were relatively homogeneous in terms of age and social background. Sociology at Tockerington had a more modest research reputation but was a long-established department in a high reputation research-intensive university with an attractive residential campus nearby a popular city with good leisure facilities. Students here were socially and educationally homogeneous with predominantly middle class school leaver recruitment.

Fenton and Wilton were both post-92 universities, the former located in an inner city and part of a large industrial conurbation and the latter located in a more semi-rural 'de-industrialised' area some miles away from the nearest city. Sociology at Fenton was a small and relatively insecure staff group with only limited research activity. At Wilton, sociology was a 'field' within the university's school of humanities and social science with some research-active staff, but overall a mainly teaching focus. As noted previously, both Fenton and Wilton were type A settings though with strong elements of type C. They had predominantly local recruitment, including above-average numbers of 'non-traditional' and mature students. Fenton had significant numbers of students from ethnic minorities.

Bilton was the project's one example of a pre-92 university, which approximated the characteristics of our type C setting, with a diverse set of students – around one-third with 'non-standard' entry qualifications – recruited mainly locally with a large number living at home. It had higher than average proportions, for sociology, of mature, ethnic minority and male students.

As already noted in Chapter 3, entry grades varied from a required 360 at Tockerington to between 160 and 230 at Fenton and Wilton, reflecting a mixture of institutional prestige and location and the perceived reputation of sociology at the institution.

In the theoretically more 'open' sociology offerings at Bilton, Fenton and Wilton, patterns of module choice revealed that most students tended to choose relatively coherent and traditional programmes of study. Such patterns of choice, which may reflect the advice and guidance of academic staff, are also a significant indicator – despite the theoretical openness of the curriculum – of the maintenance of strong course boundaries, and often also of strong disciplinarity. In Bernstein's terms, either the 'collection codes' remain substantially intact (although not unchanging and permitting a range of 'joint honours' offerings of 'sociology with' various other social science and humanities subjects) or, where a tendency towards more 'integrated codes' is apparent, the 'control' of sociology over these new offerings – such as 'crime and deviance' or 'media and society' – remains strongly evident.

Business studies

According to the 2000 business studies subject benchmarks statement there were around 7,000 UK honours programmes with business or management in the title. HESA data indicate that more than 11 per cent of the total undergraduate population were enrolled in business studies in both three- and four-year courses, including many sandwich courses with periods of time, up to a year, spent on placements (although of late the sandwich element appears to be a declining feature of provision).

The first degrees specifically in business studies appeared at the end of the 1960s in what became the new polytechnics. Overseen by the Council for National Academic Awards, degree schemes in the subject were emblematic of the innovative vocationalism of the new institutions. The degrees can be described as characterised by Bernsteinian 'integration' of a range of subject-based and thematic course modules around the 'integrational idea' of studies 'for business'. They are generally housed within a substantial business studies school or department, with a curriculum controlled by it. A number of core modules such as strategic management, marketing, financial management, information systems, statistics and economics now feature centrally in most courses. In pre-92 institutions, outside the polytechnic tradition, business studies has been a somewhat different animal, coming later to the scene and tending to continue a more pick-and-mix provision from a range of more loosely integrated, but still freestanding subjects located in separate departments, representing a curriculum organised, in Bernstein's terms, as a 'collection code'.

This polarisation of business studies teaching programmes between institutions to some extent mirrors a polarisation in research patterns pointed out by the ESRC demographic review (Mills *et al.*, 2006). While:

> Subjects such as Design, Creativity, Travel & Tourism only featured in the lower rated schools; those like Strategy and Economic Modelling only featured in the higher-rated schools.
>
> (Mills *et al.*, 2006: 48)

Also the more traditional disciplines and sub-disciplines such as accounting and finance, economics, management science and organisational behaviour are concentrated in the business schools with the higher Research Assessment Exercise (RAE) scores. The newer and more applied disciplines, such as human resource management, information management, marketing, law, strategy and general management tend to predominate in the schools with lower RAE scores. In the former, the main teaching focus tends to be on lucrative MBA programmes and postgraduate research training with undergraduate business studies being something of a 'poor relation' in terms of local priorities.

Reference to 'business' in disciplinary terms therefore requires caution. According to the ESRC demographic review, business and management remains an 'importer' discipline and is more affected than sociology and the biosciences by the competition with the private sector in the recruitment of staff. In other words, the staff of business departments and schools are likely to have very diverse backgrounds compared with their counterparts in sociology and biosciences. Not only are they likely to have academic backgrounds in – and possibly continuing loyalties to – a range of other social science disciplines, but they are also more likely to have work experience from outside the academic world.

The most central elements of the business studies subject benchmarks are given in Box 4.3. It is noticeable that the purpose of business education is seen as part preparation for a career in business and management but also as enhancing wider skills and personal development. The 'encouragement of positive and critical attitudes towards change and enterprise' is also emphasised. For all this, the emphasis of business studies can fairly be described as continuing to be more a matter of studies for business than a critical study of business.

Box 4.3 Subject benchmarks – general business and management 'typical standard', 2007

On graduating with an honours degree in general business and management, students will typically:

- have a wide knowledge and understanding of the broad range of areas of business and management and the detailed relationships between these, their application and their importance in an integrated framework

- consistently demonstrate a command of subject specific skills, including application of knowledge, as well as proficiency in intellectual skills

- have a view of business and management, which is influenced by a variety of learning sources, including guided learning, team work and independent study

- be distinguished from the threshold category by their enhanced capacity to develop and apply their own perspectives to their studies, to deal with uncertainty and complexity, to explore alternative solutions, to demonstrate critical evaluation and to integrate theory and practice in a wide range of situations.

Three of the business studies cases – Husthwaite, Wistow and Weighton – represented type B settings – and the remaining two – Bramham and Bugthorpe – type C. In terms of the characteristics of the parent universities, as we have already noted in Chapter 3, Husthwaite and Weighton were pre-92 campuses and Wistow, Bramham and Bugthorpe were post-92.

The Husthwaite business school offered a number of undergraduate programmes in business. The foci for the SOMUL project were the single honours business administration (with a year in industry), accounting and finance, industrial relations and human resource management and management science programmes. The curriculum was modular in a full sense, in that students could mix and match their options. In year 1 half the credits were compulsory and the remainder optional. In subsequent years routes were relatively tightly structured. As in other subject areas, because of student preferences and/or resource constraints, actual choices of students were usually a good deal more limited than the theoretical range of courses potentially on offer. Thus, of the business studies cases, Husthwaite lay more at the 'closed' end of curriculum organisation and, reflecting its institutional origins and reputation, the student body in business studies was socially and educationally homogeneous, composed mainly of middle-class school leavers.

In contrast, at Bugthorpe, a post-92 institution with a more heterogeneous intake and a course typical of those in the 'polytechnic' tradition, the curriculum was more 'open' and catered flexibly for a mainly local clientele. There was a part-time route available for students and considerable student choice across relatively open curriculum boundaries. In terms of student numbers, business studies was very important to this relatively small university situated on the edge of a large industrial conurbation.

Husthwaite and Bugthorpe represented arguably the extremes of the variations across the five business studies cases. Weighton, the other pre-92 university, had a small and quite remote campus dating from the 1960s. Students were again relatively homogeneous although here the majority were fairly local and working class in origin. The programme was a combined degree in business and computing. Most modules were optional and taught jointly to students taking a range of programmes. Compared to the other business studies cases, business studies at Weighton was relatively small.

Bramham and Wistow, though both post-92, were very different from each other, the former providing a type C setting and the latter a type B. Business studies at Bramham was a large separate faculty that had been highly rated in the national teaching assessment exercises. The focus of the SOMUL project was on the part-time version of the undergraduate business studies degree programme. The curriculum was relatively 'closed' in terms of choice but rather flexible in terms of both attendance patterns and duration. The students were mature adults leading busy lives and with quite a wide variety of educational backgrounds. Students at Wistow, in contrast, were socially and educationally homogeneous, consisting of mainly middle-class school leavers and drawn from the region rather than the quite attractive immediate locality of the university. The business studies programme was located in an institute of business and law. The curriculum of the undergraduate business degree was relatively 'closed' and attracted particularly large cohorts of students.

Given that business was identified as a typical 'importing' discipline in the ESRC demographic review of the UK social sciences, one would expect the diversity of staff backgrounds to impact upon their views regarding subject culture, teaching and research, and students' approaches to learning. However, this impact was mediated by the characteristics of the different institutional homes for business. In particular the subject/institutional diversity described above seemed likely to generate more 'conventional' academic perceptions and expectations among the staff of some institutions while in others, the less academic background of the teaching staff (who took up academic jobs as second careers or who taught alongside continuing non-academic activities in the business sector) suggested more practical and innovative concerns and a curriculum 'for' business rather than 'of' it.

Institutional and subject differences in staff subject identities

Our interviews with academic staff across the project's three case study subjects provide a good deal of further data to continue our overall exploration of the differences between subjects and their implications for the student experience and what is learned. The interviews covered the different career trajectories of staff, their perceptions of subject culture and students' subject identity, as well as more general views on changing institutional and policy environments. In all three of our subjects the move to modularity and semesterisation, coupled with market pressures for new courses as well as new kinds of student, has undoubtedly put pressure on traditional disciplinarity. How significant have these pressures been? What subject differences are evident? What differences exist between different types of institution?

We can first note the importance of the differences in the career trajectories of academic staff in our three subject areas. In ways that we have to some extent already noted, career patterns in biosciences and sociology contrast sharply with business studies. Patterns in biosciences are relatively typical of those for physical science more generally. Career patterns in sociology are somewhere in between those in biosciences and business studies. While there are differences between departments, both biosciences academics and sociologists tend to be research oriented and, in some departments, very strongly RAE-driven.

The strong common professional identity in biosciences is marked by unambiguous training areas and widely shared common career patterns (postdoc abroad, research fellow, etc.), illustrated by the following staff biographies:

> I got a first class in Microbiology with Biochemistry and Physiology and I carried straight on . . . to do my Ph.D. From that point on I went on to do a postdoc at [another] university, in the USA. I was there for about five years, where . . . I started on the field of work in which I research now. From that point I then went to [another] University in the . . . Then I took up a lectureship here.
>
> (Warthill lecturer)

> I've been ten to twelve years. I did well I suppose, a very traditional scientific thing. I did first degree in physics at [one university and my] Ph.D in maths at [another] . . . then I went into biophysics and biochemistry in my post graduate studies . . . did a postdoc in the States for five or six years, then I did another one in Switzerland for five or six years, and then I came here.
>
> (Givendale lecturer)

The shared career backgrounds of staff in biosciences are a significant factor in the strong shared subject identities of staff. Such shared identities are powerful factors in the maintenance of subject cultures and boundaries within universities, although in such a multifaceted subject field it is noticeable that academic staff do sometimes appear more comfortable with interdisciplinarity than their sociology counterparts:

> One of the things that helped me to get this job was the fact that I had experience in a lot of different fields, so they, from a research perspective, they could see me fitting in with a lot of different groups and here from a teaching perspective saw me as being able to cover a lot of different teaching.
>
> (Warthill lecturer)

In sociology, the increasingly shared research training experiences makes it broadly similar to biosciences. In both subjects these shared staff backgrounds and an associated strength of subject identity have important implications for the student experience, including a well-defined projection of a subject identity and a usually strong relation between research and teaching in both pre-92 and post-92 institutions.

The markedly different pattern in business studies is evident in staff perceptions of career patterns and promotion criteria, a different relation between research and teaching and a more uncertain subject identity. In Weighton, for example, most staff appear to position themselves primarily as teachers and often lack a research background. A similar pattern was observed at Bramham. Business departments in Husthwaite and Wistow presented a higher research profile, although in the case of Wistow, one respondent suggested that the conversion to a research culture is perhaps a fairly recent phenomenon:

> It's changing . . . I've been here for ten years now and that was . . . my first teaching post because before that I had been in business – it was very much an emphasis on teaching and not very much on research.

In all five business studies departments our interviews with teaching staff suggest that a somewhat uneasy relationship between research and teaching can be exacerbated by an RAE-driven emphasis on research in contexts dominated by a teaching culture. Although in some ways a similar situation was observed in other subjects in post-92 universities, the situation in business studies is rendered more problematic by the relatively lower level of conventional academic qualifications among staff (a major contrast with the two other subjects, even in similar types of institution). The broader picture provided by the ESRC review cited earlier is confirmed by our survey of staff in business studies: the field is largely recruiting from a range of relevant disciplines (who do not themselves have undergraduate business degrees) or directly from the business sector (the second career route). The latter group of (predominantly teaching) staff was found to be prominent in the departments we visited, with career trajectories largely lacking any conspicuous research base. This female lecturer is typical of many:

> I [first] worked for a very short period of time in a sales position, selling postage meters, very exciting, hard-edged stuff. That was about three months, but then I moved into a Marketing Consultancy and Executive Search consultancy position as a junior consultant, so I would have been really carrying out market research plans for local companies in this region and also advising and training local companies with regard to marketing. I stayed there for about two years and then I actually moved into industry, in the food industry as a Marketing Manager within a Frozen Food company.
>
> (Husthwaite, female lecturer)

Sometimes this category of staff started on teaching positions, sometimes on a part-time basis alongside other activities before being made permanent teachers. Although, as we have seen, some departments are seeking to raise their research profile and this involves recruiting staff with higher academic qualifications and a research profile, this is not always possible for some departments. As the ESRC demographic review notes:

> As one respondent puts it: 'Finding people with appropriate professional backgrounds who also have experience of or aspirations to undertake research (which, broadly speaking, is the ideal combination for lecturing in this field) can be difficult.'
>
> (Mills et al., 2006: 48)

Staff views on student engagement, instrumentalism and subject identity

As a vocational subject, business studies contrasts with biosciences and sociology, with implications for student engagement and student instrumentality. What might be expected to be a single higher education discourse on these issues is in fact revealed as a series of, to some extent, subject-related staff discourses. Despite some clear differences in all three subjects, staff views on students were driven by two shared broad areas of concern: the marketisation of higher education and the widening of participation.

Both of these are quite often seen in negative terms. In the case of the former, academic staff sometimes saw a tendency to a customer orientation among students leading to a narrow instrumentalism and a largely 'surface' approach to learning. Widening participation is seen by some to have brought poorly prepared students into higher education, forcing teachers to adapt their pedagogy often without much support from the institution. Each of these tendencies is seen by some staff as damaging to the health of their subject. For example, students may be seen as working hard but showing little engagement with the subject:

> You might have 20 per cent of them who are very good and you know, actually really read and really begin to sort of have a feel for the subject and feel quite strongly motivated and have a kind of political consciousness that allows them to engage with it in some way that they find more transformative in some way. But the rest I think find . . . that they just want to make sure that they get a 2–1 that's very important and then . . ., they didn't really know why they chose to do it in the first place, and by year 2 they're beginning to get worried about what kind of job they could do with a sociology degree.
>
> (Tockerington lecturer)

Instrumentalism in the above case (in a highly reputed institution) refers to the attitudes of students seemingly having chosen the subject by default, as it were, in order to secure a place in this prestigious university:

> A lot of them have been to private schools not famous ones, but private schools. They've been thoroughly taught in small groups so they do very well at A level. They come to Tockerington because it's regarded that a degree from Tockerington is . . . a good brand that will secure their future. An admissions tutor said to me a couple of years ago, perhaps he was feeling fed up on that day, that he thinks we get some students who are encouraged to apply for

sociology because their school tells them they're not good enough to do things like English or history, so we get at least some students who are really not particularly interested in the subject.

(Tockerington lecturer)

For such students, 'where' they were studying seems to have been more important than 'what'. More generally, the notion of student instrumentalism as used by staff essentially refers to the strategic pragmatism of students under pressure to get a pass, thus giving the impression of a limited intellectual interest in the subject:

> I have very few students within the field of sociology here that I would say have really [grasped] what sociology, in my perspective, . . . is all about and appreciated it. It's usually a kind of thing that has to be done, its not something that has really people materially engaged with. Obviously there are exceptions . . . but in a class of 40 students you may get two, three, four or five students you think 'oh they're getting to grips with the questions' and the rest it feels like kind of mechanical in the way they approach it.
>
> (Fenton lecturer)

In such locations, the combination of sociology with programmes (criminology, media studies, etc.) which are more 'attractive' to the new categories of students being targeted is portrayed by some staff as responsible for a merely grade-focused attitude to sociology. A number of students on these programmes even stated that they get 'too much' sociology.

The five business studies departments had much more diverse student intakes than the sociology and biosciences departments. This is partly explained by the type of institutions represented, but also by the vocational nature of the subject, which attracts a greater number of mature students seeking an enhancement of or a career change. Business schools are also large recruiters of international students at undergraduate level. Such student diversity was seen by staff as a challenge to their pedagogical practice, leading to widespread concerns regarding students' orientations, approaches to study, etc.

Staff interviewed in business studies were largely agreed that students do not engage fully with their degree programmes, although explanations for this differed within departments. For one Husthwaite lecturer, part of the problem was seen to relate to the fact that university has become a 'means to an end' while in the past, she assumed, students attended because they were committed to a particular subject:

> I was shocked at how calculating they can be. I don't mean that in a nasty way but just they do work out exactly the minimum they need to do. They'll look across the different grades they need to get. What's the minimum they can get to be compensated under the credit work framework, all these sorts of things. They're extremely businesslike in their approach to it.
>
> (Husthwaite lecturer)

Like many of her colleagues, for this lecturer the trend was a direct consequence of the widening participation agenda, although not all staff agreed. Others believed that this agenda has generated a more complex picture of students' approaches to their studies:

> Again I think the younger students are probably here because they just picked a degree and they're doing the course, and I think I'd say the majority of the mature students, say over 25s, they've got a fairly clear focus of why they're here and that's that.
>
> (Bugthorpe lecturer)

A small number of academic staff took the view that course structure, the mode of assessment, but also the subject culture, are equally responsible for the inclination towards instrumentalism:

> The mere fact that they've chosen business studies as a subject would tend to indicate that their focus of attention is on career opportunities or job hunting. If you choose to study history or if you choose to study Irish Literature then you're more academically oriented towards that particular subject and so you'll tend to find that the people that choose to study business studies have pound signs in front of their eyes, they see the career in Accountancy looming, they see their career in Law looming, or they see themselves managing their own business. I think that however ... that might be what initially attracted them to the course but it's up to us then to make the academic side of the subject interesting enough to them for them to want to pursue the study of their academic theory, the foundations of course.
>
> (Weighton lecturer)

Student instrumentalism is by far the main characteristic attributed by staff to students in all three subjects, but our interviews confirm that staff do not necessarily have in mind exactly the same phenomena in using this term. Business studies academics are the only ones to suggest that this may be the result of the subject's inner identity. It is also the only subject where instrumentalism is seen overwhelmingly by staff as increasing over the three years of an undergraduate course. This appears to be corroborated by our questionnaire data, which show that business studies students' engagement with their studies (measured by indicators such as time spent reading for the course, books bought, time spent discussing the course with others, etc.) does not increase over the duration of their course, whereas in biosciences and sociology it does.

As in business studies, in sociology some lecturers, particularly in universities more open to non-traditional students, tend to associate instrumentalism with the pressure of the socio-economic environment in which students operate:

> They had a job, a part-time employment and in fact part-time employment can turn out to be quite a large number of hours. So although they are full-time students in many respects they are only here on a part-time basis and they're very much drop in, do their classes and they're off somewhere else.
>
> (Bilton lecturer)

> You know our students that have got here are shoestring and they're struggling . . . here to get this piece of paper because at the end of the day it's a way for them not to be doing the poorest paid, most insecure, awful kinds of jobs which a lot of them have or will do if they don't get degree.
>
> (Lecturer, Wilton)

In sociology, concerns over instrumentalism are specifically discussed as bound up with the issues of a possible dilution or fragmentation of the subject. We know from other recent studies (e.g. Halsey, 2004) that many sociology staff believe that there has been some decline in student quality, and around 75 per cent are concerned about an increased risk of 'fragmentation' of the subject (see also Scott, 2005). Negative implications are sometimes seen as arising from modularisation and the 'marketisation' and 'democratisation' of learning and teaching (Letherby, 2006). Interdisciplinarity is treated with circumspection by many: while working with colleagues from other fields is seen as positive for research, many sociologists believe that interdisciplinarity could become a threat to subject identity when it means broadening the spectrum of undergraduate programmes towards criminology, cultural and media studies.

On average, students in biosciences enter with higher entry qualifications than business studies or sociology students and the polarisation between elite universities and recruiting ones does not appear to generate the extent of discourses on student engagement or on widening participation that it does in sociology. In our staff interviews with bioscientists the issue of a narrow strategic instrumentalism among students is, however, touched upon in all departments and is often seen as associated with (i) the fees policy, which generates 'value for money' attitudes among students, and (ii) a college culture that perhaps fails to encourage critical thinking and a spirit of enquiry:

> I don't think our students when they first come to us are aware of how critical having a wider range of these sort of . . . I struggle to call them academic abilities, because I think they go beyond academic abilities, I think they are just life abilities, you know, the ability to notice what's going on around you to like read a newspaper. They don't read, they don't do that, they don't read at all . . . they will read if we say to them, 'Look, here are some books and some journals that you might want to access for this module' or 'Here's a really interesting website that you might want to have a look at'.
>
> (Langtoft lecturer)

In biosciences, especially in the newer universities where it tends to be taught on more specifically vocational programmes – for instance in health – concerns about instrumentalism were linked by the staff we interviewed to students' busy lives as well as the narrower professional objectives of students:

> Yes, I think there's a lot of them now who are doing the bare minimum and they are being very tactical . . . I've noticed that in the first year, for instance, in the Biochemistry module, they have three phase tests, an essay and an interpretative exercise . . . to do as their coursework. And you know, if they pass the coursework then that's the module for them. So in the very last phase test, which is the last assignment as it were, is the, is a very poor attendance

... they've done the calculations. You know, 'I've passed. It's not going to count towards my degree so I'm not even going to bother turning up', seems to be the attitude. We have tremendous problems with attendance at tutorials, at Levels 1 and 2.

(Ulleskelf lecturer)

The overall staff discourse on student intellectual engagement and attitude at work is a shared one in biosciences. Everywhere there is the same tendency among older staff to compare current students with the students of 20 or more years ago, producing the same nostalgic discourse.

How weakened is the influence of subjects?

The important issue arises of how justified are the more negative of the above staff views on student instrumentality and subject identities. The possibility, as voiced particularly by a younger business studies academic, is that many of these views may reflect a lack of understanding of the current student world:

I think the problem is when you talk to university academics, what they forget is, they were always the most engaged. They were always the brightest and the most committed in the year, and they compare current students against themselves. And they forget ... that within their own year group, you know there was ... you know you shouldn't be comparing students to yourself. Because you were a very select part of it. You were the one that was going to be, to become an academic you know. It's not the majority of students.

(Fridaythorpe lecturer)

The fact is that historically subjects never have been as powerful or significant for students as sometimes assumed. We can note, for example, research from four decades ago such as Becker *et al.*'s (1968) account in *Making the Grade* or the relatively low student commitment to subject evident in a study such as Marris' (1964) *The Experience of Higher Education* – student instrumentalism has been an ever present feature of higher education. It would seem that a good deal of over rosy nostalgia is evident among sections of older academic staff and even among some younger staff, too young to have directly experienced the assumed earlier conditions.

Certainly there are clear indications of the relatively limited subject identity of some students and obvious diversities of provision. And these are to be expected and in many respects welcomed as a demonstration of flexible provision. But this does not entirely counteract what remain of the shared career patterns and strong common professional subject identities in biosciences and sociology that feed through strongly into, albeit diversified, courses producing subject-related 'mediations' of outcomes. Such strong shared identities even allow academics to be polyvalent in their teaching: some teaching a substantial part of their time outside their area of specialism, provided that what they teach can be seen as remaining viable as 'sociology' or 'biochemistry' or whatever tribal identity is possessed by the particular academic.

The lack of a conventional disciplinary research culture in quite the strong terms that exists in biosciences and sociology makes business studies different. But here again there must be some doubt as to whether this amounts to quite the problem that business studies staff suggest. Arguably, great strengths arise from the emerging disciplinarity of business studies and its increasing association with 'communities of practice'.

The continuing importance of subjects

Whatever the recent possible attrition of the impact of subjects may be, given that students are still mainly recruited to universities via subject, the importance of subject identity and related notions of disciplinarity persists.

One indicator of the continuing importance of disciplines for students in our questionnaire survey data is seen in student reasons for entry into higher education. Among a range of reasons identified, more than 80 per cent of students in our three subjects answered: 'It was a subject that interested me' (Table 4.4).

Across all three subjects, the single most important factor in students' choice of university was their interest in the subject. This was particularly true for sociology students, where 87 per cent regarded the subject as important or very important. No other factor received anything like this level of endorsement by the sociology students. Over half the sociology students (52 per cent) also wanted to remain close to family and friends, this being less relevant to business studies (30 per cent) and biosciences students (32 per cent). For business studies students 'job prospects' was actually the most important

Table 4.4 Factors influencing university choice (percentage indicating a factor was important or very important)

	Business studies	Biosciences	Sociology
It was a subject that interested me	82	88	87
It was a subject I had done well in previously	62	72	53
The job prospects after graduation seemed good	84	61	43
The reputation of the course or institute seemed high	56	70	41
The geographical location suited me	69	52	66
The social life seemed good	54	51	37
Suitable accommodation was available	48	48	33
I felt the standards expected would not be high	16	16	13
I already knew some people here	19	16	14
It meant I did not have to move house	21	22	43
I could remain close to family and friends	30	32	52
I could obtain work while studying	33	25	39

factor, being endorsed by 84 per cent of the students as important or very important against the 82 per cent who rated subject interest the same way. Interest in the subject was the factor most frequently rated as important or very important (88 per cent) by students in biosciences for whom having done well in the subject previously was also significant (72 per cent). Seventy per cent of biosciences students also scored the reputation of the course or institute as an important factor; much higher than those doing business studies with only 56 per cent and the even lower 41 per cent for sociology students. This may reflect the fact that biosciences students were more likely to move away from home for their higher education, thus gaining a much greater choice of universities. The requirement on biosciences students to have studied related subjects prior to admission to university also probably explains the importance of 'having done well in the subject previously' for these students. Thus, for most students, while subject of study is not the only factor determining choice of university, it is nearly always one of the most important ones.

Subject benchmark statements

A further strong indicator of subject relevance arises from a consideration of the extent to which students regard a selection of 'outcomes' drawn from subject benchmark statements as capturing the outcomes of their own education in the subject area of their study. How far and in what terms do students endorse these?

We sought to capture student endorsement or otherwise of subject benchmark statements by constructing a composite of key statements drawn from the three subject areas. The results are seen in Table 4.5.

We have already indicated that for many students academic and subject identities will not necessarily emerge as a primary aspect of student identities, so we would not expect this. The high level of student endorsement visible overall stands out. However, since the questionnaire items were drawn up by combining the benchmark statements of all three subjects, the conclusion to be drawn from this is not simply an endorsement of the specific subjects but also of the more 'generic' of all three subjects. Subjects may still be important but as a means to the achievement of more generic learning outcomes rather than as ends in themselves.

Aware that over recent decades, a growing emphasis on generic and 'transferable skills' has come from national government and from industry, many staff we interviewed expressed scepticism and sometimes outright suspicion about the implications of such an emphasis for the independence and integrity of subjects (also see Holmes, 2002). However, our findings might be seen as at least a partial vindication of the emphasis and a backing for views such as Albrow's (1986) that subjects can be vehicles of generic skills in ways not necessarily in tension with subject concerns in the way some academic staff suggest.

If the overall high level of endorsement by students of the kinds of learning outcomes emphasised by subject benchmark statements stands out in Table 4.5, there are also some interesting subject-related differences. It is noteworthy, for example, that business studies

Table 4.5 Similarities and differences in student endorsement
of benchmark outcomes across the three SOMUL
disciplines (%)

Student endorsement of benchmark statements – year 3 students	Business studies	Biosciences	Sociology
A systematic understanding of key aspects of my area of study	95	99	96
The ability to deploy accurately established techniques of analysis and enquiry within my discipline	84	94	70
The ability to sustain arguments and solve problems using up-to-date ideas and techniques from my area of studies	86	87	86
An appreciation of the uncertainty, ambiguity and limits of knowledge	79	86	90
The ability to manage my own learning and to make use of scholarly reviews and primary sources	88	96	100
The capacity to communicate information and ideas, problems and solutions	91	94	98
The capacity to exercise initiative and personal responsibility	90	92	90
The ability to cite evidence and make judgements about its merits	88	90	100
The ability to recognise the ethical dimensions of research and advances in knowledge	69	85	82
A view of my subject area that is predominantly influenced by guided learning	78	86	69

Table 4.5 (continued)

Student endorsement of benchmark statements – year 3 students	Business studies	Biosciences	Sociology
A wide knowledge and understanding of a broad range of area and the detail relationships between these, and their application and importance	82	89	86
Self-awareness and a capability to operate effectively in a variety of team roles including leadership	82	65	65
The ability to access information from a variety of sources and to communicate the outcome both orally and in writing	92	96	100
The ability to plan, execute and present an independent piece of work (e.g. a project) within a supported framework in which qualities such as time management, problem solving as well as interpretation and critical awareness are evident	94	99	98
An understanding of ethical issues and the impact on society of advances in knowledge	73	85	92
The ability to record data accurately, and to carry out basic manipulation of data (including qualitative data and some statistical analysis when appropriate)	80	91	80
Well-developed strategies for updating, maintaining and enhancing my knowledge	74	89	75

students score best on 'team work' but score less well on ethical awareness compared with either biosciences or sociology students. Sociology, as might be expected, scores well on awareness of social diversity and on written communication and the ability to assess information, although – perhaps somewhat worryingly in terms of the employability of students – report less strongly on techniques of analysis.

Conclusions

Subjects remain central to the identities and concerns of academic staff. They are also clearly important to most students providing, as we have seen, the main reason for their choice of university. However, unlike their teachers, except in professional fields such as engineering or medicine, students' engagement with their subjects at university does not for the majority of them constitute a process of 'becoming' a sociologist, or historian or mathematician, etc. Or at least it does not in the sense of acquiring a professional or occupational identity. Courses are selected by students because they seem more or less interesting rather than because they necessarily provide a long-term professional future. But the study of a subject at university can also be valued as a means to a desirable end, whether this be simply the acquisition of a credential, or the acquisition of sets of employable skills and competences, or the development of a more informed and confident personality. But there may be alternative ways of achieving these same ends.

One of the main reasons for attending to the characteristics of subjects is to raise the question of the extent to which the impacts of different subjects are amenable to mediation by organisational and social factors that are the focus of other chapters of this book. Or put more crudely, universities can 'mess' with some subjects more easily than they can with others!

Quite a number of the teaching staff interviewed during the course of the SOMUL project seemed to be of the view that their subjects were in fact being 'messed with' to a greater or lesser extent. The source of this seemed to lie both with the backgrounds and expectations of the students themselves and in the imperatives of national and institutional policies. These particularly concerned goals of employability and social equity, which led to pressures to combine areas of knowledge that cut across subject boundaries, to emphasise learning outcomes that were independent of subject content, to change recruitment criteria so as to widen participation and to proliferate degree titles in order to secure greater market share.

Some would argue that a potentially more differentiated and more student-centred higher education will better serve a diversity of student and societal needs. Against this there is also the possibility of a loss of the previous benefits associated with disciplinarity and an increasingly polarised higher education, in which there is a 'pecking order' of traditional disciplinary degrees that stand above more performative- and skills-oriented courses, the latter being, in the memorable phrase coined by Alison Woolf, 'great for other people's children' (Woolf, 2002).

As a vocationally orientated subject business studies is inherently 'performative' and Mode 2-ish. A business studies programme typically integrates different disciplinary inputs. On the other hand, while offering 'scientific careers' as a strongly 'performative' vocational outcome for some of its students, our representative 'science' subject area biosciences is nevertheless characterised by continuing strong disciplinary controls, although controls that are affected by a rapidly changing knowledge base where boundaries between disciplines and sub-disciplines such as biology, biochemistry and micro-biology are continually being redrawn and different combinations of them are usually available in university curricula, often leading to different named degrees. Sociology, our representative social science subject, with a relatively strong disciplinary shape is associated with far fewer direct vocational outcomes than biosciences. It has nevertheless recently embraced new 'applied' areas such as 'crime and deviance'.

In sociology its integrity and coherence is believed by some staff to be threatened by a fragmentation of the discipline – the outcome of increasingly partial or 'standpoint' sociologies as well as student demand for more applied approaches, especially in newer institutions. However, in contrast with the fears of some of the academic staff we interviewed, we found only limited evidence of dramatic change. At the same time there appeared some manifest benefits from new course offerings in meeting student needs. This said, there still remains a shared recognisably sociological curriculum and a related sociological student experience fostered especially by shared staff orientations.

While there are clear differences between our three subject areas, there are in fact common features, which lead us to suggest that all three (and in universities of all kinds) can perhaps be described as involving – here combining Bernstein's two terms – 'subject mediated integration' alongside more traditional disciplinary control.

A 'subject mediated integration' permitting greater flexibility and responsiveness to student needs is evident in all institutions. At the same time such 'subject mediated integration' – assisted by both course design and patterns of student choice – has prevented the kind of free for all in a radically modularised, new higher education with tendencies to 'MacDonaldisation' (cf. Parker and Jary, 1995) – a situation perhaps already reached in the USA. Gibbons *et al.* (1994) regarded the massification of higher education as one pre-requisite for and correlate of an increasing presence of Mode 2 knowledge forms. These authors may have a case, but we would argue that this need not mean 'massification' with the pejorative overtones sometimes implied. The debate here has too often been wrongly presented in unhelpful over-polarised, positive and negative, either/or terms of 'old' versus 'new' and 'collection' versus 'integration' codes.

The balance between subject specific and more generic elements in student preferences and in the educational experience provided within particular degree courses is at the heart of curriculum reforms in many parts of higher education. The findings of the SOMUL study suggest that the relation between the subject-specific and the generic is perhaps less problematic and less a necessary source of major tension than is often suggested. With many students emphasising the import-ance of the generic as well as the subject-specific aspects of their higher education experience and outcomes and, as our examination of benchmarks suggests, a greater compatibility between subject and generic outcomes can be said to exist.

Thus, in one sense subjects are the 'great survivors' adapting to different institutional circumstances and student preferences. However, the mechanisms of survival can differ. In a discipline such as sociology, shared values and professional control by the subject community ensure the continued transmission of a core body of knowledge, though a body of knowledge that itself is quite adaptable to different institu-tional and student goals. The biosciences are in some ways a cluster of disciplines capable of combination in different ways to meet different needs and circumstances and sharing a number of common properties, especially in respect of epistemology and methodology. However, while 'open' to some degree within the field, the curriculum boundaries with other fields of knowledge are rather strong. Few would regard business studies as a 'discipline' at all in traditional terms. Courses in this field are intrinsically interdisciplinary but generally 'integrated' in terms of a common ideology of 'study for business'. While both sociology and biosciences courses *may* be vocational, degree courses in business studies are necessarily so. Thus, in their different ways, subjects continue to set the boundaries to what may be learned at university. But as we shall see, they do not tell the whole story.

This chapter has attempted to contribute to the further elaboration of the volume's overall portrayal of the character and outcomes of contemporary higher education as a blend of commonalities and diversities. Subjects represent experiences, knowledge and frequently values that are shared between 'members' of the subject community and which separate them from non-members. However, in all three of the contrasting subjects examined here, each appears to be sufficiently adaptable to different needs and circumstances while maintaining common properties. And differences, where they exist, do not on the whole fall into neat academic/applied dichotomies or follow simplistic distinctions of institutional status. In the terms we have introduced, a variety of 'subject mediated integration', and a variety of student orientations, can be accommodated within courses, without sharp institutional differentiation.

Later chapters enlarge on this portrayal of higher education. In Chapter 5 we explore how student orientations and student learning outcomes are further mediated by wider social as well as organisational factors. In subsequent chapters we examine how student identities and conceptions of 'self' impact on or are otherwise related to formal and informal learning outcomes.

In Chapter 3, in our typology of learning settings in higher education, we noted variations in students' engagements with higher education. In part these reflected the organisational and social characteristics of the different settings, but also differences in the orientations of individual students. In other words we can find diversity both between and within study programmes but a diversity that is mediated by the defining features of particular subjects.

In the next chapter, we extend this analysis arguing for the tenability of a diversity of student orientations that neither reflects nor requires an over-attenuated institutional diversity. Despite a national obsession with reputational differences between universities, the findings of the SOMUL project suggest that the experience of study in all categories of university can be life changing. To a large extent students construct their own worlds within higher education and meet their own needs. It perhaps was always this way. Staff concerned over student instrumentality and a lack of engagement with the subject should perhaps give greater credence and attention to the personal outcomes and generic skills that students insist they obtain.

Chapter 5

The students

Backgrounds, lifestyles and forms of engagement

Introduction

Alongside the commonalities and diversities of higher education's institutional settings and the ways in which knowledge is organised within subject-based degree courses, commonalities and diversities can also be found among the students who populate these institutions and courses. We noted two sources of student diversity in Chapter 2: diversities reflecting the backgrounds of the students (diversities 'imported' into higher education) and diversities in the lives and experiences of students once in higher education (diversities 'constructed' within higher education). In this chapter, we explore both sorts of diversity and attempt to relate them to the diversities in institutional settings and subjects examined in Chapters 3 and 4.

The chapter reports institutional and subject differences in student backgrounds and student lifestyles. It examines students' views on what they learn and their 'personal' as well as 'subject' identities and it explores the extent to which student self-narratives vary with academic contexts, including institutional 'reputation' and physical infrastructures as well as modes of curriculum organisation.

We utilise two typologies introduced earlier, the typology of learning settings used to explore differences *between* courses and/or institutions and a typology of student orientations developed by Jary and Lebeau (2009) to explore differences *within* particular courses and/or institutions. Overall our data suggest high levels of student satisfaction and positive perceptions of higher education and personal change. The data also indicate that students are approaching university learning in a variety of modes and levels of engagement and with different degrees of integration, most of which possess validity.

As seen in earlier chapters, our data from five contrasting cases in each of three subjects indicate a good deal of differentiation in terms of student social backgrounds, student orientations and student experiences. But they also point to many commonalities. Our data do not indicate quite the sharpness of the differentiation between 'traditional' and 'non-traditional' students or between 'old' and 'new' universities suggested by some commentators. Rather than the stark institutional polarisation of student conditions and experiences, or clear discontinuities with previous eras sometimes suggested as the reality of contemporary 'mass' higher education, a recognisable though not unchanging experience of UK higher education can be identified. But there are also some large differences, particularly perceptible when subjects are compared, reflecting a complex mix of perceived reputation of courses and institutions, as well as students' circumstances, life histories and orientations.

Student socio-economic backgrounds – what students bring to higher education

Table 5.1 uses national student data to summarise the main features of the student populations in biosciences, business studies and sociology.

As can be seen, the biosciences attract a greater proportion of students from a higher socio-economic background than sociology or business studies. Students in biosciences also tend to be younger, and a greater proportion of students enter university on the basis of traditional qualifications. Sociology, also broadly recruiting within the 'traditional' UK higher education intake (predominantly middle class, white, 18–20 and A levels entry qualification) has the greatest overall preponderance of female students. Business studies has a greater range of ethnic diversity, more specifically in Asian participation, which is at twice the level of the other two subject areas.

Table 5.2 presents a demographic profile for the project's 15 cases using the project's survey data.[1]

The main differences between the project's 15 cases and the national student data lie in the higher proportion of female students responding to the project's surveys and the much smaller proportion of business studies students with A levels or Scottish Highers. The latter discrepancy is likely to be largely due to the inclusion of one part-time case among the business studies programmes. While the other cases do not differ massively in terms of types of entry qualifications, there will of course be considerable differences in the grades required (as indicated in Chapter 3). It should also be reiterated here that cases were selected to offer the widest possible range of features in terms of social

Table 5.1 National subject profiles of students in biosciences, business studies and sociology (%)

| | Social economic background | | | Age | | Gender | Highest qualification | Ethnicity | |
	High	Low	Unknown	< 20	21–24	Females	A level/ Scottish Highers	Asian	White
Biosciences	65.9	24.3	9.8	91.4	4.7	57.9	91.2	5.5	86.3
Business studies	55.0	28.1	16.9	87.8	8.0	46.7	85.9	15.1	70.5
Sociology	62.1	22.8	15.0	85.3	6.4	67.3	86.0	7.1	81.8

Source: Adapted from UCAS dataset 2004. UK home students, full-time degree level study

Table 5.2 Demographic profile: the project's cases (%)

	Gender	Age		Highest qualification	Ethnicity
	Female	Mean	Standard deviation	A level/Scottish Highers	White/white other
Business studies					
Bugthorpe (C)	52.1	28.6	8.7	20.9	56.1
Husthwaite (B)	54.4	21.3	4.2	77.5	69.8
Wislow (B)	49.1	21.0	2.0	81.6	94.5
Weighton (B)	68.7	21.1	2.4	61.9	100.0
Bramham (C)	68.7	30.9	7.9	29.5	97.4
All business studies students	56.9	23.5	6.4	63.5	87.5
Biosciences					
Warthill (B)	68.4	20.9	4.9	94.7	88.2
Langtoft (A)	53.6	21.3	4.4	83.6	73.2
Ulleskelf (C)	61.4	22.7	5.3	71.8	42.0
Fridaythropre (B)	84.2	21.1	2.6	91.7	93.3
Givendale (B)	58.6	19.8	1.5	91.3	80.3
All biosciences students	66.9	21.1	3.9	85.6	76.8
Sociology					
Wilton (A)	88.9	24.4	8.4	79.4	88.9
Holme (B)	85.7	22.6	5.5	87.8	75.5
Fenton (A)	78.7	22.0	7.2	88.0	66.7
Tockerington (B)	86.7	21.4	3.6	93.3	91.3
Bilton (C)	73.9	23.5	8.8	71.6	80.7
All sociology students	**80.9**	**22.8**	**7.2**	**82.8**	**78.9**

Source: Survey data – first and final years

and organisational mediation, and that our survey data necessarily reflect these contrasts.

Using our typology of learning settings in terms of students having a shared and socially relatively homogenised (type B), shared but more socially diverse (type A), or more individualised (type C) university experience, it appears that traditional residential university experience provided by type B settings is generally accompanied by a 'traditional' student demographic profile. Type B contexts gather, for instance, a larger proportion of students from a high socio-economic background than the other types. In relation to age, reflecting their expected more typical traditional student body, type B settings also have a narrower overall age range profile, while type C have a larger stretch in overall age range profile.

Again, as expected, type B institutions have the highest proportion of students entering on the basis of traditional entry qualifications, with type C having the lowest proportion entering on this basis.

The gender profiles are also of interest. While, there is some difference in the gender balance for types A and B, these lie relatively close to the gender balance for UK higher education. But type C exhibits a large imbalance in favour of females. Clear differences are also evident in the level of ethnic diversity across the three types, with type B exhibiting markedly lower ethnic diversity than types A and C.

The 'mediating' implications of the above demographic patterns, especially socio-economic status, on student lifestyles and experiences will now be addressed and related to institutional types. However, it can be said at the outset that the idea that universities in general can be portrayed simply as a uniformly 'middle class' culture hostile to working class 'habitus' is belied by our data. Distinctive institutional values and practices within and across subjects appear to reflect a range of contextual realities in the formation of what is now commonly coined 'institutional habitus' (Reay *et al.*, 2001). It is also apparent from both the UCAS and questionnaire data that the general relationship between structures and agency is one in which structures 'enable' as well as constrain, and are also interpreted by individuals creatively (e.g. see Giddens, 1991).

Students' personal and collective higher education experiences

Turning to the lives of the students while at university, we find further evidence of both commonality and diversity across UK higher education. Using the sets of data referred to above, along with interview data, we now look at student experiences and lifestyles, including study patterns, patterns of residential accommodation, the incidence of term-time paid work and time spent socialising within and outside of university.

What we will need to consider is what is involved in 'becoming' and 'being' a student, and also what is involved in being a particular type of student. Being a student is something that must be learned. And there are alternative versions of what being a student means and contrasting opportunities to adopt the several versions available in different settings.

Student accommodation

It is widely assumed that university residential accommodation is an important factor in the student experience (Brothers and Hatch, 1971; Christie, Munro and Wager, 2005). The traditional English experience of university has been associated with living away from home and is widely perceived as a life and identity changing *rite de passage*. It is also a supporting factor in maintaining the highly stratified nature of English higher education. If students mainly attended their local institutions, the relative competitiveness for places at different universities would change dramatically.

Students who attend university without leaving home used to be in a minority in most institutions. As Holdsworth (2006: 495) in an empirical study finds: 'residential status is a key demarcating factor in how successfully students feel they adapt to being at university', reflecting 'both the practical problems faced by these students as well as difficulties in incorporating a student habitus while living at home'. Holdsworth's (2006) study indicates that students living at home less often report themselves as 'enjoying a good social life' and as taking part in extra course 'university-based activity'. What has begun to change in recent years is that in some universities such students are now in the majority.

Our data from individual interviews and focus groups confirm the significant role of shared institutional residential accommodation in forming relationships with other students in the early stages of the student experience, including relationships beyond subject or course affiliations. These relationships often prove to be enduring and the subsequent sharing of a flat or house with fellow students (more often from the same hall of residence in year 1 than from the same course) results in long lasting friendships, which interviewees stated they expected to continue beyond graduation and as such are more important for residential students in maintaining social networks than with peers from their subject group. It is clear that differences between institutions and between subjects in these respects are important social mediators of university learning.

However, our data from institutions offering limited student accommodation do not support Holdsworth's findings and suggest that while the residential pattern can be source of inequalities and 'habitus conflicts' in residential universities (feeling of exclusion of a working class student living at home in Tockerington where 80 per cent of first-year students live in halls), networking and social life also characterise the student life – albeit differently – in predominantly 'commuting' institutions.

More specifically, a clear distinction between type B and types A and C institutions is apparent from Table 5.3. Almost half of students in type B institutions compared with around a third in type C and a fifth of type A institutions reside in institutional property. In addition, compared to type A and C, students in type B are much less likely to stay in the parental home. A general distinction exists between what might be termed 'residential/living away from home' and 'commuting institutions'. This distinction has pertinence in relation to all three of our subject groups. Overall, type B settings are more likely to occur within universities that exhibit what may be considered a more traditional pattern of undergraduate accommodation, university halls or other university maintained accommodation in year 1, with a shift from institutional to shared provision in subsequent years. Living together provides opportunities for 'playing together', for spending considerable amounts of time together and for forming close relationships with other students studying a range of subjects. For students in type C settings, the largest shift is in the proportion setting up home with partners and children over the course of their studies, while for type A, there would appear to be a shift both to shared accommodation but also an increase in those returning to the family home. However, it should be noted that many type B institutions recruit more and more locally despite being predominantly 'residential', such as Holme on our sample. This is likely to impact on the student life, and in particular on the use of facilities and societies on campus.

Our survey data (Tables 5.3 and 5.4) show the shifts in residential patterns that occur between first and final years. Figures in **bold** are for first-year students; those in *italics* are the final year. The differences between types of setting are dramatic. For the students who find their way into a type B setting, around 70 per cent will be in halls of residence in the first year and in shared accommodation with friends in later years. Changes are less dramatic for students in type C settings but there is a move away from halls and parents to sharing with friends or living with a partner in later years. In type A settings, there appear to be drops in the proportions in halls and increases in proportions in private accommodation with friends or parents. Another way of looking at the data in Table 5.6 is in terms of the amount of time likely to be spent with other university students as a result of shared accommodation. In year 1, the proportions of students 'living with' other students are 43.5 per cent in type A settings, 78.9 per cent in type B and 28.3 per cent in type C. The equivalent figures for later years of their courses are 46.4 per cent, 77.7 per cent and 26.3 per cent.

The complexity of the underlying patterns is further seen in Table 5.4, which provides case-by-case details of student accommodation and by subject group. Seven of the cases may be said to reflect a traditional experience as indicated by at least three out of five (and in some cases at least four out of five) students spending first year in 'halls' or other institutional accommodation. The patterns are largely independent of the subject studied. (The very low proportions of Bramham students in institution-maintained accommodation reflects the part-time nature of this study programme.) What these figures of residential patterns indicate are the diversity of students in the different case studies in terms of factors such as stage in the life course (e.g. living with parents or partners), living away from home (and leaving old friends and making new ones), 'independent' or 'dependent', continuity or discontinuity with life before university. The residence patterns tell us much more than where students live.

The significance of first-year residential accommodation in halls of residence is seen in the following remarks from students:

> And it was very good and I enjoyed it very much and it helped me settle in. Meeting people and making a few friends . . . and getting used to everything, and because there is a lot to think about, you know, you don't need the stress of thinking about your bills and how to get into uni in the morning and all that.
>
> (Warthill, female)

Table 5.3 Student residence (percentage of students in different types of accommodation)

Where are you living?	Type A		Type B		Type C		Sociology		Business studies		Biosciences	
Halls or other university accommodation	**25.7**	*10.7*	**69.0**	*7.7*	**18.2**	*7.2*	**31.2**	*14.0*	**56.1**	*5.6*	**56.6**	*10.2*
Alone in private accommodation	**4.0**	*3.6*	**3.6**	*2.8*	**6.1**	*6.8*	**2.6**	*3.2*	**5.1**	*4.4*	**4.4**	*3.8*
Private accommodation with friends or students	**17.8**	*35.7*	**9.9**	*70.0*	**10.1**	*19.1*	**13.0**	*43.0*	**10.3**	*49.4*	**11.1**	*66.2*
Private with parents/relatives	**36.6**	*42.9*	**14.6**	*14.8*	**41.2**	*31.8*	**38.3**	*26.9*	**17.8**	*22.5*	**22.1**	*14.6*
Private with partner/children	**15.8**	*7.1*	**2.9**	*4.7*	**24.3**	*35.2*	**14.9**	*5.1*	**10.7**	*18.1*	**5.8**	*5.1*

Source: Survey returns: first and final years. Figures in **bold** are for first-year students only, figures in *italics* are for second and subsequent years

Table 5.4 Student residence patterns across the 15 cases (%)

	Institution maintained		Own home		With friends or other students		Parental/ guardian home		With partner or children	
	First	Final	First	Final	First	Final	First	Final	First	Final
Business studies										
Bugthorpe (C)	30.0	3.8	10.0	7.7	10.0	11.5	10.0	42.3	40.0	34.6
Husthwaite (B)	77.1	10.5	2.1	10.5	4.2	31.6	14.6	18.4	2.1	13.2
Wislow (B)	65.7	0.0	4.4	0.0	14.6	50.0	13.1	43.8	2.1	6.2
Weighton (B)	32.4	0.0	8.8	0.0	8.8	55.6	44.1	33.3	5.9	3.7
Bramham (C)	4.2	8.7	8.3	8.7	0.0	6.5	16.7	23.9	70.8	60.9
Biosciences										
Warthill (B)	87.1	24.4	3.2	6.8	0.0	60.6	6.5	4.1	3.2	4.1
Langtoft (A)	25.7	0.0	2.9	0.0	37.1	75.0	28.6	25.0	5.7	0.0
Ulleskelf (C)	11.8	0.0	9.8	100.0	5.9	0.0	54.9	0.0	17.6	0.0
Fridaythorpre (B)	76.3	0.0	0.0	0.0	2.6	86.2	21.1	10.3	0.0	3.4
Givendale (B)	80.3	0.0	4.2	0.0	11.3	93.3	2.8	6.7	1.4	0.0
Sociology										
Wilton (A)	25.0	0.0	0.0	0.0	16.7	100.0	33.3	0.0	25.0	0.0
Holme (B)	60.0	41.7	0.0	8.3	13.3	25.0	13.3	16.7	13.3	8.3
Fenton (A)	16.7	11.8	2.1	5.9	18.8	41.2	54.2	23.5	8.3	17.6
Tockerington (B)	84.6	12.1	0.0	5.0	15.4	78.4	0.0	4.5	0.0	0.0
Bilton (C)	25.8	0.0	4.5	0.0	7.6	100.0	40.9	0.0	21.2	0.0

> I think it's the best type of place to be in your first year. Yes, a lot of my friends now are from there. I live with people who lived there and I'd say it was the best way to have met them that way.
>
> (Langtoft, male)

Relationships made in first-year residence often carry over into subsequent years:

> Well, first year, most of my friends were in OTC and in halls but then in halls you're in like a corridor with friendly people, so you basically know everyone. Then second year, I was in a house of nine, so I still had quite a lot of housemates and loads of friends from OTC and then joining the canoe clubs I had that as well and started making friends with all my course mates as well and now it's pretty much the same.
>
> (Givendale, female)

As suggested earlier, staying in halls in year 1 can be regarded as 'normal' at some universities, to such an extent that commuting students may perceive themselves as different and disadvantaged, as 'other', but overall, commuting students were prompter to mention travelling time, family commitments, finances and their possible impact on their studies, as factors affecting their student experience positively or negatively:

> You have to be a lot more self-disciplined with living at home because there's so many distractions, you can cut yourself off if you're in a student house into your room and do your work and at home you've got everyone around you wanting, wanting to talk.
>
> (Langtoft, female)

> I live at home, it's hard because I have to leave the house at half seven and I get here for nine o clock, so like it is quite hard. But then if I lived out I know I'd be in debt, and I'd rather stay away from the debt.
>
> (Ulleskelf, male)

> I was like if I don't do studying now I won't do it when I get home because I'll be absolutely shattered. So I made sure I did it on the train and I stayed late in the library and I did loads of extra work. I got so much better grades doing that than when I lived in halls.
>
> (Langtoft, female)

Other students, however, are positive about commuting:

> I say 'okay 7 o'clock this evening I'm going to be on the computer, no disturbance please'. I'll be in the front room, on my laptop, on the internet, doing my research, doing my work, getting my job done. And then about three or four hours later my wife will probably come in and bring me a coffee and say 'take a break now'.
>
> (Ulleskelf, male)

What seems particularly significant in a context of regionalisation of the catchment area of most universities is the impact of the dominant accommodation pattern. A diversity of accommodation options chosen in year 1 (as in most type A cases in our sample but also increasingly in 'residential universities') inevitably leads to more individualised options in years 2 and 3. By contrast, where the dominant university-maintained residential pattern prevails in year 1, shared rented accommodation in years 2 and 3 appears to be the dominant pattern. Different universities valorise different versions of a 'normal' student experience. For many, the traditional pattern of residential accommodation in year 1 and shared private accommodation with other students in years 2 and 3 provides the archetypal 'total student experience' with the university as the centre of student life. 'Being a student' in a broadly similar way to everybody else in these respects may become important to students. Other things being equal, students who do not fit with this pattern can potentially suffer by obviously being different and standing outside the mainstream of university life. There is less opportunity to 'learn from each other'. This can be a source of difficulties for a growing number of students experiencing a predominantly commuting student life at traditional institutions.

Even within institutions in which commuting is a well-established pattern, living at home is also a source of potential difficulties, but most of these are actually related to the fact that students living at home are more likely to be from lower status homes and less often have fathers with professional and managerial jobs (Holdsworth, 2006: 497). Managing two different worlds may be a source of extra tensions. The routines associated with becoming and being a student are rendered uncertain. Students become differentiated by and from other students on the basis of living at home. In the longer run, leaving home may also be important in generating 'cultural capital', leading to greater cultural adaptability and enhanced employability.

On the other hand, this should not distract from the fact that a majority of commuting students do cope and that these students – retaining old friendship networks and perhaps with domestic responsibilities – sometimes simply do not want the traditional student experience, as our later analysis of student identities will show, preferring a more focused academic or a more 'instrumental' relation with the university. Responding to Bourdieu and Wacquant's (1992: 127) assertion that middle class students, possessing the right kind of cultural capital, enter 'a social world', of which they are a product, 'like a "fish in water"', Holdsworth (2006: 506) notes that all students have to work to fit in, to making new friends. A 'strategic, active habitus' is necessary.

We should also note, however, that some of the learning settings provided by the project's cases have so few students living together that the 'commuting' outsiders constitute the vast majority (for example, at Langtoft or Bugthorpe). At these institutions, such students are not 'missing out' on some fuller version of student life enjoyed by their peers. It seems no longer legitimate to regard such students and the institutions they attend as 'deviant' and 'inferior' cases. As we shall see in subsequent chapters, learning opportunities and achievements occur in all sorts of settings. Differences do not have to be ranked to imply a stratified higher education experience, though there may be pressures to do so.

Study patterns

Further aspects of the student experience are class contact time, study patterns, socialising and paid term-time employment. A survey undertaken for the Higher Education Policy Institute (HEPI) in 2006 (Bekhradnia, Whitnall and Sastry) provided national data on the time students devote to study. It revealed large differences between individual subjects and between different universities offering the same subject. For the three subject areas that are the focus here, the HEPI report indicated total median study hours per week of 25.4 in the biological sciences, 22 hours for social studies, and 21 hours for business studies. However, these overarching subject figures disguised very significant institutional differences within subjects. Thus, biological studies courses varied from mean hours per week of 43.7 hours down to 19.1 hours, business studies from 26.6 down to 17.1 and social studies from 33.4 hours to 17.8 hours. And, of course, the hours spent by individual students would vary as well.

The SOMUL survey data on self-reported time spent in personal studying and coursework, for both first years and final years combined, broadly parallel the HEPI patterns of subject group and institutional differences (Figure 5.1). Distinct subject differences and also clear differences within subjects are evident. Biosciences have by far the greatest self-reported contact time, although there are differences between cases. In addition, wide differences in individual patterns were also evident in our students' interviews. A weak positive correlation existed between the overall amount of self-reported contact time and the amount of self-reported study time: the greater the contact time, the greater the amount of private study and conversely the lower the contact hours the lower the amount of such study.[2]

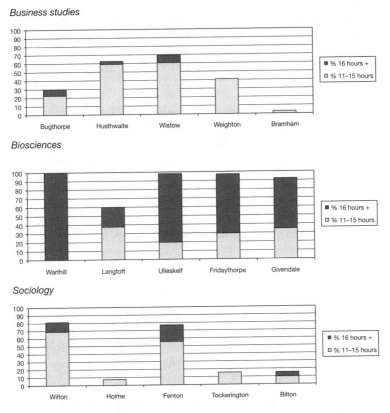

Figure 5.1 Student contact hours; subject comparison of percentages between 11–15 hours and 16+ hours

As can be seen from Figure 5.1, study contact hours tend to be higher in biosciences courses. With the exception of Langtoft, close on 100 per cent of students have more than 11 hours per week of study contact and most have over 16 hours. The laboratory-based nature of this subject area is probably largely responsible. For both business studies and sociology, differences between individual institutional cases are substantial but there are few students having 16 hours or more contact time in these subjects. Thus, we can conclude that biosciences students tend to spend more time with each other than do business and sociology students. The business and sociology students, in contrast, have more flexibility and more opportunity to combine study with other, non-student activities. However, it must be recognised that most students devote considerable additional hours to their studies and definitions of study and non-study time are not always clear-cut.

The following comments from students illustrate something of the nuances of their real world concerns and anxieties in relation to study time. Some students recognised the complexities of definition and hoped to improve what they saw as the inadequacies of their own levels of engagement:

> Does that include staring out of the window? Usually about three hours if I can. Three hours a night, it's not much, I need to do more, and I'm trying to increase it now.
>
> (Warthill, male)

> There's no day this term that we've had completely off and I don't think there was any days that we had completely off last term either. Actually occasionally we did get Wednesdays off last term. In the second year we usually had one day off a week.
>
> (Warthill, female)

> The first semester we had I'd say a lot of free time. We probably only had about 15 hours a week. And I was surprised at that. But we have had more practicals this semester and more seminars and more lectures. So it's probably some weeks been about 25 hours.
>
> (Fridaythorpe, female)

> I go through phases of being really good, you know, coming home and reading my notes and reading extra bits in textbooks and stuff and then it sort of, you know, goes by the wayside again, you know, I forget.
>
> (Givendale, female)

At the opposite end, there were students who said, for example:

> In my second year, I completely drowned myself in work, at the library every day after lectures and then until ten o'clock at night before going home. And I made myself ill doing that.
>
> (Warthill, female)

As well as hours of study our SOMUL data also allowed us to explore wider aspects of patterns of study. Under the rubric of 'learning communities', initiatives that seek to develop a shared experience for students on similar programmes, are now an accepted part of institutional provision at many institutions in the United States (Goodsell and Tinto, 1994; Shapiro and Levine, 1999). Our examination of module patterns suggests that where students spend a lot of time either in class or in socialising with the same groups of fellow students, this enhances opportunities for a shared rather than atomised experience. The presence of a 'common core' as especially in biosciences, where students study all their modules together, provides greater opportunity for bonding and getting to know fellow students. Furthermore, this shared experience of class contact does not disappear in later years. In biosciences especially there is often also considerable crossover between different named degree programmes and thus students from a number of different single honours programmes may continue to 'share' a number of modules. A further aspect for biosciences courses is the amount of time spent in laboratory work. Not only does this add to the total number of study hours experienced by students, but these are generally quite interactive and sociable hours. These are times when students get to know each other, when relationships, which may continue beyond the doors of the laboratory, develop. Business studies and sociology courses generally have no direct equivalent.

It is worth observing that student contact hours are a function of two things. The first is the number of teaching hours that the university makes available to them, i.e. the students' timetable. The second is the number of hours that students choose to turn up for! The latter is a function of many things, not least the other things that are going on in the lives of the students, their commitments outside of university as well as their activities (both work and recreational) within it. One important aspect of this is the time students spend in paid employment during term time.

Paid employment

Table 5.5 reports student responses to the question of whether or not they had taken up paid employment during their time at university. There is a clear association between subject and the amount of term-time part-time work – with business studies students generally reporting more hours than sociology students who generally report more hours than biosciences students. However, in addition to differences between subjects, there are also differences within subjects.

Table 5.5 Regular term-time paid employment (excluding work placements) (%)

	Business studies	*Biosciences*	*Sociology*
First year	49.4	36.6	46.1
Final year	62.4	33.3	55.4

Figures 5.2 (a), (b) and (c) report hours of part-time work in the different institutional cases. The presence of the part-time cohort in business studies may go some way in explaining the relatively high proportion working more than 16 hours per week. It is also evident that fewer students in more selective and residential institutions undertake paid work than at recruiting and commuting institutions. The proportions of working students are lower in biosciences and decrease from first to final years, possibly reflecting the demands of final-year projects.

To convey something of the general context of term-time part-time work, it is useful to examine some of the comments contained in interview transcripts. Part-time work can mean many different things. Here are a few illustrations from biosciences students:

> I work every Saturday and Monday in a little shop back home. So my weeks, at the moment, are working on a Monday and then driving back down here Monday night. Uni Tuesday, Thursday, Friday. Drive home Friday, work Saturday and Sunday and Wednesday are supposed to be my days off but because I get one day off here and one at home it's . . . I'm never kind of relaxed or anything because when I get back down here, because it's quite late on a Monday usually, I've got lectures in the morning so I've got to make sure that I've done all my work for my lectures . . . even

(a)

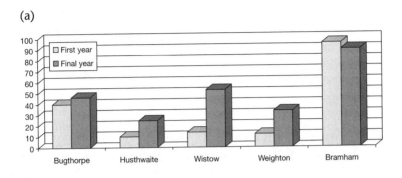

(b)

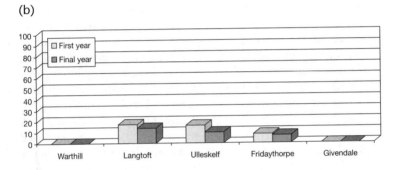

(c)

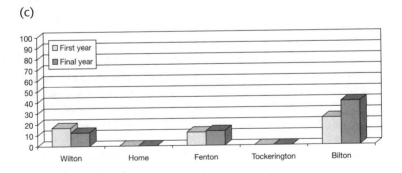

Figure 5.2 Percentages of students doing 16+ hours of paid employment per week, first year and final year: (a) business studies; (b) biosciences; (c) sociology

though I drive home, it's not always convenient to take all my books with me. So I spend the week really just getting back into routine, doing all my work, and then go home at the weekend and just . . . usually my day is preparing to come back down.

(Ulleskelf, female)

I'm a bus driver now. I'm driving for seven hours on a Saturday after a very long Friday afternoon. And by the time I get back on a Saturday night it is about nine o'clock and I'm completely wiped out. Come Monday I'm not even fully recharged and I'm back in again. So I'm more or less constantly tired . . . it's much easier for a full-time worker without doing education, to be honest. I mean for a person like me who's going to have to support a wife, a child and the parents, although they're pensioners, as well as I've still got to support my child and my wife and myself . . . [A]s soon as the lectures and the exams are finished, I'm working five days a week/six days a week, and maybe even looking for overtime, even on a Sunday so that I can get as much money in during those four/five months. So I can have, I can have a relaxed four or five months into studying. I mean I've already said this to my boss, I said 'look my study comes first, either you give me just the Saturday work and Sunday work otherwise I'll just pack it in, I don't care'. Because I've worked so hard getting so far. And I'm not going to pack it in just over a bus driver's job. Working for £6 an hour. It's not worth it.

(Ulleskelf, male)

My dad's widowed and so I'm on like maximum loan and I pay for my rent as well . . . I only have £800 left over of that loan, so all throughout my university career, I've had a job and working like two nights a week . . . and that . . . money doesn't go that far. So I've not been able to do as much of the partying as other people have and I haven't been able to go out because I've been working. I've recently finished that . . . I haven't got a lot of money but it's the time issue obviously. So I'm living on the breadline just to finish . . . I quite enjoyed my job. I really enjoyed my job, but it just means that it's been a worry sometimes like. So I have applied for the hardship fund and I can imagine that I'll have to do it again at the end of March and I have been successful and I did get help, but it's one of the things that that's a big worry is money and . . . it's jeopardising what you're thinking about in the day.

(Fridaythorpe, female)

Of course, not all students need or want to work during term time – and this applies to students across institutions. Some are concerned about the effect on their degree, for others parental support is provided. In addition, there are those who choose to work only during the vacation times, especially summer, to help support them the following year, or pay off debts accrued the previous year. Again some illustrations from biosciences students:

> I've never considered working. Even at home I didn't have part-time jobs. I'm not sure how I'd balance it anyway.
>
> (Warthill, female)

> My parents paid . . . for my tuition and my accommodation. And then . . . I live off the student loan. But there's one condition that I don't work. I can't get a job during term time because I am a student. That is my job.
>
> (Fridaythorpe, female)

> I probably should have done at some point, or I could have done, but I chose not to . . . I don't particularly need to work because I get an allowance and the loan.
>
> (Warthill, female)

> I tried to work at the beginning of the semester. I had a job in a club at the weekends and a part time in a shop that it had carried on from the summer. But there was a lot of pressure to do extra hours . . . and I couldn't cope with it. So I just got rid of them both, it's my final year and I'm not, not messing it up.
>
> (Langtoft, female)

> I worked last year . . . that affected my uni work quite a lot. So I'm not working this year . . . I'm not really that much more skint, because my dad's started giving me a weekly allowance which I didn't get last year.
>
> (Fridaythorpe, female)

One student succeeded in negotiating more parental support after the improvement in performance when she stopped her term-time job:

> I was working in B&Q for a while as well. So I was doing all that and socialising . . . till February and I started off doing 20 hours

and then cut down to 16 I think . . . that was during term time . . . they were okay in that I gave them the dates of my exams . . . and booked a holiday out of my holiday allowance, so that I could revise on a Saturday and Sunday before the first exams. I quit in February as a sort of an experiment to show my dad, that if I didn't work and had more time I could get better grades and it worked thank God.

(Givendale, female)

And another Givendale student questioned the real value of term-time work after trying it in first year and had decided to concentrate on their studies:

I've tried to avoid that because it's quite an intensive full-time course. I tried to get some work at the start of the first year . . . but I just couldn't actually fit the time in with the full-time course . . . Because a lot of the time, like the work during term time and stuff, you kind of, because it's only a couple of hours here and there, you spend more time travelling there and from there. So the actual time or money you get from it, isn't that great.

(Givendale, male)

What these comments from students reflect is the diversity of experiences and the diversity of meanings associated with term-time work. We also found examples of students who suggest that they undertake paid work partly because work experience may be a significant element for their CV.

For all the indications that paid term-time work is a function of financial strains and would not be a preferred option without this, the evidence that it invariably detracts from study outcomes is not as strong as sometimes assumed. There is, for example, evidence that students spend more time in leisure activities such as watching television than they do in undertaking paid work.

A subject perspective on integration and engagement

As well as differences related to social background and to the organisational and social setting in which their higher education takes place, students of course differ as individuals, possessing their own distinctive plans and orientations and their lifestyle and engagement also differs according to the subject they study and related expectations.

In Chapter 3, we introduced an eight-fold typology of student orientations developed by Jary and Lebeau (2009) to explore differences in attitudes and experience within a specific subject, beyond contrasted institutional contexts. Based on a framework devised by Francois Dubet (1994), this typology was built on student interviews collected in the five sociology cases in the study. Here we offer a brief outline of key findings from this typology in order to suggest the potential strength of the subject or the course that students take in the shaping of their identity and experience.

The typology is constructed around three variables (personal project, integration, vocation or engagement) presented by Dubet as central to understand individual ways of being as student in mass higher education systems. The eight types of student experience – identified across our sociology sites – result from a combination of these dimensions.

Type 1 (Project +, Engagement +, Integration +) represents the traditional 'ideal' student though perhaps not the most representative today – characterised by a clear project as well as subject engagement and involvement in student activities. Although an orientation of this type is by no means predetermined by institutional and organisational mediations, institutional structures may facilitate the orientation, for example: 'spatial markers' (self-contained campus, departmental common room, departmental library, sociology society, etc.) may support strong identification with the university; social and education

Table 5.6 SOMUL typology of student orientations – sociology

	Vocation (Engagement) +	Vocation (Engagement) +	Vocation (Engagement) −	Vocation (Engagement) −
Project +	1 The archetypical student	2 The engaged non-traditional experience	3 One form of strategic engagement	4 Second form of strategic engagement
Project −	5 Open-minded engagement	6 Detached engagement	7 Brand seeking orientation	8 A case of anomy
	Integration +	Integration −	Integration +	Integration −

Source: From Jary and Lebeau, 2009

backgrounds (e.g. with good A levels and graduate parents) may give confidence and clarity about personal objectives; institutional and subject reputation may attract students with particular forms of cultural capital. We might also expect students of this type to exhibit 'deep' rather than 'surface' approaches to learning and to endorse strongly the subject benchmarks set for sociology.

Type 2 (*Project* +, *Engagement* +, *Integration* –) was found to reflect the experiences of many mature students in our sample. They may be similar to type 1 students in the relatively high levels of subject engagement and in the clarity of the personal project (e.g. to change status or job) but will frequently have much lower levels of integration with their courses and university (due to family commitments, etc.). Where such students socialise at university it is usually with other mature students. But for many, university life might be relatively isolated.

Types 3 and *4* refer to behaviours of strategic engagement (*Project* +, *Engagement* –, *Integration* + or –) of students with low subject engagement who reported strategies regarding their choice of programme in relation to expected future prospects, including employment. Such students have a clear particular or general professional project, but express relatively limited personal interest in the subject.

Institutional and curriculum organisation appear to be relevant factors, where relatively low subject engagement (type 3) and also weak integration (type 4) may be influenced by a more open modular curriculum organisation (i.e. weaker 'classification' and 'framing' with more choice and hence more variation available to students). In both of the examples provided above, students were studying sociology as one part of a joint degree, with a consequent possible dilution of the strength of subject identity.

Type 5 (*Project* –, *Engagement* +, *Integration* +) consists of students who are engaged with their subject or subjects and are integrated into their departments and/or institutions but where a definite 'personal project' is less in evidence. We found some resemblance (particularly in the character of the confident intellectual engagement with the course and in a drawing on pre-existing cultural capital) between this type and the stereotype of the 'bourgeois' student in Bourdieu's *Inheritors* (Bourdieu and Passeron, 1979).

Type 6 (*Project* –, *Engagement* +, *Integration* –) offers a similar profile of high engagement but the relatively low levels of integration mark this off from type 5. This pattern also characterises those mature students (for example at Wilton, and Bilton) who are doing sociology for the sake of studying, who are really enjoying the subject but who cannot become more integrated because of external constraints or because the age difference operates (they say) as an excluding factor.

Type 7 (Project –, Engagement –, Integration +) characterises a particular 'elite' form of instrumental orientation, associated with admission to a 'high reputation' university. The 'personal project' is not greatly emphasised, though implicitly there may be a high valuation of the social capital to be acquired through the contacts made at such institutions. There is little pronounced engagement with the subject. The orientation is illustrated by many Tockerington students who systematically minimise the role of the subject in their student lives and in their careers.

Type 8 (Project –, Engagement –, Integration –) is the polar opposite to type 1, which Dubet presents as an 'extreme' manifestation of a mass higher education system and is associated with a 'depressive' student experience – students who may have made a 'wrong' choice, enrolled on courses with high drop out rates, exhibiting low integration because of socio-cultural barriers.

Unsurprisingly, we have no direct illustration of this orientation from our interviews. Such students are less likely to respond to questionnaires or to present themselves for face-to-face interviews. However, the existence of anomic disengagement as a student orientation was mentioned in our interviews and feedback sessions with academic and support staff so its absence in our data should not be taken to imply its absence in reality.

Using our adapted version of Dubet's tri-dimensional conceptualisation of student experience and engagement suggests that a range of factors generate potentially contrasted ways of being students within the same subject and sometimes within the same institution. We have not carried out a similar analysis to that for sociology of our other two subjects but in line with our discussion in Chapter 4 we would expect to find stronger personal projects in biosciences and business studies, and somewhat greater integration for biosciences where class contact hours are higher. However, we would also expect to find the same overall range of student orientations across institutions and subjects.

The eight types can be regarded as conceptual spaces over which students' orientations range, such that a differentiation of student orientations and experiences exists – including changes over time – that is in part related to the institutional differences and variations in curriculum type that are central in our focus on 'social and organisational mediation'. It may also be related to differences in social backgrounds and lifestyles among students while at university. In other words, some student orientations may be partly a product of an interaction between the settings in which they study and the social and cultural capital that they bring to that study. Thus a type 1 orientation is more likely to be found in traditional 'selecting' rather than 'recruiting' universities and in what we have previously termed type B learning settings; types 2 to 4 are more commonly found in type A and C settings. However, while in part related to institutional characteristics, examples of our student types are found to occur across all institutional types, though their consequences may differ in different types of learning setting. It is also suggested that, with the exception of type 8, each of the student orientations can be regarded as an entirely tenable way of accessing and experiencing higher education. As we have seen, students are largely positive about their experiences and the outcomes of higher education. Endorsement of generic elements in subject benchmark statements by students in responses to our questionnaires (see Chapter 4) suggest generally high levels of student satisfaction across the eight types.

Across the project as a whole, we do not dismiss outright the views of a significant number of academic staff we interviewed that there is a declining commitment among students (and also therefore greater challenges in teaching – see Letherby, 2006). However, the generality of our research findings – the student rather than the staff voices we report – does not support a strong picture of low commitment to study or unsatisfactory outcomes. Academic staff or 'faculty' seem eternally to have voiced regret that student orientations and aspirations are different from their own. However, comparisons with the findings of earlier studies (e.g. Marris, 1964, as well as Becker et al., 1968) do not support assumptions about an earlier 'golden age' when student orientations were markedly different from the range to be found today.

Conclusions

As discussed in earlier chapters of this book, UK higher education is characterised by considerable diversity, both in terms of the types of universities and in terms of the types of subjects and courses taught in them. And as this chapter has shown, it is also characterised by considerable diversity among its students.

It is a commonplace to see these diversities in terms of hierarchies, of 'top students' being recruited to 'top universities' and thereon to 'top positions' in business and the organs of the state. It is a viewpoint that rests on a notion of 'meritocracy', that those who are advantaged deserve those advantages by virtue of their superior learning, knowledge and skills. Against this is the 'problem' of the differential recruitment to universities according to social background with higher education performing a 'status confirmation' function (Brown and Scase, 1994). And certainly, the skewed patterns of recruitment reflect the fact that many of the country's most prestigious institutions are under recruiters of 'non-traditional' students. Our data confirm the continuing significance of social background – of class and ethnicity – in influencing the recruitment to courses but they do not indicate the sharpness of differentiation between 'traditional' and 'non-traditional' students suggested by some commentators. The SOMUL data from five contrasting departments in each of three subjects show that to some extent a differentiation of student orientations and experiences exists between and within institutions, including variations in curriculum type, but also that a good deal of overlap and commonalities between institutions occurs.

Undoubtedly students are faced with difficult choices: do they choose the social standing and so-called 'academic excellence' of certain high prestige 'traditional' universities? or do they prefer the more culturally congenial, more geographically convenient, cheaper, perhaps 'safer' location? It has of course to be acknowledged that many students have little choice in the matter. They enter the 'best' places that their entry grades give them access to.

The widening of access to elite universities is a legitimate continuing goal of higher education policy. However, rather than an automatic assumption that such entry is a best option for all students, there is an issue of whether such a policy emphasis risks devaluing what other higher education institutions have to offer. The culture and habitus of such institutions may better fit the needs of some students, providing an option that may also be perceived as involving less financial and cultural risk. This said, non-traditional students also need to take into account the undoubted advantages in terms of the cultural and social capital accruing from attendance at elite institutions. Given these dilemmas, there is a good deal to be said for not encouraging any increased – more polarised – differentiation of institutions, and for preserving existing continuing commonalities across courses, subjects and institutions.

Our data indicate that, despite all the issues, students mostly cope! Our SOMUL and other data suggest generally high levels of student satisfaction and positive perceptions of higher education and the personal changes with which it is associated. Our data also suggest that students are approaching university learning in a variety of styles and levels of engagement and with different degrees of integration, but that most of these have viability. There are differences between universities and there are differences to be found within them. The central question of the SOMUL project concerns the extent to which these differences in context and process are associated with different outcomes of learning. It is this question to which we now turn in Chapters 6 and 7.

Notes

1 It should be noted that response rates varied from site to site so there can be no assumption of representativeness in our samples. In relation to gender, for biosciences the percentage of females is larger in the survey than the HESA data, and there are smaller gender differences between the type A, B and C cases in the survey than for the HESA data. It is apparent that business studies respondents and students in type C are less likely to have entered on the basis of traditional qualifications than suggested from the HESA data. Also the survey data suggest somewhat less ethnic diversity, both by subject and type, than would be expected from the HESA data. Such differences must be taken into account in interpreting our data.

2 Langtoft, one of the type 'A' cases, includes a part-time cohorts and the relationship between study and contact may be expected to differ from the patterns exhibited by full-time cohorts. When only Langtoft responses are analysed, a significant positive correlation of a similar magnitude was observed.

Chapter 6

What students learned at university

The previous three chapters have considered the diversity of the student experience of higher education in terms of the contexts provided by different university settings and different fields of study and in terms of differences between students in respect of their backgrounds, lifestyles and orientations to higher education. Now we move on to the question of 'what was learned' and the extent to which there were differences in the outcomes of learning according to differences in contexts of study and types of student. In the present chapter, we utilise some established theories of learning in higher education and the research instruments, which have been developed as part of them, in order to pose questions of 'what was learned' that in principle cut across differences in subject content. Of course, the students learned more or less substantive knowledge of bioscience, business studies and sociology but this learning can also be conceptualised in more general terms of cognitive development. This is the approach adopted here, one which we believe is particularly appropriate given the 'generalist' traditions of higher education in the UK and the generally looser relationship between the subject studied and future career discussed in Chapter 1.

This chapter, therefore, outlines the key concepts used in the questionnaire surveys of the SOMUL project: students' conceptions of learning; their approaches to studying; their personal and educational development; and their broader views of personal change while at university. It begins by describing the research background to each of these concepts of 'what is learned at university' and presents a heuristic model to link them together into a holistic view of students' cognitive development. The account of the quantitative analyses and results will be deliberately informal for the sake of readability. A more formal account of the analyses and results has been published elsewhere (Edmunds and Richardson, 2009).

The data from the SOMUL project can be looked at from three different viewpoints. First, we have evidence about the relationships among the different measures. Second, we have evidence about the relative importance of a student's subject of study and department as predictors of their conceptions of learning, their approaches to studying, their personal development and their personal change. Third, the SOMUL project obtained responses from two cohorts of students at two different times in their experience of higher education, from first-year students to final-year students and then to alumni. It is therefore of interest to ask whether there are significant changes across this period in students' self-reported conceptions of learning, approaches to studying, personal development and personal change.

Conceptions of learning

Much research on the conceptions of learning that are held by students in higher education has been based on the analysis of interview transcripts following the general principles of phenomenography. This is 'a research method for mapping the qualitatively different ways in which people experience, conceptualise, perceive, and understand various aspects of, and phenomena in, the world around them' (Marton, 1986: 31; see also Marton, 1994). Säljö (1979: 19) asked 90 people aged between 17 and 73 at educational institutions in Sweden what 'learning' meant to them. He found five different conceptions of learning:

1   Learning as the increase of knowledge.
2   Learning as memorising.
3   Learning as the acquisition of facts, procedures, etc., which can be retained and/or utilised in practice.
4   Learning as the abstraction of meaning.
5   Learning as an interpretative process aimed at the understanding of reality.

Säljö described Conceptions 1–3 as 'reproductive' conceptions of learning, and he described Conceptions 4 and 5 as 'reconstructive' conceptions of learning.

Martin and Ramsden (1987) used Säljö's scheme to classify 60 first-year history students at two universities in the United Kingdom. Their conceptions of learning were distributed between Conceptions 2 and 5 but were concentrated in Conceptions 3 and 4. (No student exhibited Conception 1.) Nevertheless, there was a direct relationship between the students' conceptions of learning and their academic performance at the end of the year: those students who achieved the lowest grades all exhibited Säljö's Conceptions 2 or 3, whereas those students who achieved the best grades all exhibited Säljö's Conceptions 4 or 5. In other words, students' conceptions of learning are linked to their academic attainment.

To investigate conceptions of learning in large samples of students, it would clearly be useful to employ some quantitative instrument that could be efficiently administered and scored. Vermunt and van Rijswijk (1988) devised the Inventory of Learning Styles (ILS), a questionnaire containing 144 items in 16 subscales. The first section was concerned with the study activities that were involved in the processing of course content and the regulation of learning, and the second section was concerned with study orientations and conceptions of learning. The latter included five subscales measuring different conceptions of learning: Construction of Knowledge, Intake of Knowledge, Use of Knowledge, Stimulating Education and Co-operative Learning. Vermunt (1998) developed a revised version of the ILS that included the same five subscales, except that the latter were described as 'mental models' of learning rather than as conceptions of learning.

Vermetten, Vermunt and Lodewijks (1999) selected 50 items from the ILS concerned with processing or regulation activities and 50 items concerned with mental models or study orientations. They gave this instrument to 276 students at a university in the Netherlands at the end of their first and third semesters. The test–retest reliability of the subscales was good, but there was only one significant change between the first semester and the third semester across the five subscales that measured mental models: the students showed a significant (though fairly modest) decline in their scores on intake of knowledge. This suggests that the experience of higher education may have little impact on students' conceptions of learning.

Richardson (2007a) obtained an English translation of the mental models section of the ILS and used it in a survey of students who were taking courses by distance learning with the UK Open University. He found that the five subscales were both homogeneous and reliable, but that the subscales concerned with Construction of Knowledge and Stimulating Education could not be differentiated from each other in the students' responses. In the SOMUL project, we used 12 items taken from three of these subscales. Each item consisted of a statement, and the students indicated the extent of their agreement or disagreement with the statements on a five-point scale from

Table 6.1 Defining items of the conceptions of learning subscales

Subscale	Defining item
Construction of knowledge	I should try to look for connections within the subject matter without having to be told to do so
Intake of knowledge	I prefer teachers who tell me exactly what I need to know for an exam
Use of knowledge	For me, learning means acquiring knowledge and skills that I can later put to practical use

'disagree entirely' to 'agree entirely'. The defining items of the three subscales according to analyses of the data from the SOMUL project are shown in Table 6.1.

Approaches to studying

Interview-based research carried out during the 1970s found that students in higher education tend to adopt two different approaches to studying: a deep approach based on grasping the meaning of their course materials and a surface approach based on memorising the course materials for the purposes of assessment. A deep approach tends to be associated with good academic performance, but a surface approach tends to be associated with poor performance. The same student can exhibit different approaches to studying in different learning situations. In general, the choice of one approach rather than another is related to their perceptions of the content, the context and the demands of different learning tasks (for a review, see Richardson, 2000: Chapter 2). This pattern of results has been confirmed in surveys using questionnaires to measure students' perceptions and approaches to studying (Richardson, 2007b).

Nevertheless, students still vary in their approaches to studying, even when variations in their perceptions of their courses have been taken into account (Sadlo and Richardson, 2003). Marton (1976) suggested that this was because students vary in their conceptions of learning and in their conceptions of themselves as learners. In particular, he argued that students who adopt a deep approach take an active role and see learning as something that they themselves do, but those who adopt a surface approach take a passive role and see learning as something that just happens to them.

Table 6.2 Defining items of the approaches to studying subscales

Subscale	Defining item
Deep approach	I look at evidence carefully to reach my own conclusion about what I'm studying
Surface approach	I often have trouble making sense of the things I have to learn

Van Rossum and Schenk (1984) carried out a study with 69 psychology students at a Dutch university. They asked the students to read a short text and then to describe how they had approached the task of reading the text and how they approached their studies in general. Van Rossum and Schenk were able to classify the students into Säljö's five conceptions of learning. Most of the students who showed Conceptions 1–3 had adopted a surface approach to read the text, but most of the students who showed Conceptions 4 and 5 had adopted a deep approach. In other words, the approaches to studying that students adopt in particular learning tasks are linked to their underlying conceptions of learning.

As mentioned above, researchers have devised a variety of questionnaires to measure students' use of different approaches to studying (see Entwistle and McCune, 2004). In the SOMUL project, we used ten items taken from the Approaches to Learning and Studying scale that was devised for use in the ESRC TLRP project on Enhancing Teaching–Learning Environments in Undergraduate Courses (see www.etl.tla. ed.ac.uk/publications.html) at the University of Edinburgh. These were intended to measure the extent to which students tended to adopt a deep approach or a surface approach to studying at university. Once again, each item consisted of a statement, and the students indicated the extent of their agreement with the statements on a five-point scale. (Two new items were included, but these proved not to be useful.) The defining items of the two subscales according to analyses of the data from the SOMUL project are shown in Table 6.2.

Personal and educational development

North American researchers have carried out investigations into the processes of intellectual development in higher education (e.g. Perry, 1970; Belenky, Clinchy, Goldberger and Tarule, 1986; Baxter Magolda, 1992). However, work in the United Kingdom has focused

Table 6.3 Defining items of the personal and educational development subscales

Subscale	Defining item
Cognitive skills	Critical analysis
Mathematical skills	Ability to analyse numerical data
Self-organisation skills	Self-discipline
Social skills	Leadership skills

more upon the acquisition of generic skills. Lawless and Richardson (2004) constructed the Personal and Educational Development Inventory (PEDI), which asks students to rate the extent to which their studies have enabled them to develop in each of 26 areas. They found that the PEDI was a psychometrically robust instrument according to a survey of more than 3,000 alumni from the UK Open University. The 26 areas defined four domains: cognitive skills, mathematical skills, self-organisation and social skills.

In the SOMUL project, we used 14 items from the PEDI, supplemented by two new items. The items were examples of particular skills or abilities, and the students responded by indicating how much they felt they were developing each ability on a four-point scale from 'not at all' to 'a great deal'. The defining items of the four subscales according to analyses of the data from the SOMUL project are shown in Table 6.3. One interesting result was that the item relating to computer literacy (which Lawless and Richardson defined as a mathematical skill) proved to be more closely related to the social skills subscale, suggesting that students regard computers as a means of social communication rather than as mathematical devices.

Personal change

The project team felt that there were other dimensions of personal change that should be considered beyond the acquisition of generic skills. We therefore devised an entirely new scale consisting of 12 items focusing on how students had changed as people since they entered higher education. Once again, each item consisted of a statement, and the students indicated the extent of their agreement with the statements on a five-point scale. Analyses of the data from the SOMUL project suggested that this scale was measuring three aspects of personal change concerned with academic identity, personal confidence

Table 6.4 Defining items of the personal change subscales

Subscale	Defining item
Academic identity	I am very committed to the subjects I've studied here and would like somehow to continue to read/study them in the future
Confidence	I feel that I am now able to get on with a much wider range of people
Social networks	The qualification is the main thing. University has not changed me that much*

* Item to be scored in reverse

and social networks. Some of the items showed negative relationships with the scale to which they belonged, and so they were scored in reverse (so that a high level of agreement yielded a low score and vice versa). The defining items of these three subscales are shown in Table 6.4.

A heuristic model

Figure 6.1 shows a heuristic model to indicate how we think these different facets of learning and development are linked to one another. The arrows represent putative causal relationships, so that students' conceptions of learning are assumed to affect their approaches to studying, and both their conceptions of learning and their approaches to studying potentially affect their personal development and personal change. The model is presented simply as a framework for validating the instruments that we employed. It deliberately excludes the contextual factors (both academic and social) with which the SOMUL project is mainly concerned. In principle, of course, these can influence all of the components shown. Moreover, it provides only a snapshot of the links between learning and development at a particular point in the students' academic careers, and it excludes the feedback processes whereby personal change and development might prompt students to modify their conceptions of learning and their approaches to studying over the course of their degree programmes.

The research design

Students were recruited from five departments teaching each of three disciplines: bioscience, business studies and sociology. As was

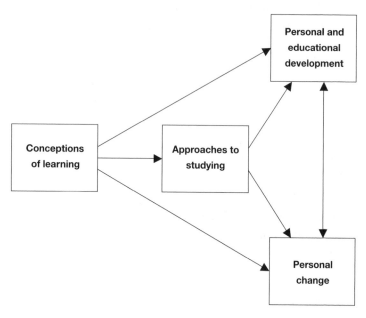

Figure 6.1 A heuristic model of learning and development in university
students

Source: Richardson and Edmunds, 2007: 4

explained in Chapter 4, the disciplines were chosen to reflect variation
in the hard/soft and pure/applied dimensions of Biglan's (1973)
taxonomy of academic subjects. The departments within each discipline were chosen to exhibit variation in the structure of the
undergraduate curriculum (open versus closed) and in the homogeneity or heterogeneity of the student population with regard to age,
gender, ethnicity and social class. In most departments the undergraduate programme lasted for three years, but some of the business
schools included an additional year (the third year) spent on work
placement.

    In each department, a questionnaire containing the four instru-
ments described above was administered to students in the first
year (the 'entering students') and the final year (the 'exiting students')
of the undergraduate programme. A similar questionnaire was given
to the same students two years later (when the entering cohorts
were in their third year of study and 12–18 months after the exiting
students had graduated). This design enabled a 'longitudinal' study of

Table 6.5 The research design

	First year	Third year	Final year	After graduation
Entering students	•	•		
Exiting students			•	•

Note: The bullets indicate when the two cohorts of students were surveyed

changes over 4–5 years to be carried out in just 2–3 years (see Table 6.5). Wherever possible, the questionnaire was administered during normal classroom activities. However, since many of the graduates were no longer engaged in formal education, their version of the questionnaire omitted the scales on conceptions of learning and approaches to studying, and it was administered by means of a postal survey.

Relationships among the four scales

The results of the SOMUL project provided broad support for the model shown in Figure 6.1. First, the students' scores on the conceptions of learning subscales explained 38 per cent of the variation in their scores on the approaches to studying subscales. In particular, those students who regarded learning as the construction of knowledge or as the use of knowledge were more likely to adopt a deep approach and were less likely to adopt a surface approach. Conversely, those students who regarded learning as the intake of knowledge were more likely to adopt a surface approach and were less likely to adopt a deep approach. This pattern is consistent with the findings of Van Rossum and Schenk (1984) in showing that students who hold reproductive conceptions of learning are more likely to use a surface approach to studying, whereas students who hold reconstructive conceptions of learning are more likely to use a deep approach to studying.

Second, taken together, the students' scores on the conceptions of learning subscales and the approaches to studying subscales explained 17 per cent of the variation in their scores on the personal and educational development subscales and 19 per cent of the variation in their scores on the personal change subscales. This confirms the hypothesised links between conceptions of learning and approaches to studying, on the one hand, and personal development and change, on the other hand. However, these were in fact relatively weak relationships, which suggests that contextual factors may be much more important determinants of the amount of personal development and change that students experience during their time at university.

Finally, the model shown in Figure 6.1 includes the possibility of an interrelationship between personal and educational development and personal change. (This is indicated by the double-headed arrow.) This suggestion was supported by the fact that the students' scores on the personal and educational development subscales shared 25 per cent of their variation with their scores on the personal change subscales. However, this too represents only a relatively weak relationship, suggesting that there is relatively little overlap in the aspects of personal change and development at university that these two scales are tapping. Both seem to be necessary to provide a clear picture of the students' experience.

Variations with age and gender

Students taking different subjects in different departments vary in terms of age and gender, variables that were not in themselves the main focus of the SOMUL project although they were of course part of the larger interest in the diversity of student cohorts. In addition, students who are surveyed in their first year of study, in their final year of study and after graduation will by definition be at different ages on these different occasions. However, the project was concerned with differences in students' conceptions of learning, approaches to studying, personal development and personal change that specifically result from their experience of higher education and not simply from the processes of maturation or ageing. It was therefore necessary to adjust the results statistically to remove the possible effects of differences in age and gender. In fact, both of these variables influenced the students' scores on the various scales.

First, the older students tended to obtain higher scores than did the younger students on the subscales measuring construction of knowledge, deep approach and academic identity. In contrast, the younger students tended to obtain higher scores than did the older students on the subscales measuring intake of knowledge and surface approach. This pattern is consistent with previous evidence that older students are more likely than are younger students to hold reconstructive conceptions of learning and to adopt a deep approach to studying (Van Rossum and Taylor, 1987; Richardson, 1994).

Second, women tended to obtain higher scores than men on all three conceptions of learning scales concerned with construction of knowledge, intake of knowledge and use of knowledge. This might be taken to imply that female students hold conceptions of learning that are more elaborated than are those of male students. However, Van Rossum and Taylor (1987) found that the distribution of conceptions of learning according to Säljö's (1979) scheme was similar in male and female students. In the SOMUL project, women also tended to obtain higher scores than men on the subscales concerned with self-organisation, social skills and confidence. It is of course quite possible that age and gender relate to some of the larger contextual factors examined by the SOMUL project. Mature women students, for example, are particularly likely to be balancing multiple identities – for instance, as wife or mother, worker, student – and developing multi-tasking skills of self-organisation as a result.

Variations across academic subjects

When the possible effects of age and gender had been statistically controlled, there was no significant difference among the students taking biosciences, business studies and sociology in their scores on construction of knowledge. However, on both intake of knowledge and use of knowledge, the business studies students tended to obtain higher scores, and the sociology students tended to obtain lower scores, with the biosciences intermediate. This might suggest that the curriculum in business studies fosters a conception of learning that focuses upon the reproduction and application of what is learned rather than one that focuses on understanding. In contrast, there were no significant differences in the students' scores on deep approach or surface approach: students in all three subjects were more likely to report a deep approach than a surface approach. This suggests that the curricula in all three subjects were successful in promoting a desirable approach to studying.

In terms of personal and educational development, the sociology students tended to obtain higher scores than the biosciences and business studies students on cognitive skills but lower scores than the biosciences and business studies students on mathematical skills. This may be the result of more abstract or theoretical content and less of an emphasis upon mathematical content in sociology degrees. However, there were no significant differences in the students' scores on self-organisation or social skills. In terms of personal change, there was no significant difference among the students taking the three subjects in their scores on confidence. Nevertheless, on social networks and academic identity, the biosciences students tended to obtain higher scores, and the business studies students tended to lower scores, with the sociology students intermediate. This may reflect the fact that the biosciences curriculum attaches importance to laboratory work in groups and to the idea of entering a profession.

Variations across departments

When the possible effects of age and gender had been statistically controlled, there were also significant differences across the five departments in each of the three academic subjects:

- The students in the different bioscience departments showed significant variation in their scores on use of knowledge and mathematical skills.
- The students in the different business schools showed significant variation in their scores on intake of knowledge, social skills, social networks, confidence and academic identity.
- The students in the different sociology departments showed significant variation in their scores on intake of knowledge and mathematical skills.

Nevertheless, in none of the three subjects did students in the different departments show significant variation in their approaches to studying.

It is perhaps more important that, although the quantitative instruments used in the SOMUL project differentiated among students taking the three subjects of study and among students in the five departments in a readily interpretable manner, even those differences that did achieve statistical significance were relatively modest in their magnitude. This suggests that idiosyncratic contextual factors may be more important than more formal aspects of the curriculum or the institution in determining students' conceptions of learning, approaches to studying, personal development and personal change.

In Chapter 3, we suggested a simple typology of departments based on the diversity of the student population and whether the students' experience was shared or individualised. This generated three types of contexts for the student experience: in type A, a diverse group of students share a largely common experience; in type B, broadly similar kinds of students come together to share a largely common experience; in type C, students have only limited contact with their peers (e.g. because of their non-academic commitments), and so they have a largely individualised experience, and the diversity of the group is relatively unimportant. In the 15 departments participating in the SOMUL project, there seemed to be three examples of type A, eight examples of type B and four examples of type C. Table 6.6 shows the mean scores on each of the subscales obtained by students in the three types of department. These have been statistically adjusted to control possible confounded differences in age and gender. (The latter procedures removed the possible direct effects of age and gender upon individual students' subscale scores but did not affect the contributions of these variables to institutional diversity.) Superscripts in the table are used to identify statistically significant pairwise differences. A significance level of 0.01 was used to reduce the likelihood of

Table 6.6 Adjusted mean scale scores for three types of institution

	Type A	Type B	Type C
Conceptions of learning			
Construction of knowledge	4.05	4.05	4.03
Intake of knowledge	3.38[a]	3.66[a]	3.86[b]
Use of knowledge	3.68[a]	3.73[a]	3.93[b]
Approaches to studying			
Deep approach	3.61	3.67	3.69
Surface approach	2.48	2.50	2.67
Personal and educational development			
Cognitive skills	3.35[a]	3.16[b]	3.20[b]
Mathematical skills	2.43[a]	2.72[b]	2.73[b]
Self-organisation	3.27	3.27	3.24
Social skills	3.01	2.99	2.93
Personal change			
Academic identity	3.30	3.32	3.13
Confidence	3.63	3.61	3.57
Social networks	3.56[a]	3.65[a]	3.21[b]

Note: Pairs of mean scores on the same subscale with different superscripts are significantly different according to *post hoc* tests ($p < 0.01$). All other pairs of means are not significantly different from each other.

spuriously significant results (i.e. Type I errors) when making large numbers of statistical comparisons.

There were significant differences among the three types of department on five of the 12 subscales. First, students in type C departments tended to obtain higher scores than those in type A or type B departments on both intake of knowledge and use of knowledge. This suggests that students in type C departments are more likely to hold conceptions of learning that focus on the reproduction and application of what is learned rather than one that focuses on understanding. And this would fit the conception of a greater instrumentality among such students, their greater emphasis on credentials and meeting course requirements. Once again, however, there were no significant differences in the students' scores on deep approach or surface approach. Students in type C departments tended also to obtain lower scores than those in type A or type B departments on social networks. It is hardly surprising that students, whose experience of higher education is shared with others, report more social development than their counterparts whose experience is individualised.

Second, students in type A departments tended to obtain higher scores than those in type B departments on cognitive skills. This suggests that learning among a heterogeneous student population is conducive to a student's cognitive development. This is consistent with the evidence (primarily from the United States and primarily concerned with ethnic diversity) that heterogeneity in the student population is conducive to students' cognitive development (e.g. Gurin et al., 2002, Chang et al., 2006). Curiously, however, students in type A departments tended to obtain lower scores than those in type B departments on mathematical skills. This suggests that learning in a heterogeneous student population is somewhat less conducive to the development of a student's understanding and use of mathematics. In both respects, the students in type C departments obtained scores that were similar to those obtained by students in type B departments and significantly different from those obtained by students in type A departments. In other words, students learning in an individualised setting showed a similar pattern to those learning with broadly similar kinds of students in a shared setting.

The effects of the different learning contexts implied by the typology will be discussed further in Chapter 7 where more attention will be given to the views expressed by students in interviews and focus groups. On the basis of the survey data, however, we can note that differences in the outcomes of learning between the three types of learning setting existed, were generally in the expected direction, but were generally quite small.

Variations across cohorts

When the possible effects of age and gender had been statistically controlled, there were no significant differences between the scores obtained by the entering students in their third year and those obtained by the exiting students in their final year. This is not at all surprising, as in most departments (except for some business schools) the final year for the exiting students *was* their third year of study.

As mentioned earlier, only the personal and educational development scale and the personal change scale were administered in the follow-up survey of the exiting students during their second year after graduation. Even so, there were no significant differences between the scores obtained by these students as graduates and the other three sets of scores. In other words, current students and graduates report similar levels of personal development and change as a result of their experience in higher education.

All four instruments were administered to the entering students in their first year of study, the entering students in their third year of study and the exiting students in their final year of study. The first-year students obtained scores that were very similar to those obtained by the third-year and final-year students, except on cognitive skills, where the latter students tended to obtain higher scores than the first-year students. In other words, students who were in their third or final year of study tended to report a greater development of their cognitive skills than students who were in their first year of study.

Nevertheless, none of the other comparisons between the first-year students, on the one hand, and the third-year and final-year students, on the other hand, was significant. In other words, the quantitative instruments used in the SOMUL project found little evidence for any significant differences from first-year students to alumni in students' conceptions of learning, their approaches to studying, their sense of personal development and their sense of personal change.

Conclusions

The observed relationship between students' conceptions of learning and their approaches to studying is consistent with the idea that students' choice of approach is determined at least in part by their conceptions of learning. In contrast, approaches to studying showed no variation across academic subjects or departments offering the same subject, suggesting that contextual factors are less important. (Even so, the *perceptions* of the academic context held by different students in the same department might well induce different approaches: Richardson, 2007b.) There is a far weaker relationship with students' reports of personal change and development while at university, suggesting that contextual factors play a greater role in this case. Indeed, there were significant variations across both disciplines and departments in this regard. The students' reports of their personal and educational development differentiated among students in the three types of educational setting that were identified in Chapter 3.

Nevertheless, there was remarkably little variation in the students' scores between the first year of study, their final year of study and the second year after their graduation, apart from a slight increase in the reported development of their cognitive skills between the first year and the final year. In short, the questionnaire surveys of the SOMUL project have found little evidence for real changes in students' conceptions of learning, approaches to studying, personal development and their personal change. This is consistent with the findings of the study by Vermetten *et al.* (1999) mentioned earlier in this chapter. However, in an interview-based, longitudinal study of students at one university in the United States, Baxter-Magolda (1992) found clear evidence for development in their conceptions of learning and knowledge. As will be seen in Chapter 7, similar evidence was obtained from the interviews and the focus groups in the SOMUL project.

One possible explanation is that development of this nature is simply less apparent in questionnaire-based investigations. For instance, it is certainly the case that students come to university with their own expectations or implicit theories regarding how they will develop and change as a result of their studies. It may be that these expectations persist throughout their degree programmes and that they refer to these expectations when they are asked to complete questionnaires about their experience of higher education (cf. Ross, 1989). An alternative explanation, of course, is that in the mass system of higher education that exists in the United Kingdom in the first decade of the twenty-first century students simply undergo far less personal development and change than has traditionally been assumed.

Chapter 7

What else students learned at university

Introduction: what else students learn

In Chapter 6, we looked primarily at the 'academic side of student life', at the student as 'learner', at different approaches to study, and at how these related to differences in what was studied and where it was studied. Significant differences were reported but also some commonalities. Overall, we might conclude from the above analyses that students have more in common across different subject fields and institutional types than is currently thought.

Chapter 6 also commenced a discussion about personal change associated with student life, which we continue in this chapter. As we have noted at several points previously, the 'residential tradition' of English higher education (traditions differing somewhat in the other nations of the UK) was for a long time its defining feature, especially when compared with its different European counterparts. Ideologies from Newman onwards have noted the 'gifted amateur' aspect of British life or, in Halsey's terms, the importance of 'character formation', 'liberal education' and the 'collegiate ideal of education' (Halsey, 1961). These facets of the university experience contrast with the stronger traditions of credentialism and vocationalism in much of continental Europe (Gellert, 1998). In consequence, for the graduate from an English university, greater importance may attach to 'who you are' rather than 'what you know'. There is now quite substantial research evidence to indicate that UK graduates are far less likely than their counterparts from other European countries to utilise their knowledge and skills in subsequent employment (Schomburg and Teichler, 2006; Brennan, 2008).

Contemporary developments of these traditions have been the widespread discussions about 'transferable skills', 'graduateness' and the attempt to capture the essence of 'what graduates have learned' through official statements such as subject benchmarks and programme specifications.

In a sense, where Chapter 6 looked at the nature of 'being a student', Chapter 7 looks at the nature of 'being a graduate'. How have people changed from their non-graduate personas? All of this raises questions of 'identity', a much discussed concept in contemporary social science. We begin the chapter by summarising some of the recent discussions of 'student identity' before going on to present the views of the students themselves about how they have changed, how they have 'managed' their often 'plural identities'.

Student identities

Two conceptions of identity are central in the general sociological and psychological literature on the subject:

1   *Personal identity/self-identity/self-concept* – shared but variously nuanced concepts in social psychology and individual psychology as well as in sociology.
2   *Group identity/social identity* – concepts in social psychology and sociology.

The former refer to the corporeally located personal/individual sense of coherence of self, e.g. of agency and disposition or attitude. The latter refers to sometimes relatively 'ascribed', often politically and ethically highly salient, felt membership of a social category such as ethnic, national or class identity. Strong relationships often exist between actual or perceived group/social identity and personal/self-identity, not only in relation to the relatively ascribed aspects of social identity associated with 'social origins' but also in connection with areas of 'achieved' social status – including occupational/vocational identity – and in relation to peer group and life style choices including 'identity politics' (e.g. Giddens, 1991; Castells, 2004).

Within modern societies, the acquisition of new and the dropping of old identities is seen to be increasingly possible and indeed required. Modern/post-modern identities are widely seen as a passing from an association with 'ascribed status' to an association with 'achieved status'. As such, identities are now also often viewed as involving greater differentiation and 'individuation' and as involving increasingly reflexive 'narratives of self' (Giddens, 1991) but also the potential for a pluralisation and fragmentation of self/selves (e.g. Sennett, 1998).

'Identity' – including the concept of 'self-authorship' (Baxter-Magolda and King, 2004) – as an aspect of research on personal development has had a clear place in previous research on learning and teaching and 'how college affects students' but the emphasis has been psychological or social psychological rather than fully socio-logical, although social factors figure as an aspect of this work. One strong focus – influenced by the Ego Psychology of Erikson – has been on cognitive and moral development and on challenges and responses and decisive/crisis points in identity formation (see Pascarella and Terenzini, 1991). For example, Chickering (1969), for whom 'identity' is a central construct, identifies seven vectors of individual develop-ment, including differentiation, integration and maturity. While accepting the relevance of such approaches, in the SOMUL project the focus on identity has been driven by more sociological perspectives related to social and organisational mediations, including academic or subject identities as well as 'graduate identity' and broader personal identity.

For some students, higher education is about the acquisition of a disciplinary or subject identity – 'becoming' an historian, a biochemist, a sociologist. The notion of 'academic subject identities' has been explored mainly in the literature in respect to academic staff within universities (e.g. Geertz, 1983; Henkel, 2000) and is more problem-atic in respect of students (Brennan and Patel, 2008). Within mass systems of higher education, only a small minority is heading for careers in the academic profession. For some, on the whole studying more professional subjects, the higher education experience may be about beginning to acquire a long-term occupational identity – as engineer, medical practitioner, accountant – but for the majority serious engagement with their academic subject of study may not continue many months beyond graduation. Thus, while a notion of 'subject identity' should not be neglected, it is important also to look more broadly at notions of identity in adult life and, more especially, at notions of graduate identity.

As was discussed in some detail in Chapter 5, students import into higher education several well-established identities, some ascribed – gender and ethnic identities – and some achieved – a 'successful student', a 'confident person'. These may be developed further during higher education, or they may be 'parked' for its duration, or they may be maintained either separately or interactively, or they may be destroyed (at least in the case of achieved identities). Which of the above happens may be a function of the orientations and life circumstances of the students themselves, the subject and institutional contexts of their studies, and the interaction of all of these; in other words 'the social and organisational mediation of identity'.

Different approaches to the conceptualisation and investigation of student identities have been explored more fully in one of the SOMUL project's working papers (Jary and Brennan, 2005). Here we just refer to a particularly useful discussion by Holmes (1995) of the concept of 'graduate identity', specifically in relation to business education, but with much that relates more generally to the changing face of higher education. He suggests that:

> It is important to use the term 'identity' as it has come to be understood and used within the social sciences over recent years. The notion of identity as a 'fixed' entity is rejected in favour of the idea of the process of identity formation and re-formation. The process involves a dynamic relationship between the individual's personal sense of self and the social processes which to a significant degree determine what count as the criteria for being ascribed a particular identity. Thus an identity cannot be decided on solely by an individual, as a personal act of choice and will, but must always be subject to affirmation (or dis-affirmation) by others.
>
> (Holmes, 1995: 7)

The important point here is that 'identity' is an increasingly negotiated entity. It must be both personally and socially owned and recognised. For example, the graduate attending a job interview must convince others that he/she is or has the potential to become a 'successful' lawyer, banker, media consultant, IT specialist or whatever.

In this context, Holmes notes that the concept of 'identity project' (Harré, 1983) can be:

> used as an approach to reconsidering the process of becoming a graduate. An identity project is the continuing process by which a person seeks to attain and maintain uniqueness and individuality (personal being) while also being socially recognised (social being). This involves the 'appropriation' by the individual of the characteristics of socially and culturally (and therefore discursively) legitimated identities. From this follows a stage of

'transformation', making personal sense of the socially acquired understanding, in terms of personal experience. The 'publication' of the actor's claim to the identity, the public expression of the characteristics associated with the identity leads, if successful, to 'conventionalisation' into the personal biography and social order. So the 'moral career' (Goffman, 1961) of the graduate is one achieved through the transition through a set of hazards, leading to esteem, reputation and self-worth, or loss of these – 'spoiled identity'.

(Holmes 1995: 7)

One of the things that discussion of student identities does is to switch attention away from notions of capability and competence to more subjective notions of 'confidence' and 'aspiration'. In particular, group identities inevitably imply reference points but for many of today's students a considerable choice of reference groups presents itself – from the 'parked' identities from their pre-university lives, from social and work-related experiences while a student, from political or community engagement, or from the academic/professional content of their studies. In other words, students have some considerable degree of choice over their 'identities' that they take with them into the world beyond higher education. How such choices are exercised has been an important focus of much of the SOMUL research.

Students' perceptions of how they had changed

In Chapter 6, we looked at some summary data on students' perceptions of how they had changed. Here we look at these data in rather more detail before going on to report on the way students elaborated on these things during the interviews and focus groups. First, however, we consider those students who did *not* feel they had changed at all, or who felt they had experienced very little change during their experience of higher education. Table 7.1 presents the percentages of students in each of the 15 cases who perceived little personal change and who, instead, emphasised the importance of the qualification as the valued outcome of higher education.

The first point to make is that the figures are mainly quite low and an indication of a generally positive outcome of higher education in this respect, the one exception being the students on the part-time business studies programme at Bramham where 68 per cent felt there had been little personal change and the qualification was the most

Table 7.1 Students perceiving little personal change and emphasising the qualification (%)

	Type A institutions	Type B institutions	Type C institutions
Business studies		Husthwaite (32) Wistow (24) Weighton (33)	Bugthorpe (49) Bramham (68)
Bioscience	Langtoft (11)	Warthill (16) Fridaythorpe (20) Givendale (11)	Ulleskelf (43)
Sociology	Wilton (26) Fenton (29)	Holme (18) Tockerington (9)	Bilton (28)

important thing. More generally, it was students in type C settings who were more likely to feel this way and, in terms of the three subjects, it was business studies students who were the more likely to express such a view. Perhaps a greater instrumentality is to be expected among business studies students and the somewhat less engaged (and generally older) students in type C settings. But it is important not to allow interesting differences between subjects and types of setting to disguise the larger picture. And here we can note that with the exception of one type C course in business studies, 50 per cent or more students on each of the remaining 14 case studies rejected the notion that their university experience had been mainly about the qualification and that they had been little changed by it. At 10 of the 15 cases, this view was rejected by over 70 per cent of the students.

Overall, most students felt that they had changed considerably as a result of their higher education, though different students at different places emphasised different aspects of change. Table 7.2 reports the percentages of students in the three types of educational setting who felt they had changed to a significant extent in a number of different ways.

From Table 7.2, we can see that students who had a type C experience differed from the others in a number of respects. They reported lower gains in self-confidence and were less likely to expect to retain university friendships after graduation. They were more likely to feel that they 'never fitted in' and very much more likely to feel that the 'qualification was the main thing' and that life outside of university remained the more important aspect of their lives. They were, however, compared with other graduates, rather more likely to believe that they had a clearer view of the future then when they commenced their course. As many of these students were mature students living busy lives outside of university, some of these features may be expected and understandable. As older people with more life experience, they may well have been more self-confident when they started their courses and have less to gain in this respect. And the achievement of a 'clearer view of the future' may reflect a finding from previous research that type C students may enter higher education both to escape the present

Table 7.2 Student perceptions of how they had changed (by type of learning setting) (percentage of students that 'agree for the most part' or 'agree entirely' that they have changed)

Students perceptions on how they have changed	Type A	Type B	Type C
I now have a much clearer view of what I want to do in the future	47	46	53
I am a much more self-confident person than the person I was when I came here	72	74	62
I feel that I no longer have much in common with friends outside of university	19	17	14
I am very committed to the subjects I've studied here and would like to continue to read/study them in the future	52	47	45
I can't imagine losing touch with some of the friends I've made here	72	70	46
I would like to remain associated with the university in some way	28	88	23
My time at university has really changed the way I see the world	41	55	52
My life outside university remains the most important to me	40	42	69
I feel that I am now able to get on with a much wider range of people	67	78	67
I never really fitted in here. I'll be quite glad to leave	9	6	14

and past and to obtain a clear view about a desired future (Brennan and Shah, 2003).

Students from type B settings were much more likely to want to retain an association with their university and were also more likely to feel able to get on with a range of people. Again, the importance of the university 'brand' in type B contexts and its approximation to the 'residential ideal' of higher education in England may go a long way to explaining the first of these findings. Type B settings tended to have fine campuses with good facilities and an active student culture for students to enjoy. With regard to the second point, however, we must point out that type B settings were by definition characterised by relatively low diversity of students. Thus, the 'range' of people with whom students were feeling 'able to get on' was somewhat more limited than the range found in other types of university setting.

Type A students were broadly similar to students with a type B experience but were somewhat more likely to have a continuing commitment to their subjects and rather less likely to feel that university has changed the way they saw the world.

All of that said, there are important commonalities in the reported effects of the student experience, irrespective of type of setting. Thus, looking at 'what was most important' for each type, there was commonality in two of the top three most endorsed statements: these concerned the gains in self-confidence and feeling able to get on with a wide range of people. The third 'most important' thing was, for students from type A settings, the maintenance of university friendships after graduation, for type B students, remaining associated with the university in some way, and for type C students, life outside university remained of high importance. A continuing commitment to the subjects studied in higher education – and by implication the acquisition of a 'subject identity' – was important to fewer than half the students sampled.

There were also some significant differences between students according to the subjects studied. Perhaps most noticeable from Table 7.3 is the much lower commitment to their subject expressed by the business studies students. But the business studies students were very likely to believe that they were now able to 'get on with a much wider range of people' as a result of their time at university. The world outside university was more likely to be important to these students. Bioscience students, on the other hand, were more likely than others to want to remain in contact with their university after they had graduated. Sociology students were more likely to emphasise a

Table 7.3 Student perceptions of how they had changed (subject differences) (percentage of students that 'agree for the most part' or 'agree entirely' that they have changed)

Students perceptions on how they have changed	Business studies	Biosciences	Sociology
I now have a much clearer view of what I want to do in the future	50	52	45
I am a much more self-confident person than the person I was when I came here	68	69	63
I feel that I no longer have much in common with friends outside of university	18	27	20
I am very committed to the subjects I've studied here and would like to continue to read/study them in the future	32	62	54
I can't imagine losing touch with some of the friends I've made here	60	68	58
I would like to remain associated with the university in some way	26	44	29
My time at university has really changed the way I see the world	48	52	58
My life outside university remains the most important to me	55	35	46
I feel that I am now able to get on with a much wider range of people	70	65	68
I never really fitted in here. I'll be quite glad to leave	7	6	10

changed world view. But, as we have noted, self-confidence and friendships tended to be emphasised by students, irrespective of the subject they had studied.

On certain aspects, subject of study seemed to matter little. Final-year students who felt 'glad to be leaving' university and who felt 'they had never really fitted in' were most likely to be found in type C settings. On the other hand, commitment to their university and to their subjects of study were significantly lower for business studies students, pretty much irrespective of the type of setting they were in.

As already noted, friendships were much less important to students in type C settings. But they were also more important to bioscience students, irrespective of the type of setting.

As we have discussed previously, the attitudes and engagement of individual students differ, both within subjects and within the three types of university setting. In other words, some students will have a type C experience in a type A setting. In some places, this can result in what we have termed the existence of 'parallel universities' where different types of students have different types of university experience alongside each other. Thus, overlain on the differences related to setting type and subject of study are differences according to individual student characteristics such as age, living arrangements, social background, amount of term-time work undertaken, and so on. Differences of these kinds and in the orientations to study of individual students were examined in Chapter 5.

Student voices

During the interviews, students often referred to the personal impact on them of university. For a majority, this was viewed as large and related to things such as living away from home and becoming more mature, confident and responsible as the following examples illustrate.

For many of the sociology students, personal change was a product of both the content of their studies and the larger experience of being at university. Sarah was a mature sociology student at Fenton (type A). For her, study and home life were continuously interacting:

> There are not many modules that you really feel you can't tap into in some shape or form there is something about my life that fits with just about everything really and I think that – it allows you to express your own opinions in a way that I think most academic subjects don't allow you to. There's a real scope for testing your construction of the world, all that kind of thing . . .
>
> . . . it has changed the dynamic of our family considerably . . . my relationship with my husband has changed. Mostly for the better I would have to say. I think there have been some huge personal improvements in our relationship. But having been at home full time there is this huge flux of domestic issues that now we have to address. One of my modules is Gender in Society so I'm now kind of 'oh yeah! And why is that my job?' you know.

So you know I'm kind of looking at things and pushing him to help me a little bit more and he's more than willing to do that so that's lucky that you know it hasn't caused any sort of major fireworks.

Whereas at Holme (type B), Catherine, another final-year sociologist but this time a young school leaver, placed much more emphasis on the overall life at university, which as we have noted, at type B settings is generally rich and varied:

I've met some wonderful, wonderful people who are so different and diverse. Different outlook on life, different social backgrounds, different sort of aspirations there in life. I think you know just being with them obviously changed you as a person. Members of just the department itself you know sort of gives you an – you know different appreciation of what sort of life and what you want out of – but I definitely think people, people are sort of very important.

Interviewed again in the year after she had graduated, Catherine was this time emphasizing the 'generalist' features of a traditional non-vocational UK undergraduate experience. Again, subject of study does not seem to be important but qualities such as breadth and flexibility are perceived to provide an excellent basis for life ahead:

If you have an idea that you very much want to go down a route, sort of like you know like a doctor or a lawyer and doesn't want to do anything other than that, then it's all well and good to do a degree that's completely specific. And if you just want a well rounded good degree that gives you a vast quantity of skills and touches upon such a wide range of subjects which opens many doors, doesn't matter what you want to do, it's a brilliant, brilliant degree. It's a brilliant educational basis to have because it leads on to so many things, to complement so many things. And I think its very sad that people are trying to pigeonhole children and young people so early into what you know into what road or what route they should be doing when really if you're going to, isn't it sadly, it maybe its more beneficial I haven't decided to quit yet but you know in today's society you're not likely to have one job, you're likely to have more than one job according to your career.

Karen, a mature sociology student at the same university had experienced conflict between the two aspects of her life, those inside and outside of university:

> Yeah my parents were so proud! My God they've waited for 25 years to be proud in front of the children! . . . my relationship with my partner broke up. He found it very difficult to accept that I actually had a brain after all, that I could actually do these things so I think he felt threatened by me going into further education and the relationship broke down as a result of the fact that I wanted to talk on an academic level and I suddenly discovered that I could actually say things that I hope are interesting or even thought provoking or whatever and I think he didn't like it. I mean it wasn't obvious, that you know the relationship broke down because you've gone to university and things like that but it made life very difficult . . . some people say you'll never do it at your age or why are you doing it at your age. And the other half of the people, I mean that say oh well I couldn't do it, I'm you know I'm really proud of what you're doing. So I've got kind of 50:50. Some support and some are really like dismissive of saying oh you're too old for it, you know you should be going out and getting a proper job and all the rest of it. I get a lot of that.

Linda, another final-year student at Holme, had also experienced change which, if not a source of actual conflict, had led to her drifting apart from previous friends and her life before university:

> Second year I found that really, really hard because I felt that I had so much that I wanted to talk about but I had no one from my outside university life that would understand what I was saying. And I did find that frustrating. I found that very, very hard. I couldn't – it makes you sound so bad really because from my point of view I've changed from being a sales adviser to being an undergraduate you know. I know that I've changed. I know that I've changed and my friends tell me I've changed but they can't tell me how. Apart from I can have more intellectual conversations. Without actually knowing that I've done it, outside friends I don't see. I don't see because I don't feel now that I've got anything in common. I can't switch from going, one person to being another.

I can't do that. So people that I meet now know me for who I am. People who knew me before I don't hardly see them . . .

. . . What does it mean to be a student? Something to be very, very proud of. From my point of view. Something to be proud of. Something that you've achieved. Something that you work hard at. Something that does change your life.

Students in bioscience and business studies attending type B settings also spoke about wide-ranging personal changes resulting from attending university, but tended to place rather less emphasis on the impact of subject content. Samir was a bioscience student at Givendale (type B). Like other students at type B settings, he tended to emphasise things such as confidence, independence and 'people' skills:

The whole package of discovering in detail the ins and outs of a subject fascinating to you while growing as a person, i.e. living away from home, maturing and meeting such a wide variety of new people, some of which turn out to become life long friends (hopefully!) . . . I think I find it easier to meet new people and get on with them and also like living with different people . . . I'd probably just say like developing me as a person. Like I think if I hadn't, say like to some of my friends way back from Hull that did go straight into work from A levels, and didn't . . . and have kind of stayed at home and might still be living with parents and things, I think I have definitely developed as a person, so I'm more rounded and had that experience of kind of living out of, you know, another city, away from parents.

Paul was a business studies student at Weighton (type B). For Paul, university had helped him to focus his life and, like so many other students, he attributed the changes in his life to the people he had met while at university:

Um, it's an experience. I think it's a life changing experience to be honest. It really is. It changed me a lot as a person. Um, I think for the whole overall experience I think it's a brilliant thing to do. It gives you such a different outlook on life as much as anything. Um, develops you as a person and obviously the educational side as well you know . . . Um, it's when I actually sit down and I focus on it and I think and I'm thinking right this is what I need to do and I think I'm targeting myself a lot more. I'm able to concentrate a lot more on what I want to do. I'm a lot more focused you know. It really is you know the people I've met because they are from everywhere. I didn't really realise to be honest how different people would be from different areas but it's been really good. It has been really good so. Mainly the people have changed me.

The above quotations are from final-year students who had experienced the 'shared experience' of university life characteristic of the student experience at a type A or B university setting. The experience of university in a type C setting is, as we have noted, more individualised while students attempt to juggle the competing commitments of university, home life and, frequently, paid work. While familiar themes of independence, confidence and communication skills emerge as perceived learning outcomes, more academically-related factors are more often mentioned as the main sources of change.

Linda had studied business studies at Bugthorpe (type C), one of many locally-based mature students on the course:

I've learnt some IT stuff since I've been here. One of the modules was IT based and although I had used sort of basic spreadsheets training and things like that, I'd learned a lot of new formulas and sort of things. Yeah, it has been hard. I wouldn't you know say it's been easy in any way, shape or form. But then I enjoy coming here. I will miss that. Coming here every week. I won't miss having to do the work at home and trying to fit it in!

As for many mature students, the stage in the life-course has implications for what they do after graduation. This was clearly the case for Linda. On asked whether she might consider further study, she responded cautiously:

. . . maybe if I had done it when I was younger when I didn't have family commitments and you know, like parents getting older and I had been a bit more kind of ambitious and done something else with it. But I don't know. At the moment I just feel like I need a break from it for a while just to kind of recover my state of mind. And then I think, perhaps when my little boy is a bit older then I might think more career for myself.

In some ways, Bugthorpe presented some of the characteristics of what we have termed a 'parallel university' where different kinds of students experienced different kinds of university life alongside each other. Roberto, a young school leaver who had left home in order to go to Bugthorpe, remarked that:

> I've definitely changed but I don't know if the change came because I am doing my degree. I think it's more because of the people and the new environment you get and so you change. I don't think it is because of the degree. Mmm. It was more like a gradual improvement but it was. The big change could have been the beginning when we arrived here. Because we didn't know anything so we were not sure if we were really accepted.

But the lack of much by way of campus life at Bugthorpe and the large proportion of students who quickly disappeared back home after lectures meant that even for the young school leavers away from home, the balance between the 'subject experience' and the 'wider experience of university' seemed to be weighted firmly with the former. Bugthorpe students all seem to emphasise what Becker termed 'the academic side of college life'.[1] This is what four of them had to say.

> Babett: I would say I learned to work independently. And I learned to find connections between different topics. And I learned to make decisions and what other possibilities what we have. And I learned to work on a structured way maybe. Like you must start with a little step and then you can go on.

> Abby: Um. What have I learned. Just basic management and business methods, procedures, policies. The lot. But what else have I learned is I've also improved on my time management and skills such as presentation skills. And writing skills. And organising – not just my time but working along with people and organising tasks.

> Linda: A bit more confidence I think. I think the confidence has come more because as I've done assignments, I've realised that I'm getting quite good marks . . . Yeah. I think – like I say, I think my confidence has grown, definitely. And what I've been learning on the course I am able to link into what's happening at work and I can – I don't know – my eyes have been opened really. Looking at different management styles and you know looking at people at work and seeing how they're operating and how it fits in with some of the theories that we've been learning about.

George: I just develop my skills, knowledge and my experiences so I would be able to adapt it to any situation, you know, my way. So you know if it has to be a job that they want to train someone they want me to do so I think I will try to do my best you know. Even if I have to do it with a few mistakes so I will recognise my mistake and try, you know, do better than, you know – it's a big question . . . Oh yeah. I've got new skills. I've got now experience, you know so. Even like my interpersonal skills so I'm not really the same person anymore. So I've got probably another way of, you know, judging people, seeing things different. Probably because I did work as a supervisor as well. So I think I will be doing better now than where I was before. I think it was quite a good experience . . . So like I said I get on quite well with my lecturers so. When I've got anything, I always ask them so we have had more like, not really student to a lecturer conversation but it's more something so . . . even outside, you know, no more class.

For young students away from home for the first time, change is multi-dimensional with the emphasis firmly on the non-academic sides of university life, especially if attending the traditional type B university setting, rich in a whole range of extra-curricula opportunities and experiences. In the more individualised type C settings, and for older students balancing study with a range of other life commitments, the course and academic aspects of university figure more strongly in the still substantial perceptions of personal change that attach to the university experience.

It should not be thought, however, that all students perceive their university experiences as being a source of major personal change. Some students are effectively having a type C experience, irrespective of the nature of the university setting, because external commitments leave little time, energy or opportunity for them to avail themselves of the non-academic aspects of university life. Some of the following quotations are from students for whom the experience of university appeared to have a relatively limited impact.

Lusia was a final-year sociologist at Tockerington (type B). She was a mature student who had originally studied architecture, lived in Paris and had had a year in Copenhagen. She summed up her time at Tockerington with the following words: 'I feel I have a non-student life but I study.' Davina was a final year in bioscience at Ulleskelf (type C) and commuted daily from a neighbouring town. Her engagement with the university was limited: 'I don't do anything within the university environment. No, my social life is all in [nearby town], with my friends. So it's like two separate things really.'

Helen, another final-year sociologist at Tockerington (type B), felt that she had changed through experiencing a 'gap year' and this was being built on while at university:

> I think I would have matured in the same way anyway without going to university but my confidence I think has come through, come through meeting new people. I think that's the major thing. Meeting people from different backgrounds really makes you more aware of the fact that it's a bigger world with lots of different people in it sort of thing.

Experiences like Helen's prompt the thought that it may be 'leaving home' rather than 'going to university' that is the source of the major impact on many young people. Leaving home for a 'gap year', for 'military service' or even for 'prison' may have just as much personal impact as leaving home to go to university! Or even more!

Amal was a final-year bioscientist at Warthill (type B) and compared his university experience rather negatively with his schooling:

> But I don't think, you know, like when I left school I thought school has really shaped my personality. It's made me a better person, it's made me a stronger person and I know more because of it. And I don't think that I could say the same about university. Like I think I came in thinking a certain way and being a certain person, right, and I might have learned one or two lessons, but besides from that I haven't changed much.

Amal was an international student from the United Arab Emirates and felt surrounded by people who had never travelled internationally:

> Like I came in here and I find some people had never, you know, left the country or have never left the tiny place that they're from and they don't know anything beyond that. So you can't discuss anything more beyond their mental thinking, or you can't say something because then they'll start, you know, attacking you for.

Jennifer, a first-year bioscientist at Fridaythorpe (type B), felt that university had been a narrowing rather than a broadening of her horizons:

> I think I would have expected more involvement in important issues and things because, I mean, stereotypically students are quite active in those kind of a . . . in that kind of a respect. I think I would have expected to broaden my horizons more and I think actually what's happened is I've narrowed them. I mean I live a life of going out, going to rugby, going to uni, staying at home. So I think that's been the biggest thing. I definitely haven't really broadened my horizons a huge amount and I think that was what I was hoping for out of university.

Jennifer was another student who had had a gap year and then at university lived with six people who had never lived away from home:

> I mean having gone from being fairly independent and on my own most of the time when I was travelling, to come back and be around 36 people basically in a block most of the time is, is hard work.

While Holme was in some respects one of the most stereotypical of the type B university settings, a well-established university with a good reputation and attractive to school-leavers with good A levels, individual students could be found who confounded the institutional stereotype and had their own personal stories and circumstances that made a different 'sense' of the university experience. Mike, a first-year sociologist at Holme, commented:

> The degree as far as I'm concerned is a paperwork exercise. I need to get the certificates and the qualifications to work in the areas, to be taken seriously in working in the areas that I want to work in.

A mature student, recovering alcoholic/drug addict, Mike saw studying as a means to becoming a drug addict counsellor, so spent lots of his time doing relevant work/work-experience (in a night shelter, etc.). He felt excluded from the non-academic side of the university experience because he couldn't drink. He has had to have a huge identity change to get to where he is now:

I was – I'm in recovery from drug and alcohol addiction. I was addicted to heroin and crack cocaine. And by the time I was 30 that caused massive problems in my life. My life fell apart but I ended up begging on the streets of Oxford. I lost all my material possessions and I then went through a course of treatment over the next five years. It didn't work when I came back home I carried on to drink and to do drugs and then three years ago I went into another rehabilitation centre up in Scarborough and my life changed. I am not sure exactly what happened but I stopped drinking, I stopped doing drugs and I found that there was a big hole in my life. I left school with no qualifications at the age of 16 and felt stupid because I couldn't read or write very well. It didn't occur to me the reason that I couldn't read or write very well was because I never did it. I started to have an interest in reading books, I read a lot of science fiction and I found as a consequence of that my spelling improved which came as a surprise to me. I always wanted to, I always suspected that I haven't actually fulfilled my potential academically and that kind of nagged at me. And I decided I needed to be computer literate that was the first thing I wanted to do, so I did a course in computer skills. I got myself computer literate. Then I got accepted to do an Access course at Scarborough and while I was on the Access course, I found out that I was a visual learner and that was the reason I didn't read or write very well at school because I never wore my glasses. I also found that I'm quite a creative person and I found that I could express myself creatively in writing which did wonders for my self-worth. I found that I had a talent for writing. I just became hooked – I just became hooked on studying! It was just amazing to think that I actually would be able to be in a position to come to university was like a major surprise to me. It – I felt my self-worth come up. I became quite obsessive towards studying.

Mike's story is interesting for the contrasts it provides with the predominant social orientation of student life at many type B universities. As with many mature students, it was the fact of being at university at all that was the major form of personal meaning and impact. What, for many younger middle-class students, was an expected and seemingly inevitable life stage was for students such as Mike an achievement of major significance – irrespective of what was studied and what was experienced while at university.

While we have discussed in this and other chapters the different kinds of experiences that are provided according to the social and organisational mediating factors present in particular cases, we have also reflected that for some students, the experience of university study is something that is lived in parallel with other lives, lives quite full of other responsibilities. Thus, in response to questions about their sense of self-identity, some students would point to the possession of several.

Karen, who had graduated from Holme with a sociology degree, commented about her identity as follows:

> Yes, yes I would say I'm a student. But in the context you know my primary role is obviously my family and obviously I'm a mother and so on and so forth but that's almost forgotten. When somebody asks you something you don't know if you're going to say oh I'm a housewife or I'm a mother because that's not the way you generally respond. When people say to you 'well what are you doing now', they tend to mean or in my experience they tend to mean work wise you know, so on and so forth what are you doing with your disposable time if you like. So yes I would auto-matically say that I'm a student and but then having said that, that's if – if something had to go if you know what I mean if there were family pressures or some or this would go not the family if you know what I mean.

When asked about identity change as a result of her studies, Karen continued:

> No because I felt that was the latent student in me all the time that sort of never went away if you know what I mean. So you know whether this will perish. Its like for example I was – well I was talking with my mum and we're on the phone and I said to mum I said 'well I can't talk anymore, got to put the phone down, cos I've got to go and do this, I've got to go back into the library'. 'Oh she said oh you know I feel sorry for you' and I said 'well mum you know I like doing it'. So you know it's almost like a masochistic thing. I actually quite enjoy doing it. So you know I've sort of taken that on I'm quite – about an identity that I've taken on I quite like. It's not a negative thing . . .
>
> . . . I do feel that my experience has left me like that in a way because when I'm discussing with people who its part of their

family, its part of just who their identity with their connections are is that everybody goes to university in the family. I don't feel I'm part of them because that's not my experience. But equally I don't feel that I'm part of the same experience because as I say nobody has ever been before so it's quite – quite an unusual position to be in. So therefore when you were saying about the student identity and non-student identity it's almost like a mantel that I put on depending on who's company I tend to be in.

Hayley, another Holme final-year sociology student, was quite explicit about it: 'No I have two lives.' And when asked about her other life:

Home and quietness. Like yeah if go home I'm like I go home just to be with my family like to see my mum and dad not really to go out and have fun with my old friends no. It's really it's just to go home and see my family and yeah.

Conclusions

In pointing to the differences in the personal changes associated with higher education between types of students and types of university settings, it is important to attempt to balance the significance of the differences between them with the undoubted similarities. We thus find that students overall place more emphasis on the social and personal aspects of change than they do upon the academic. New identities are less connected to subject affiliations and more to do with people and institutions, with personal confidence rather than knowledge and skills. However, some students point to their academic experiences as a major source of personal change whereas others point to the more general experiences of life at university and of leaving home for the first time as the major source of change. University life as a whole seemed to be more important than academic experiences for students at type B institutions. And sociology students seemed more likely than others to locate the sources of change within their academic studies. None of this should be taken to imply a general lack of importance attached to the academic; it was just that other aspects of university were often regarded as even more important.

What is clear is that for a majority of students, the experience of university is associated with the achievement of greater self-confidence, independence, communication skills, understanding of other people and maturity. Some students, particularly older ones, have already achieved many of these things well before they have ever entered university. But such traits are in any case multi-dimensional. The self-confidence that comes from travel and living away from home is something different from the self-confidence that comes from getting good grades and a university degree. These then seemed to be some of the main features of a 'graduate identity' among the students from the 15 case studies of the SOMUL project. Following Holmes, they were more about 'confidence' than about 'competence'. They were more about the acquisition of 'social and cultural capital' than the 'human capital' associated with knowledge and skills. More generally 'reflexive' changes in student identities (Giddens, 1991) are evident but so too is the weight of previous more ascribed identities. Also, as noted in other surveys of university learning (see Pascarella and Terenzini, 1991), and pointed out by one student cited above, there is also the issue of whether changes in student identity are the outcome of university experience or simply of 'growing up'. Plainly both are involved. And as Holmes (2001) suggests, the 'affirmation' of both 'imported' and 'new' identities occurs within higher education as part of what can be termed 'identity projects'.

The diversity of today's students means that different students are looking for different things, or will be affected in different ways by otherwise similar experiences. But the settings and the opportunities for learning also differ. Not all universities provide the wide range of extra-curricula social experiences that appear capable of transforming the lives of many young students. But nor do all universities provide the diversities of people and circumstances, nor the potential for balancing multiple and complex identities, which can also be an important source of learning and personal change. And not everyone experiences major personal change as a result of going to university. But most do.

Note

1   'The academic side of college life' is the sub-title of the well-known study by Howard Becker and associates: Becker, H., Geer, B., and Hughes, E.C. (1968) *Making the Grade: The Academic Side of College Life,* New York: Wiley.

Chapter 8

Diversities and commonalities in the student experience

Introduction: 'What' you study or 'where' you study

The two key decisions faced by potential students are what to study and where to study it. Increasingly, these decisions are being informed by public information – often in league table form – of the strengths and weaknesses of different universities and of different study programmes within them. But how far do these differences matter, in terms of the outcomes of learning for individual students?

While the increasing diversity of the student experience in UK higher education cannot be denied and is illustrated at many points in the preceding chapters of this book, the significance to be attached to many aspects of this diversity is open to question. As we noted in Chapter 7, most students attach considerable importance to the friendships they made at university and to the confidence they believe they have acquired there. Commitment to the subject of study is important but less so than these more social aspects of university life. There are exceptions. Students, especially mature students, with substantial domestic and work commitments, have little time to spare for the non-academic aspects of higher education. Family and friends are generally close by so the incentive to build up new relationships may be rather weak. Most programmes of study have a few such students who, in any case, may not be looking for new friendships and may have acquired self-confidence through a wide range of previous experiences. However, in programmes of study where such students form the majority (our type C settings), the opportunities to achieve these social and personal changes may be limited for all students. In this sense 'where' you study does matter. It will be a different experience according to the characteristics of the local student culture.

Another sense in which 'where' one studies seems to matter lies in the huge importance attached to institutional loyalty and identity from students who had experienced their higher education in type B settings. Such students were much more likely to want to retain contact with their *alma mater* after graduation. As we have already noted, type B settings were generally to be found in more prestigious 'pre-92' universities with mainly school-leaver students away from home for the first time. With more time to devote to the social and leisure side of university life and with generally better campus facilities to enjoy, it is perhaps not surprising that these students seem to reveal a greater fondness for their institution than others. Additionally, these students may also be aware of the long-term value to them of their institutional 'brand' and of the social networks that they have joined while at university. To a considerable extent, these institutional settings continue to provide the 'elite reproduction' functions well described by Bourdieu and others. For these students, 'what' they studied may be quite unimportant. These are the bioscience students from Warthill and the sociology students from Tockerington who are destined for 'top financial jobs' in the City of London. Paradoxically, rather fewer business studies students seemed destined for such jobs. Studying the 'wrong thing at the right place' seems to be a much better option than studying the 'right thing at the wrong place' in British higher education and society.

All of that said, the data collected from the students participating in this project do not on the whole support the perceptions of many university teachers that there is a growing instrumentality among the student population. At 10 of the 15 case sites, more than 70 per cent of the students rejected the notion that higher education was mainly about getting the qualification and not about important personal change. Perhaps not surprisingly, it was on business studies programmes where the greater instrumentality was found. The same was true of type C settings, though here the important factor may be the greater maturity of many of the students. They were at a stage in their life course where personal change and development was no longer such a key element. By comparison, for young students straight from school and living away from home for the first time, the experiences of university life could provide a catalyst to personal growth.

For most students, personal change was a reflection of the broader social experiences of attending university. Sociology students were an exception. Particularly in the interviews, many spoke of the personal impact their studies had had on them. And this was true irrespective of the kinds of students or the kinds of university setting. For the older sociology students, studies could help make sense of personal biographies. For the younger students, it could be a way of comprehending an adult world and one's place within it.

Conceptions, approaches and personal development

Turning to the 'academic side of student life', to the different approaches to study and learning, although some interesting differences were reported in Chapter 6, there were also some important commonalities. This suggests that differences related to subject studied and institution attended exist, but are not necessarily as important as factors that impinge on what students learn as is commonly thought.

For example, as we reported there was no significant difference among students across the three subjects in their scores on Construction of Knowledge, though we did find subject differences in relation to intake of knowledge and use of knowledge. Further there were no significant differences in the students' scores on the use of deep or surface approaches to learning across subjects. Similarly, when we considered personal and educational developments there were no significant differences in the students' scores on self-organisation or social skills, but there were subject differences in cognitive skills and mathematical skills in different disciplines.

We also reported in Chapter 6 that there were differences within the five departments for our three subjects. However, despite these being of statistical significance, the differences were of low magnitude, and we have suggested that certain idiosyncratic contextual factors could be of greater importance than more formal aspects of the curriculum or the institution when we assess students' conceptions of learning, approaches to studying, personal development and personal change.

We have also applied our type A, B and C contexts to the data generated from our quantitative tools, and have reported significant differences among the three types of department on five of our 12 subscales. However, once again these differences are relatively small in magnitude.

We also conducted a wider survey using our survey instruments of third-year students in our existing three subjects and six other subjects (computing, electrical engineering, film and media, geography, history and mathematics) within our original institutions, and within one new institution. The new subjects chosen extend the range of disciplines to, in Becher's (1989) terms, include hard pure knowledge (mathematics), soft pure knowledge (history), hard applied knowledge (electrical engineering and computing) and soft applied knowledge (film and media and geography). Not all subjects were taught at each institution, and not all institutions took part in this wider survey. However, we do have data from nine institutions, nine subjects and over 800 respondents. From these responses there is sufficient data to test:

(a) whether there are differences in our measures across the subjects;
(b) whether there are differences in our measures across the various institutions (shown as 'Batch' in Table 8.1);
(c) whether there is an interaction between these two effects, so that the differences across the subjects vary from institution to institution (and vice versa).

We have calculated the same measures as for the main surveys reported in Chapter 6, and we have carried out multivariate analyses of variance on these different measures. In each case we have used the independent variables of batch and subject. The top part of Table 8.2 shows the multivariate effects (i.e. are there differences in the scores obtained on each questionnaire?). The main part of Table 8.2 shows the univariate effects (i.e. are there differences in the scores obtained on each scale of each questionnaire?)

Within each part of the table, the first half uses just the independent variables of batch and subject. In the second half, we have

Table 8.1 Responses in wider survey

Subject	Frequency	Per cent
Biosciences	63	7.7
Business	35	4.3
Computing	156	19.1
Electrical engineering	26	3.2
Film and media	59	7.2
Geography	97	11.9
History	222	27.2
Mathematics	68	8.3
Sociology	91	11.1
Total	817	100.0

Table 8.2 Results from wider survey

	Batch	Subject	Interaction		
Conceptions of learning	0.022**	0.058**	0.036		
Approaches to studying	0.010	0.046**	0.044*		
Personal and educational development	0.015 (p = 0.051)	0.129**	0.073**		
Personal change	0.038**	0.022*	0.053**		
	Batch	Subject	Interaction	Age	Gender
Conceptions of learning	0.023**	0.054**	0.035	0.002	0.006
Approaches to studying	0.011	0.046**	0.044*	0.005	0.000
Personal and educational development	0.016*	0.134**	0.073**	0.003	0.066**
Personal change	0.035**	0.024*	0.054**	0.005	0.011*
Conceptions of learning	Batch	Subject	Interaction		
Construction of knowledge	0.013	0.026*	0.024		
Intake of knowledge	0.030**	0.039**	0.034		
Use of knowledge	0.021*	0.103**	0.060**		
Approaches to studying	Batch	Subject	Interaction		
Deep approach	0.012	0.057**	0.047*		
Surface approach	0.006	0.040**	0.037		
Personal and educational development	Batch	Subject	Interaction		
Cognitive skills	0.011	0.110**	0.066**		
Mathematical skills	0.011	0.244**	0.077**		
Self-organisation	0.010	0.030**	0.034		
Social skills	0.019	0.111**	0.091**		
Personal change	Batch	Subject	Interaction		
Change	0.015	0.020	0.056**		
No change	0.055**	0.021	0.049*		
Conceptions of learning	Batch	Subject	Interaction	Age	Gender
Construction of knowledge	0.012	0.024 (p = 0.051)	0.022	0.000	0.002
Intake of knowledge	0.033**	0.037**	0.033	0.002	0.002
Use of knowledge	0.022*	0.102**	0.058**	0.000	0.000

(continued)

Table 8.2 Results from wider survey *(continued)*

Approaches to studying	Batch	Subject	Interaction	Age	Gender
Deep approach	0.012	0.055**	.0047*	0.005	0.000
Surface approach	0.007	0.040**	0.040	0.002	0.000

Personal and educational development	Batch	Subject	Interaction	Age	Gender
Cognitive skills	0.011	0.107**	0.066**	0.001	0.013**
Mathematical skills	0.012	0.247**	0.076**	0.000	0.015**
Self-organisation	0.009	0.035**	0.029	0.000	0.030**
Social skills	0.022*	0.120**	0.092**	0.000	0.027**

Personal change	Batch	Subject	Interaction	Age	Gender
Change	0.013	0.024	0.058**	0.001	0.008*
No change	0.049**	0.022	0.049*	0.005*	0.007*

* Statistically significant at $p < 0.05$, ** Statistically significant at $p < 0.01$
Small effect = 0.0099, Medium effect = 0.0588, Large effect = 0.1379

repeated the analyses using the covariates of age and gender. This was to check whether apparent differences across batches or subjects were simply artefacts caused by variations in age and gender. The overall effects of age and gender are also shown.

Our aim was to include a single measure that captures:

(a) the amount of variation that is attributable to the different predictor variables; and
(b) whether the relevant effect is statistically significant.

The measure we used was Cohen's (1988) eta-squared, which is the proportion of the variance in a dependent variable that is attributable to a particular predictor variable. Below Table 8.2, we have supplied Cohen's suggestions for what would count as 'small', 'medium' and 'large' effects. So a small effect is one that explains about 1 per cent of the variance in the dependent variable, a medium effect is one that explains about 6 per cent, and a large effect is one that explains about 14 per cent.

One problem with Cohen's original measure of eta-squared is that it is based on the total variation in a particular dependent variable. This will depend among other things on the other variables in the research design. If another variable is included that generates a lot of variation that will tend to increase the total variation and reduce the proportion of that variation, that is explained by the other variables. Therefore we have reported a variant of Cohen's measure, partial eta-squared, which is the proportion of variation that is attributable to a particular predictor variable when the effects of the other variables are removed (or partialled out).

We have also indicated which effects are statistically significant at $p < 0.05$ (*) or $p < 0.01$ (**). Because there are a relatively large number of statistical tests in the table, we considered ourselves vulnerable to picking up spurious effects, and we therefore suggest that a stricter criterion of statistical significance, $p < 0.01$, should be used. So readers should focus on the double asterisks.

For our data, small effects are usually not significant, but larger ones usually are. For instance, in the first tow of data, Batch explains 2.2 per cent of the variation in scores on the Mental Models scale, Subject explains 5.8 per cent, and the interaction explains 3.6 per cent. Looking down the table, the effect of Batch is on the scale measuring intake of knowledge, where it explains 3 per cent of the variance, and on use of knowledge, where it explains 2.1 per cent.

At this point it is not possible to take the analysis any further. We have an inkling that our type A, B, and C classification may apply to departments, but not to institutions. However, it was not feasible within the remit of this project to gather sufficient data about the new departments in the wider survey to be conclusive at this point.

Nevertheless, what we can with confidence say is that there are differences among the students taking different subjects in their mental models, their approaches to studying, their personal and educational development, and their personal change. These differences are not simply due to confounded variations in age and gender. However, on three of the four scales, the effect of Subject interacts with the effect of Batch. So the exact pattern of variation across students taking different subjects varies from one institution to another.

Diverse perceptions – of students and staff

When we analyse students' own perceptions of the outcomes of their higher education experience, we find considerable commonalities as well as some clear diversities. Notwithstanding the differences between the three diverse types of university settings for learning that we have used in our analysis, certain common patterns of what is valued as learning by students were discerned across all types and subjects. These included the general superiority, in terms of importance assigned, to outcomes connected with personal confidence and social networks over purely academic outcomes. A commitment to a subject, and the development of an academic identity remained relatively low, irrespective of the case type. Furthermore commitment to their university was extremely high only for students in the type B cases. These patterns appear to fit the traditions of the British university and contrast with the more professional and vocational outcomes of continental European universities. In a recent European study (Brennan and Tang, 2008), UK graduates appeared to be taking much less subject-related knowledge and skills into the workplace following their graduation than did graduates from universities in other European countries. That said, there are also commonalities: European graduates were like their UK counterparts in rating their personal development and change while in higher education as the most important outcome of the experience.

There are also some significant differences in what students themselves report. Those in a type C setting differed from the others in a number of respects. They reported lower gains in self-confidence and they were less likely to expect to retain university friendships after graduation. They were more likely to feel that they 'never fitted in' and very much more likely to feel that the 'qualification was the main thing' and that life outside of university remained the more important aspect of their lives. They were, however, compared with other graduates, rather more likely to believe that they had a clearer view of the future then when they commenced their course.

Students who had been in a type B setting were massively more likely to want to retain an association with their university and were also more likely to feel they were able to get on with a range of people. And they were much more likely to emphasise the 'life changing' nature of the university experience. While students within a type A setting were broadly similar to students in a type B setting, they were somewhat more likely to show a continuing commitment to their subjects and rather less likely to feel that university had changed the way they saw the world.

As we have reported in Chapter 4, instrumentalism is by far the most common characteristic that staff from all three subjects attributed to their students. However, this is manifested in a number of different ways, and staff are not always referring to the same sorts of behaviours, and there appear to be subject differences. Academics in business studies, alone among our disciplines, attribute the phenomenon to the subject's inner identity. Further, this is the only subject where instrumentalism is perceived to increase during the three years duration of study, a perception corroborated by our questionnaire data from students, and one not found in similar data gathered from sociology and biosciences students. Instrumentalism is also linked by academics in sociology and business studies with the socio-economic environment experienced by their students, who by comparison to those in biosciences are from poorer backgrounds and continue to struggle financially. Even where students are comparatively better off in biosciences, there is still a perception of a narrow instrumentality that has a financial basis linked to getting 'value for money' given that they are paying fees. This is also associated with a minimalist approach to study, a lack of enquiring spirit, and to a certain extent the narrow professional objectives of programmes with strong vocational orientations, and as in the case of sociology to the fragmentation of the discipline.

While there certainly are concerns expressed by academics about instrumentality and the lack of subject identity, as we have pointed out, the historical power and significance of disciplines to students may be overstated by both academics with a long history themselves and vicariously by their younger counterparts. Although we observe in certain instances relatively weak student identity with subjects, there may be positive conations of this phenomenon linked to curriculum flexibility. Further, as we report in Chapter 4, for most students in our three subjects, the subject remained very important, in particular in their choice of institution. We also find evidence of subject relevance from the high level of endorsement of generic learning outcomes as expressed by subject benchmark statements, although there are subject-specific differences. The views expressed by staff may be in part an expression that the aspirations and orientations of students are not the same as their own or wishful thinking rather than simply being a reflection of a lack of intrinsic engagement with subject.

Engagement is a significantly more complex notion than most academics suggest. There is certainly likely to be a relationship with students' individual social and cultural assets, but institutional characteristics are also important and maybe more so than the subject per se. Our application of the Dubet typology in Chapter 4 to sociology suggests that there is a complex relationship between the three variables of 'personal project', 'integration (academic and non-academic)' and 'vocation or engagement'. We have argued that student orientations may in part emanate from an interaction between the settings in which they study and the social and cultural capital that they bring

to that setting. So, for example, we find that Dubet's Type 1 orientation (the archetypical student) is more likely to be found in type B
settings, and his Types 2 to 4 (non-traditional, and two forms of
strategic) in type A and C settings. However, we also acknowledge
that while there is some relationship to institutional characteristics,
each of our student types are to be found in all settings, albeit with
different consequences for learning.

Student differences and 'parallel universities' – diversities or hierarchies?

As was noted at the outset of this book, higher education in the
UK is frequently characterised as a good example of a 'vertically differentiated' system, where reputational differences between institutions
are steep and 'where' you study is at least as important as 'what' you
study. The 15 case studies of the SOMUL project covered almost the
complete reputational range of UK higher education. They included
pre-92, post-92 and post-2000 universities. In terms of league tables,
the SOMUL range went from the top 10 down to the 90s.

In Chapter 5 we have considered the backgrounds, lifestyles and
forms of engagement of students between and across disciplines,
using secondary analysis of data from UCAS and HESA, and our own
primary data. It is the picture from the primary data that gives us the
greatest insight into student difference.

Reputational differences between universities clearly count for
much. There is greater demand for the courses of institutions with the
strongest reputation, and their graduates enjoy significant career
advantages. But it is not self-evident that students learn more or
different things. Within the SOMUL project, we have attempted to
understand the diversities of higher education in the UK without
recourse to the standard discourses concerned with 'top', 'pre-92', 'post-
92', 'world class' terminologies. We have explored higher education
diversity in terms of the student experience and the outcomes for
learning that derive from variations in that experience. We must now
consider the extent to which diversities of the latter sort map onto
diversities of the former hierarchical sort.

We can group the elements of diversity in the student experience in
terms of the characteristics of subjects of study, the way these studies
are organised, the characteristics and backgrounds of the students and
the different forms of student engagements and orientations. We can
also consider the different elements of the student experience: time

spent studying; time spent on other university activities; time spent outside of the university.

On the first of these – time spent studying – there are subject differences (with laboratory-based bioscience students spending the highest number of hours) but otherwise there seem to be no large differences between students or between institutions. Where there is a difference between students and institutions is in the time devoted to other university activities. Here, there appears to be a significant trade-off for students with external commitments and a lot of time spent on them. For these students, the experience of higher education is, as we have noted, a largely 'individualised' one. They have neither time – nor perhaps inclination – to spend time in university bars or at university societies. They have busy lives off campus and time spent at university is almost entirely devoted to study-related activities. It is also the case that such students are most likely to be found in what we have termed type C higher education settings. In turn, these settings seem most likely to be found within post-92 universities, catering for mature students and others who have followed less conventional routes into higher education. These universities are also less likely to possess the facilities to provide an attractive university social life. Another reason, therefore, for spending more time off-campus is that there are fewer things to do 'on campus'.

In contrast, we find that many students experiencing our type B settings – overwhelmingly within pre-92 universities – devote considerable amounts of time and attach significant importance to the non-academic side of university life. For these students, the new friends made and the new institutional loyalties represent the most important achievements of university life. Thus, for students in the higher reaches of the university hierarchies in the UK, it may be the acquisition of social capital and the institutional 'brand' that distinguishes them from their fellows who attend 'less advantaged' institutions. It is also the case that there is likely to be more 'fun' to be had at the former institutions, especially for the young and unattached.

In terms of the academic side of university life, we find considerable commonalities within subjects, irrespective of the institutions attended. Academic content is determined more by the values of the subject tribes than by the status of the institution attended. There are some diversities within approaches and orientations to study, but these follow subject and student characteristics rather than the reputational hierarchies of institutions.

We might conclude, therefore, that institutional hierarchies are important when higher education is performing its external social selection function. It does matter where you study in terms of the social and economic value attached to your credentials. But in terms of the broader socialisation functions of higher education, diversity cuts in different ways. The experience of higher education will be different according to the stage of the life course in which it is occurring, in terms of the external commitments of the individual student, and in terms of the subject studied and how the studies are organised by the particular university. It is not possible to reduce these diversities to a simple hierarchy of universities, although hierarchy and diversity are not completely disassociated. There are some universities still mainly catering for young school leavers and helping them to grow up. And these tend to be the older and more prestigious universities. Then there are some mainly newer universities catering in the main for local students, with a wider range of ages and backgrounds, and for whom university is mostly associated with academic study and gaining a qualification. The latter institutions are mainly providing opportunities for social mobility while the former institutions are mainly providing opportunities for status confirmation.

It may be more accurate to speak about *parallel universities*, where within one institution there are distinct student experiences. Parallel universities of both implicit and explicit kind may exist. In some institutions the primary distinction is between the experience of the commuting and residential student. In one institution there is a separate 'widening participation' campus where the same staff teach the same syllabus differently, but with the ostensibly the same outcomes. However, there is little interaction between this campus and the main site some miles distant from it. And while academic outcomes may appear largely the same, the other aspects of learning, in particular those linked to identify formation, and linked social capital attributes are quite different.

Part III

Chapter 9

Implications for institutions, academic staff and students

Introduction

Having reported a selection of our findings, what then can be seen as the implications of these for practice and policy? In arriving at our conclusions we also consider other supporting research.

We would argue that our models of organisational and social mediation of university learning and our findings about students provide useful general 'tools for thinking'. Specific substantive pointers about learning and teaching and student orientations and the outcomes of higher education can then be identified.

First, there are lessons and discussion points for academic staff and course planners, and for students. These not only have implications for the specifics of teaching and learning and students' choice of course, but also have relevance for more general teaching and learning 'discourses' in higher education. These are the main focus of this chapter.

Second, a number of challenges to current national policies and thinking also arise from the SOMUL project, especially from the student 'voices', and these are summarised here:

- The dominant hierarchical conception of diversity in current UK higher education policy discourse provides only a very limited reflection of the more complex pattern of diversities that exist and neglects the considerable commonalities that can be found.
- The policy drivers of the UK government and HEFCE have been to increase the diversity of the UK higher education system along a continuum from research intensive to teaching only institutions. However, an increased 'polarisation' of higher education threatens the economic and wider cultural and social benefits sought from an overall expansion of higher education.

- Students in general in the SOMUL study largely confirm the learning outcomes claimed in the generic elements of subject benchmark statements but this tells us only part of the story of 'what is learned at university': personal rather than narrowly academic outcomes are also important to students.
- The employability and skills agenda set down by government may not be fully shared by students. A narrow focus on employability and skills risks neglecting equally important ways in which higher education changes people's lives and the communities in which they live.
- While problematic aspects of the sometimes 'part-time' nature of the student experience (e.g. term-time paid work) must be recognised, so should the opportunities that this can provide for a wider range of learning outcomes, both employment-related and for personal development.

Some of the above are discussed further in Chapter 10. They also underpin the implications we see for staff, course planners and students that we discuss in the present chapter.

The ESRC evaluation of the SOMUL research recognised its contribution to awareness and understanding of the organisational and social context of student learning and suggested it would help institutions, as they seek to adapt, to understand the variety of ways in which students engage with higher education.

Figure 9.1 summarises our overall mapping of the organisational and social mediation of student learning. We see this map, along with our more specific A, B, C classification of institutional learning settings and our models and conceptualisations of student orientations, and the outcomes of higher education derived from Bernstein and Dubet, as having a potentially powerful heuristic value to academic staff and others seeking to enhance their overall understanding of the structures and processes of higher education.

Drawing on the so-called relational sociological theories of Giddens (1984) and Bourdieu (1977, 1988, 1998), Figure 9.1 presents higher education in terms of structure and agency. The upper three boxes of Figure 9.1 contain predominantly structural factors, while the lower level boxes list more agentic ones. An interaction of upper and lower factors is assumed in which neither structure nor agency is dominant. Movement from left to right in the figure then indicates movement through time, and can involve either social and cultural reproduction or personal change and even system transformation. Another way of

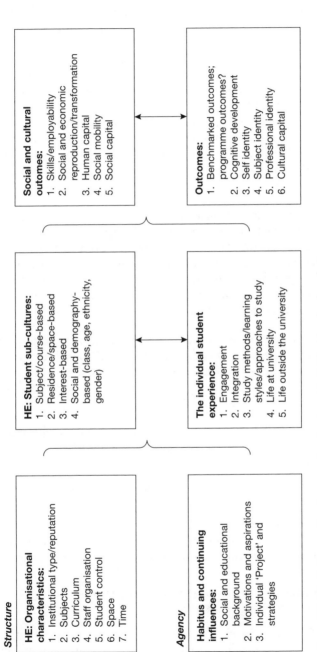

Change over time

Structure

HE: Organisational characteristics:
1. Institutional type/reputation
2. Subjects
3. Curriculum
4. Staff organisation
5. Student control
6. Space
7. Time

Agency

Habitus and continuing influences:
1. Social and educational background
2. Motivations and aspirations
3. Individual 'Project' and strategies

HE: Student sub-cultures:
1. Subject/course-based
2. Residence/space-based
3. Interest-based
4. Social and demography-based (class, age, ethnicity, gender)

The individual student experience:
1. Engagement
2. Integration
3. Study methods/learning styles/approaches to study
4. Life at university
5. Life outside the university

Social and cultural outcomes:
1. Skills/employability
2. Social and economic reproduction/transformation
3. Human capital
4. Social mobility
5. Social capital

Outcomes:
1. Benchmarked outcomes; programme outcomes?
2. Cognitive development
3. Self identity
4. Subject identity
5. Professional identity
6. Cultural capital

Figure 9.1 Mediations and outcomes: structural and individual levels of analysis

relating to such processes is what Wertsch (1998 cited in James and Biesta, 2007) refers to as the 'constraints' and 'affordances' associated with structures.

Such an approach involves a conceptualisation of higher educational processes in substantially different terms than the individualistic models that have hitherto predominated, e.g. an emphasis on 'learning styles' and 'skills' often in isolation from the socially located practices and social and organisational mediations that we see as essential.

What an agency and structure model – an awareness of agency and 'affordances' as well as 'structures' and 'constraints' – also makes clear is the potential agency of a range of agents, both singularly and collectively:

- policy commentators and policy makers;
- institutional leaders and course planners;
- teaching and learning professionals and researchers;
- academic staff, especially in their dealings with students but also in their interactions and mutual learning with other staff;
- students, not least in sharing learning with other students but especially in relation to academic staff.

In the rest of the chapter we consider the implications of our research for higher education teachers, institutional leaders, course planners, learning and teaching professionals, and for students and other stakeholders, including the employers of graduates. We have divided these into three areas:

- pedagogic issues and curriculum and organisational cultures;
- student orientations, identities and choice of course and institution;
- learning and teaching discourses.

As has been true also in the companion volumes on this series (e.g. James and Biesta, 2007), for the most part our identification of implications is not a matter of proposing simple recipes, but rather is in recommendations for action and consideration in more general terms.

Pedagogic issues and curriculum and organisational cultures

The SOMUL research brings out the elements of commonality and diversity in a rapidly expanded UK higher education system. The commonalities of the system are seen in the UK, perhaps especially an English tradition of student support describable as typified by personal 'intimate' pedagogies. The 'residential' tradition of students moving away from home and spending part of their time in university-provided living accommodation is part of this. The diversities arise especially from the recruitment of 'non-traditional' students, more likely to live at home and more likely to attend newer universities with different 'missions' than older universities. In a system in which 'excellence' is often defined as 'being better than others' and this then being associated with institutional hierarchy, pedagogic issues, curriculum issues and meeting students' needs are not always easily disentangled from such frames of reference. Our identification of three types of setting is an attempt in our analysis of diversities to move beyond an analysis simply in hierarchical terms, such as pre-92 and post-92 universities. More generally, we have seen that there remain strong commonalities across institutions, such as the cultures of subjects and students' valuation of the personal growth that higher education brings. What this means is that the specific implications we suggest from SOMUL for pedagogy and for curriculum and organisational cultures must also be viewed in the light of what we earlier identified as central general SOMUL assumptions, namely that learning is a function of:

- the social composition and life experiences (including previous and concurrent experiences) of the student body on different programmes – the social mediations; as well as
- the organisational features of programmes and their institutional contexts – the organisational mediations.

What this means is that experiences and outcomes of higher education are more than a matter of pedagogy in any narrow sense. It is also to say that those contemplating possible intervention need to consider both the 'structures' (the constraints and affordances) and the agents and 'agency' likely to operate in each particular case. Our findings suggest, for example, that each of the three A, B and C learning settings should be recognised as posing different issues and demanding different responses. Nor must it be assumed that the issues and responses will be identical within each type of learning setting. These are quite different assumptions from either a 'one size fits all' approach or the assumptions arising from any 'old' and 'new' distinction between institutional types.

With the above caveats, the following implications for pedagogic issues and curriculum and organisational cultures can be identified.

Induction and year 1 teaching

In an 'Academy Literature Review', Harvey *et al.* (2006: 5) reported that: 'students withdrew from the first year if they felt they were not integrated'. The SOMUL data confirm the importance of the early months of study and occurrence of problems of induction and adjustment for students in all settings, and for traditional as well as for non-traditional students.

A rather different issue is a 'lack of stretch' in year 1 work reported by some students. It would seem that on some courses, especially where students already possess an A level in the subject, students feel that they are able to coast or complain of lack of stimulation. However, there are also some indications that, for example, in first-year assessment sociology students who start courses without an A level in the subject perform equally as well as those who enter with such a qualification.

■ Course planners and teachers:

   a) should note that induction programmes and student support in the early months of courses and throughout year 1 are confirmed as a vital aspect of provision;
   b) should establish whether the demands made by introductory courses sufficiently match the needs of students from different backgrounds.

Teaching contact and study time

In both first and final years, biosciences courses had greater formal contact time, and students reported greater overall time spent studying compared with our other two subjects. In general, there exists a relatively weak positive correlation between self-reported contact time and self-reported independent study hours. Our reports from students also indicate overall patterns of study that suggest a virtual 'part-time' involvement by some students and relatively low weekly average hours of study. This is consistent with the findings reported for students more generally (Bekhradnia *et al.*, 2006; Bekhradnia and Sastry, 2007; and Bekhradnia, 2009). To what extent should these patterns and levels of study be viewed as problematic? Do they indicate that too little is required of students or too little regard is given for the rights of students, e.g. as 'customers' of higher education?

■ Institutional leaders, course planners, teachers and learning and teaching professionals can to some extent be reassured that the SOMUL data suggest that the concerns expressed by employers and the wider public about low teaching contact hours and levels of independent study are not shared by most students or by staff (see also a recent NUS survey – NUS, 2008). Equally, however, differences within as well as between subjects (and also international differences – Bekhradnia *et al.*, 2009), suggest that there may be benefit from a more systematic consideration of patterns of teaching contact and independent study, although such consideration should take into account all elements in the overall student experience.

Informal support for student learning

Indications exist from some university departments that well-planned informal support for learning can be a highly effective adjunct to formal teaching arrangements. For example, in one sociology department, a student officer and dedicated student support room at departmental level was especially appreciated by students.

■ Course planners and teachers should be aware that planned informal provision for support for student learning can be a vital adjunct to formal teaching arrangements.

'Studentship'

Studentship is a concept proposed by James and Biesta (2007) to sum-up the responsibilities that students should have for their own and others' learning. Students as well as staff have responsibilities in achieving collective learning outcomes. Thus, the effectiveness of seminars, for example, depends on students' attendance, appropriate preparation and active participation. E-learning is another example where increased student agency and responsibility for shared self-study activity would enhance outcomes. While we found a good deal of relatively routine use of e-learning in all three subjects, we found less indication that the pedagogic possibilities of e-learning are being widely explored. There were examples of tutor-led e-learning that were highly effective, but such provision is time-intensive for staff and could not be readily diffused across all areas of teaching. Our data suggest that while it is a growing element in students' studies, student educational use of the Internet is dwarfed by social use.

■ Students should recognise that not just academic staff have responsibilities in ensuring effective teaching and learning environments. They
too have responsibilities.

Subjects and subject cultures

Subject cultures remain a significant factor in higher education
provision. But subject cultures can also be associated with a curricular
conservatism. However, our SOMUL data suggest that the hegemony
of subjects and the demands of students may be broadly in balance.
Subjects appear to be increasingly responsive to student demands.
But equally subjects seem to have retained a measure of control
over such changes. We also found that a range of generic, as well as
subject specific, outcomes are being attained, as described by subject
benchmark statements.

A number of more specific subject specific issues also arise in relation
to teaching and learning. For example, in sociology, whether arising
from the methodological preference of staff or related to the relatively
low levels of mathematical competence of students recruited, quantitative methods appear to be losing out to qualitative methods. Williams
et al. (2008: 1003) suggest that: 'It may be concluded that the views
held by present undergraduates do not auger well for a methodo-
logically pluralist discipline in the future, or more generally for key
numeric and analytic skills sociology graduates can bring to other
professions and occupations.' For business studies, compared with
either sociology or biosciences, there are specific concerns about the
narrowness of the treatment of ethical issues.

Issues also arise from differences in the gender balance within our
three subject areas. In sociology, for example, we found female
students who welcomed both the preponderance of female students
and the prominence of the female voice within the present day sociology curriculum, but other students – including both male and female
students – viewed this less positively.

■ Institutional leaders, course planners, teachers and learning and teaching professionals should be reassured that our data suggest that the
hegemony of subjects and the demands of students appear in reason-
able balance and that in our three subjects, at least, a range of generic
as well as subject specific outcomes is being achieved. But there are
more specific subject issues that should be addressed.

Student assessment

Entwistle and Hounsell *et al.* (2007) regard 'the ways of thinking and practising in a subject' as offering 'a powerful means of evaluating the fundamental goals of a degree', which can include both course specific and generic outcomes. Ideally, student assessment should also seek to evaluate such central features of courses and encourage width of study. However, in the SOMUL research, strategic instrumentality – study and course attendance focused on areas directly involved in formal assessment – was recognised by both staff and students as a widespread feature of student behaviour and a source of dilemmas in assessment. For example, a surfeit of continuous assessment may accentuate a culture of strategic instrumentality and discourage more open-ended study. On the other hand, since students respond above all to the requirements of assessment, less assessment may still fail to encourage wider study. As Becker *et al.*'s *Making the Grade* (1968) suggests, these issues appear perennial.

■ Course planners, teachers and learning and teaching professionals need to continuously review the dilemmas associated with student assessment to seek a balance of assessment in both courses and modules congruent with both the broader and more specific learning objectives of courses.

Course structures and student option choice, including opportunities for part-time study

As seen in Chapter 4, it can be helpful to consider higher education cultures and structures as an organisation of time and space that frames, and can both help and hinder, student learning. As such, the introduction of modularity and semesterisation, a potentially new flexibility of time and space and an expansion of student option choice might have been expected. But this is not what is actually evident in our research.

Sometimes narrowness of choice arises from resource constraints but our data suggest that it more often reflects student agency, a positive preference for coherent course programmes. Such a pattern of preference is in fact something that has been evident ever since the first initiatives such as the Oxford Polytechnic Modular Scheme (Watson, 1989). This might suggest that the move to modular structures has not been worthwhile.

However, one advantage, at least from the student perspective, is that modularity has been a means by which what we have termed 'subject mediated integration' has been achieved: a way in which a previous over-dominance of subjects has been replaced by more student-centred, more market-sensitive, although still often subject-led, provision. As suggested in Chapter 4, this might be described as a 'best of both worlds', the partial decline of disciplinarity and Mode 1 knowledge but a less than total swing to a dominance of Mode 2 knowledge or even a purely 'pick-and-mix' provision. A note of reservation here, however, is that actual student choices are sometimes more limited than the theoretical ones available with the actual course patterns remaining much closer to traditional subject lines than the course titles might suggest.

A further objective of the introduction of modularity was to assist more flexible patterns of part-time study and student movement between institutions. However, there is little indication that this has occurred. It is evident that course planners still need to do more to focus on ensuring flexibility of entry and movement between courses and institutions for the minority but perhaps not insubstantial numbers of students who might wish to seek this (perhaps currently limited by the funding for part-time study).

▮ Policy makers, institutional leaders and course planners should ask why – while modular provision has helped, to an extent, to generate a new flexibility of curriculum – this has not resulted in more flexible patterns of part-time study and student movement between institutions. There is also the question of whether some new course titles are anything more than marketing devices that are hard to justify. This raises the question in some cases of whose interest a proliferation of degree titles serves?

Residential and non-residential university experiences (including part-time paid work)

The social side of university remains very important, especially in pre-92 residential universities. But with more students living at home and attending local university, commuting is now more common, often involving the combination of university and study with domestic responsibilities, part-time paid work and social lives at home. Some nominally full-time students appear in effect more like part-time students. How far do students cope? Is the experience of part-time paid work always a negative factor or are there opportunities for personal growth as well? How should institutions and teachers respond? The different collective and individual experiences and different forms of engagement found in the three settings we identified are in part associated with these different patterns of residence – in some settings we found suggestions that the institution's provision amounts almost to the existence of 'parallel universities'. In other institutions provision may have failed to respond to changing patterns of student engagement and integration. The evidence on such issues is as yet uncertain.

■ Policy makers and institutions should be alert to the uncertain implications of an increase in the numbers of students who commute from home and review how far their patterns of course provision remain appropriate.

The relation between teaching and research and the issue of part-time teaching

Both the relation between teaching and research and the status of teaching compared with research were central issues that concerned the academic staff we interviewed. While most staff, though less so in business studies than in biosciences and sociology, recognise the importance to universities of a linkage between teaching and research and some see this as the essence of a university experience, the practicalities are different.

In some departments a prioritisation of research and increased RAE and research council funding threatens to increase the gap between teaching and research by removing research-led academics from undergraduate teaching. Such teaching is often delegated to teaching only and part-time staff, which, however, typically includes research-led postgraduate students.

There is also the important issue of the general valuation placed on teaching compared with research in many institutions. In a recent online survey by the Higher Education Academy (HEA, 2009), while 92 per cent of staff thought teaching should be an important factor in promotions, only 43 per cent think it is.

Academic staff also often report difficulties in balancing teaching, research and administration, and this is especially so in post-92 universities, where research is less well-supported and part-time and postgraduate teachers are less available than in institutions with significant RAE research and research council funding.

Yet for many staff and some students the link between teaching and research remains important. Shared disciplinary research cultures are especially seen as a significant factor in teaching and learning in biosciences and sociology. This is so in both research intensive and less research-oriented institutions. In business studies, teaching receives less support from a research culture or shared research traditions. It may be that a shared experience in business practice can play an equivalent role, but in some departments the instrumentality of students seen as problematic by academic staff is associated with the lack of core research traditions in business studies.

The availability of a corps of postgraduate students as teachers in research-intensive departments and the use of part-time teaching staff in all departments raises a number of further issues. While in some departments, high-flyer researchers are allowed to contract out of undergraduate teaching, in others – including some of the most research intensive departments – it is a policy that senior staff should engage in undergraduate teaching. Also, while some students resent what they see as an over-reliance on part-time staff in their institutions, other students find the closeness of postgraduate teachers to the undergraduate experience as an advantage. Finally, where part-time teachers were employed, there was sometimes little evidence that their training and integration were adequate – a significant deficiency of the link, not only between teaching and research, but with the distinctive historic mission of the university.

■ Policy makers, institutional leaders, and learning and teaching professionals and researchers should recognise the significance placed on a link between teaching and research both by staff and students in disciplines such as biosciences and sociology. There is then an issue of what might replace this important organisational arrangement in other subject areas such as business studies that lack an equivalent research tradition.

There is also the important issue of the lesser valuation placed on teaching compared with research in many institutions. One major obstacle is the difficulty of assessing teaching and it should be an important area for research to find ways of overcoming this.

Finally, given that part-time staff play a significant role in undergraduate teaching, improvements in the integration and training of part-time staff are vital.

Student orientations, identities and choice of course and institution

Students relate to higher education in a variety of ways. Our research indicates the importance of appreciating the varied ways of being and becoming a student. Our research suggests that higher education is utilised by students in reflexively reworking their personal and social identities, in what Giddens (1991; 1992) has termed 'narratives of self'. Confidence and personal development are very important to most students although they are frequently attributed to the 'wider experience of university' rather than a specific course or subject. Sociology is something of an exception here in that personal development is often linked to what is termed by staff and students as a 'sociological imagination'. Neither subject nor professional identities have pre-eminence for students. In general, the interrelation of social and organisational structures and individual agency is strongly in evidence in the shaping of student orientations and identities, with neither predominant. The interrelation of social and organisational structures and individual agency is also again a useful model in a consideration of the broader social and cultural outcomes of higher education.

(i) Student instrumentalism

Academic staff voice concern over what is seen by some as a growing student 'instrumentalism'. But students mostly reject the notion that higher education is solely or mainly about gaining a qualification.

■ Institutional leaders, course planners and teachers should recognise the variety of viable ways in which students utilise higher education and that a majority of students in the study regarded their courses as meeting the subject benchmarks and their time at university as bolstering their personal identities.

Meeting the diverse needs of students

Alongside the three types of educational settings we identified, our eight-fold typology of student orientations (Chapter 5) indicates the range of student orientations. These relate to course objectives in different ways, but we have argued that in the main these can be recognised as valid ways of being a student within higher education. A variety of student orientations must be expected in a mass higher education system. And, contrary to what many staff assume, such variety was also far from absent in earlier eras of higher education.

In part, different student orientations are 'imported' into the academy, reflecting different social backgrounds, etc.? They can also be a function of organisational (and subject) characteristics? They may in addition be collectively 'constructed' by students on their courses and programmes. There may be different implications according to the different balance of these.

The role especially of newer institutions in meeting the particular needs of so called 'non-traditional' as well as traditional students should be acknowledged. However, the claim that a more earmarked curriculum content will always benefit such students remains undemonstrated. As the application of our student typology suggests, a diversity of student needs can potentially be accommodated within mainstream provision. There is evidence that many 'non-traditional' students cope well within traditional higher education settings (Baker and Brown, 2007). While the SOMUL research shows that there can be problems of integration and adjustment for such students, they mostly do appear to cope.

In fact there would appear to be advantages in avoiding an undue separation of traditional and 'non-traditional' students, especially when such divisions involve differences in institutional prestige. Bowl et al. (2008) argue that student types transcend 'traditional stereotypes'. And Hockings et al. (2008: 1), reporting on their TLRP research project, suggest: 'The dominant notion of traditional and non-traditional students creates over-simplistic understandings that limit the development of inclusive, engaging teaching.' An Australian study (Laming, 2007) suggests that 'regardless of backgrounds', the majority of students 'also want *all* the intangible, humanising aspects of education' as seen 'by scholars and writers from Newman onwards'.

▌ Institutional leaders, course planners and teachers 'need to be mindful of the diversity of needs, cultures and ways of being among their students, maintain high expectations of their students, and enable them to maximise as broadening an experience as possible' (Crozier and Reay, 2008). Contrary to some suggestions, our research suggests that a diversity of students can often be satisfactorily accommodated within mainstream provision.

Student choice of course and institution

Where a student studies can have more significance than what they study. Given major differences in the perceived status of provision of higher education, student 'choice' of institution can impact crucially on individual educational outcomes and 'life chances'. But students don't always select the highest ranking institution consistent with their qualifications. As Reay *et al.* (2001: 860) suggest: 'individuals applying for higher education courses are making very different kinds of choices within very different circumstances and constraints.' For some non-traditional students the local university may seem the only economically and psychologically plausible option. A central dilemma especially facing non-traditional students is balancing a psychologically, socially, culturally and economically 'comfortable', perhaps less expensive, choice of course and institution against the possibility of a more culturally challenging, potentially more economically rewarding but perhaps also more expensive, more risky choice. The dilemmas associated with the choice of course and institutions are substantial, with many students often lacking the social networks to be adequately informed of the implications of study at different types of institution. Archer and Hutchings (2000) suggest that some students on making a rough risk analysis simply decide not to go to university.

■ Both students and institutions need to be aware of the significant dilemmas associated with choice of course and institution. The suggestion sometimes is that students are guided by friends and hearsay and may not always make adequately informed choices. But equally, given the complexities of the costs and benefits involved, there is also an argument that students may often best be left to make their own choices.

Institutional hierarchy, fair access and social and economic reproduction and transformation more generally

Crozier and Reay (2008) point to greater differences between student experiences in different institutions than they find for students by social class within institutions. Given the advantages for 'employability' – factors such as cultural capital and 'screening' – and more general social advantages associated with higher status/reputation institutions and subjects promoting the fair access to elite institutions to 'non-traditional students' is important where this is their choice. However, we also concur with Crozier and Reay (2008) that, in promoting increasing institutional diversity, current government and HEFCE policy should also attempt to limit collateral 'damage' potentially arising from a further 'polarisation of institutions' (cf. Jary *et al.*, 1998).

Higher education is about 'positionality' in that a small number of elite institutions convey prestige and advantage to students who attend them. But higher education is also about positionality in a wider sense in that all institutions offer personal benefits and advantages in employability compared with non-attendance at university. More than this, although in part higher education can be viewed as the 'social reproduction' of a status system, it also offers the potential for a cultural shift and structural reshaping of this system: (i) via the circulation of individuals and increasing outside entry into elite sectors, and (ii) from an overall expansion of higher educational opportunity bringing a structural reshaping via an increased number of higher and middle ranking positions.

■ Policy makers and commentators, and all in higher education, while focusing on fair access to elite institutions, should also be alert to the potentially negative effects of an increasing reputational range among institutions. We all should avoid assuming that higher education is only a system of social reproduction, downplaying its potential for individual and social transformation.

Learning and teaching discourses

The increasing socially and economically embeddedness of UK higher education has provoked a more public and mass media-led discourse about learning and teaching alongside those inside higher education. That students are now more likely to see themselves as 'customers' has also altered the content of higher education discourse. While the 'news values' of the media have led to a distorted emphasis on many issues, it is equally the case that many staff viewpoints sometimes appear only weakly grounded in evidence.

It is in this general context that managerialism and a new accountability together with cultures of enhancement have arisen in higher education, although hotly contested. A baleful influence for many, they have nonetheless been seen by others as helping to bring about a necessary modernisation of earlier oligarchic controls that has increased the responsiveness of higher education to economic and social needs. Policy makers, institutional leaders and teachers have to learn to tread carefully in the face of the claims and counterclaims concerning the legitimacy and limitations of the 'new accountability' of higher education's new managerialism, seeking to preserve a balance between professional and managerial control.

Learning and teaching discourses and regimes of accountability and enhancement

Our interviews confirm what is apparent from other studies, that academic staff are ambivalent and divided on procedures for accountability and the value of formalised programmes for the enhancement of learning and teaching and also on widening participation. The more dialogical, less adversarial regimes of accountability and enhancement recently introduced by the QAA are welcomed by staff and are likely to be more widely supported. The role of the Higher Education Academy with its main focus on subject centres is accepted as a 'best approach' by those staff attuned to programmes of enhancement. But it has indicated that rigid polarising 'staff metaphors' – e.g. as 'bright' and 'weak', 'academic' and 'non-academic' students – restrict flexible staff responses to new contexts and new possibilities in learning and teaching (see Trowler, 2008). The SOMUL research found staff to be divided between teaching and learning and student-oriented academic staff – often also younger staff – generally receptive to new learning and teaching discourses and those – often older staff – who are largely non-receptive. Interventions aimed at bridging what is often a generation gap should be a central part of policies of enhancement.

Subject benchmarks

Benchmarking and programme specifications have the support of and are found useful by some but not all staff. A composite of benchmark statements was used in the SOMUL research. Students saw their courses as largely delivering subject benchmark outcomes. As a part of the QAA's validation and review apparatus, subject benchmarks are, however, controversial. They were introduced to inform students and employers about the expected outcomes of university learning in individual subjects. They are also intended to provide a baseline in course design and course review. Despite the reservations about subject benchmarks, their value in course design and course review was recognised in our interviews with staff.

■ Institutional leaders, course planners, teachers should note that despite reservations about subject benchmarks, in the SOMUL study these were seen as playing a useful role in course design and course review by those staff that had employed them.

Students and other external 'stakeholders' can have confidence in subject benchmarks as an overall guide to the content and outcomes of study.

Competence and generic skills

'Competence' is a key term in the development of National Vocational Qualifications; 'capability' is the term adopted in 1980 by the Royal Society of Arts (RSA) in its 'capability manifesto' for education in general and which was developed in 1988 to the Higher Education for Capability initiative. But beyond the specific association with institutionalised initiatives, the same issues have been articulated through a range of other terms. In 1984, the funding agencies for higher education issued a joint document asserting that: 'The abilities most valued in industrial, commercial and professional life as well as in public and social administration are the transferable intellectual and social skills' (NAB/UGC, 1984: 4). The Association of Graduate Recruiters (AGR) has also made its own contribution to the debate, emphasising the need for graduates to be 'self-reliant', 'aware of the changing world of work, take responsibility for his or her own career and personal development and is able to manage the relationship with work and with learning throughout all stages of life' (AGR, 1995: 4). However, Holmes suggests that an emphasis on competence risks undermining 'those very traditions valued in academia, espousing disinterested pursuit of knowledge, its production and dissemination, for its own sake'. Holmes' counter is 'that a degree carries a *double warrant*' (Holmes, 1994a, b):

> assessment in higher education is a convention of warrant, whereby the award of a degree is taken as warranting entry into the graduate occupational arena, . . . attempts to introduce a capability curriculum have been based on the assumption that the requirements for each of these social arenas, occupation and academic, are isomorphic . . . so a single, common framework of such capabilities can and should be developed and adopted.
>
> (Holmes, 1994a: 6)

The conventional manner in which the notions of 'capable people' and the 'self-reliant graduate' are interpreted is through the production of a set of 'transferable skills' or 'capabilities' (or, in the case of the AGR, 'self-reliance skills') is mistaken. Instead, 'we take the occupational arena and academia as two, separate though connected generalised 'communities of practice' (Lave and Wenger, 1991). But arguably, academia has always been concerned with 'practical' affairs of society, including the occupational (e.g. Silver and Brennan, 1988; Barnett, 1990). From our research we can ask whether there is already complementarity rather than tension between academic goals and transferable competencies? In sociology students aspirations and perceptions of outcomes and change include such central disciplinary objectives as 'critical thinking' and the 'sociological imagination' – as well as what Albrow (1986) refers to as 'humane transferability'.

■ Institutional leaders, course planners, teachers and learning teaching professionals and students should note the limitations of disembodied and decontextualised conceptions of skills and make explicit the cultivation of generic skills inherent in subject and more general communities of practice.

Capability and employability

While many graduates report satisfactory employment outcomes and may go on to employment-related postgraduate study, graduates in the SOMUL surveys also report anxieties and difficulties in obtaining what they see as appropriate employment. Higher education discourses on 'capability and employability' sometimes appear to take relatively little account of the actual practices of graduate employers. Criticising such discourses, Brown, Hesketh and Williams (2003) refer to the importance of recognising what they term the 'duality of employability'. While 'absolute employability' relates to the question 'Have students gained appropriate skills, knowledge and commitment to undertake the job in question?', 'relative employability' refers to the relative chances of a graduate acquiring and maintaining particular kinds of employment taking into account the supply and demand for posts and employers' criteria. This being so, and contrary to the claims of proponents of the 'capability curriculum', rather than always helping graduates to gain employment, innovations such as profiles of personal competence, especially where associated with lower status institutions, may only serve to increase the stigmatisation of the graduates concerned as 'less capable' than those in possession of more established forms of 'cultural capital'.

■ Institutional leaders and course planners, especially those promoting a 'capability' agenda, should be more cautious in their claims regarding employability.

The utility of models and measurement of orientations to learning and teaching

Reviewing the literature of learning styles, Coffield *et al.* (2004) suggest that the popularity and usage of learning styles questionnaires far outstrips the evaluative base. We see the SOMUL project's data as illustrating both the utility and the limitations of standardised measures of learning styles, deep and surface learning, etc., e.g. that these measure are contextual – sometimes strategic – features of student orientations to learning, not invariant dimensions of individual orientations.

■ Teachers and learning and teaching professionals especially should note the utility and the limitations of standardised measures of learning styles, deep and surface learning, etc. (see also Coffield *et al.*, 2004).

The role of practitioner-led pedagogical research

Given the pressures for evidence-based research on teaching and learning, practitioner-led pedagogical research clearly has a potentially significant role in enhancing teaching and learning. It often has the advantage of being well-placed to be richly contextual. Rather than an adjunct to a more conventional academic career, it can also be pursued as a career-reorienting route for some staff. There are examples in the SOMUL research of staff taking this route being promoted to professorial level. More often pedagogical researchers appear relatively isolated within their institutions and also lack external links with other pedagogical researchers. Opportunities exist for more cross-institutional and cross-disciplinary co-ordination of pedagogy research and also for links with more conventional academic research. For example, Higher Education Academy subject centres are now encouraging improved research networking. On the other hand, the procedures of the RAE are widely perceived as restricting progress, since practitioner research matches often falls uneasily between 'subject' and 'educational' categories.

■ Institutional leaders and policy makers especially need to further improve the provision and the rewards and recognition of practitioner and wider higher education research.

Conclusions

The implications suggested above must remain to some extent tentative. As for sociological and psychological research generally, it is characteristic of higher education research that is rarely seen as definitive. An evidence base in what is a field of social science research can never be a matter of simple formula. The SOMUL research is no exception, particularly so as higher education is a far from easy research terrain.

In an era of audit and evaluation, higher education tends to see itself over-assessed and over-evaluated, and individual departments and institutions can be suspicious of the implications of research findings for particular departments or institutions. This said, our academic staff respondents were mainly enthusiastic participants. But student volunteers for interview and for participation in focus groups proved more difficult to obtain. And for a variety of reasons, questionnaire response rates were variable between subjects. Somewhat paradoxically, they were lowest for sociologists. More generally, cohort follow-ups proved difficult, restricting longitudinal analysis.[1]

The complexity of the interplay of structures and agency in the processes and outcomes of higher education processes is reflected in our findings. Arguably, our initial aspirations for our research aimed too high. Nevertheless its sociological and multidisciplinary focus, in comparison with the more predominant individualistic psychological focus of much higher education research on student learning, has, we feel, yielded a good deal. It is in this context that we argue that our models of organisational and social mediation of university learning and our findings about students provide useful 'tools for thinking' and lead to more specific substantive pointers about learning and teaching and student orientations and the outcomes of higher education.

An issue remains about our research findings, however. Questions continue to be raised about the impact of aspects of system wide changes in higher education such as modularisaton and semesterisation, with their risks of 'MacDonaldisation' (Parker and Jary, 1995). In a recent Times Higher Education survey (Gill, 2008), 52 per cent of staff believed that universities have 'dumbed down', although 42 per cent did not. There were other strong concerns expressed, especially about resource constraints and a reduction of teaching hours. Could our more positive research conclusions focused on students as well as staff have got it wrong? A main reason for thinking otherwise is that both our own findings and numerous other surveys constantly show generally high levels of student satisfaction.

In the final chapter we examine further the implications for society. In general our own view is that while higher education in part *reproduces* economic, cultural and social capital and the related student identities, its effects are also *socially and culturally transformative* and individually liberative, providing an environment in which some students at least deconstruct and reconstruct their personal and class identities.

Note

1   The question why there has been so relatively little specifically socio-logically oriented study of higher education is also of interest. And there is a paradox about sociology specifically: why, when our belief is that departments and institutions more generally would benefit from fuller analysis of the 'sociology' of their own activities, do so relatively few sociologists show any depth of interest in the sociology of higher education?

Chapter 10

Implications for society

Why higher education matters to its students

During the course of the SOMUL project, several hundred students talked to us about their experiences of higher education, about how it had changed them and how it had equipped them for the future. Some things were broadly shared, others distinctive to the particular subject studied, or the institutional context or the circumstances and orientations of the individual student. Some of the things that were said broadly chimed with the perspectives of their teachers, of their institutions and of government policy. Other things did not.

Here is just one example, from Julie, a final-year sociology student studying at the University of Wilton. Julie was a young woman in her early 20s, from the region although not living at home. One of the things that the project was interested in was the importance attached by students to the subject they had studied, the extent to which it could be the source of new identities and loyalties that would be maintained after graduation. Thus, one thing we asked students about was whether they were considering further study in the same subject, a master's degree or maybe eventually a doctorate. In Julie's case, the answer was clear-cut. 'Definitely not.' Another line of inquiry in the same direction concerned jobs, about whether the student envisaged employment that would utilise the subject knowledge acquired at university. Again, Julie's answer was unambiguous: 'Oh no, I can't imagine what sort of job that would be. No definitely not.' And then warming to her theme, and without further prompting, she added, 'And I'll tell you this. After I've finished my last finals paper in June, I'll never open another sociology book or sociology journal ever again. Never.' After which there was a short pause, then 'And I'll tell you something else. From now, every time I open a newspaper or switch on the television news, every time from now on, for the rest of my life, when I do things like that, I'll be doing sociology. Forever.'

We reported Julie's comments, anonymously, to some of her teachers. They were impressed, excited even. They hadn't heard comments like these before. They didn't know that they could have this sort of impact. In her own way, Julie was articulating the importance that almost all the students attached to their own personal development, to the ways that they had changed as a result of going to university, changes that could not be reduced to a matter of employment-related skills and competences, important though these also were to most students. For many students, higher education had been about something more. And this was not just a function of how hard they had studied, how committed they were to their courses, how ambitious they were for the future. It was a function simply of 'being there', of being in a new environment, of making new friends, of identifying with new ideas, of developing new interests. These were not things that were necessarily captured by degree classifications or transcripts. But they were reflected by enhanced confidence, new social skills and new perspectives on the world. These were all things that were learned at university.

That Julie's teachers at Wilton seemed largely unaware of the significance of the changes occurring around them is interesting in itself. The Wilton sociologists were committed teachers but there were few opportunities for them to meet with students informally, outside of the classroom. Students were infrequent visitors to the corridors that housed the sociology staff rooms. Many of the staff room doors had signs indicating the staff member's availability to meet with students, for example between 3 pm and 4 pm every Thursday. Not a lot of time for staff who might be teaching a couple of hundred different students in the course of the week.

Thus, one of the conclusions that might be drawn from the SOMUL project is that the student voice is perhaps not always sufficiently heard. Notwithstanding the industry that has developed around student feedback, the questions asked and the analyses undertaken may sometimes 'miss the point' as far as many students are concerned. The annual national student survey seems to report mostly high levels of student satisfaction with their courses. But this simple point seems often to be missed in the near-obsessive concern with rankings and league tables. Having satisfied students is not enough, they have to be 'more satisfied' than the students from competitor universities.

One implication of the SOMUL project, therefore, is that the dominant discourse of policy makers and institutions may be missing some important perspectives on what is happening in our universities and colleges. Higher education may be more important than policy makers and institutional leaders seem to think. It may be more important than academics think. Lives are being changed, both social and cultural capital are being acquired, identities are transforming and long-term relationships and loyalties are being formed. And yes, some useful knowledge and skills are being obtained that will serve their owners well in the job market over a lifetime.

All this might sound a bit extreme, even a bit romantic, to some readers. And, of course, the SOMUL project has also been about diversity, of the institutions, courses and lives of the students, as well as in what they learn at university. As we noted at the outset, diversity is frequently conceived in hierarchical terms, in notions of 'top' universities and students. But a conclusion of the SOMUL research is that students share a lot of things in common, irrespective of where they study. At the same time, there is considerable diversity within many universities and courses as well as diversity between them. Students engage with their higher education in many different ways, reflecting their own backgrounds and aspirations as well as the nature of what is on offer, and how it is organised, in different universities and courses.

Why higher education matters to society

Political importance is attached to higher education because of its perceived contributions to a successful economy and to a just and equitable society. The first of these focuses attention on the curriculum, on the transmission of 'useful' knowledge and skills and the matching of these to the requirements of the workplace. The second focuses on widening participation and its contribution to social mobility and here the reputational ranking of universities is often given central importance. Widening participation in 'top universities' is important precisely because of this belief that these universities are superior in every way. But it does not require the obverse assumption – that all universities are the same – to question whether some universities really are better in all respects for all types of students in all possible circumstances. Social mobility is not just about gaining entry to elites. In mass and universal higher education systems, it is about the acquisition of opportunities to be different – maybe 'better'

– than parents and peers, of having choices and aspirations about what to do with one's life, including how and where to do it.

Higher education, diversity and social cohesion

As we have discussed at several places in this book, going to university has traditionally been about 'going away' from family and friends to a new kind of life with new people. Whether the new people are largely different or largely the same will vary, reflecting the type A and type B distinctions between educational settings that we introduced in Chapter 3. In the type B settings, processes of social reproduction may be discerned with students receiving what Brown and Hesketh (2004) have described as 'status confirmation'. Type A settings might be associated with social change, providing opportunities both for social mobility and for social integration, although the extent to which either is being achieved in practice remains open to question. However, today, higher education does not necessarily involve going 'away' and it can be experienced not as a life stage but as one component among others of a multifaceted and probably quite segmented period of a person's life, which may occur at different stages of the life course. We referred to this as the type C experience and have associated it with 'living with difference, and maintaining and constructing multiple identities, at university, home and school'.

Whatever the characteristics of the institutional setting and of the individual student's engagement with that setting, many aspects of the student experience do in fact seem to be shared ones. Especially in respect of type A and B settings, student experiences and their perceptions of learning outcomes were broadly similar in the various surveys carried out for the SOMUL project. Thus, leaving aside perceptions of status hierarchy, there seems to remain much by way of commonalities in the student experience in UK universities. For students in type C settings, some things are different though much is still broadly similar. And below we refer to a concept of 'parallel universities' where students from different types of setting share the same institutional context, if perhaps little else.

Some questions that arise from all this concern whether the relationship between particular types of higher education and differential social rewards are justified by the differences in experience and learning associated with the different types. Is it an example of meritocracy in action? Or is it rather the legitimisation of social differences that owe their origins to something other than higher education, for example to social class, ethnic and gender characteristics, which are unevenly distributed around the different types of higher education experience?

There is at very least a danger that by compounding notions of difference with notions of hierarchy, higher education is ensuring the maintenance of an elite reproduction function in a situation of mass enrolments. But even if that were to be the case, that is certainly not to imply that growth in enrolments in higher education has not brought about substantial social benefits. The experience of personal change brings with it a capacity for further change, over the life course. The widespread growth in personal confidence and awareness among students bodes well for notions of 'active citizenship' and civic engagement. Mobility – in both its geographical and social senses – is enhanced by attending higher education. Social cohesion may be strengthened by providing opportunities for people from different backgrounds, races and nationalities to come together and get to know each other.

However, none of these potential benefits from an expanded higher education system will necessarily be achieved if higher education is not organised explicitly to achieve them. If diversity in higher education comes to mean a collection of segmented social and educational ghettoes, differentially esteemed and celebrated, then the effects are likely to be a more segmented and divided society.

Does the experience of higher education have to be limited to one segment of it? In the United States, a majority of today's students have attended at least two higher education institutions before they attain their first degree. If we employ the consumerist language of choice, it could be argued that students might be entitled to 'shop' at more than one university for their learning and personal development. This would be one simple way of avoiding 'ghetto-isation', of making boundaries porous, of encouraging integration rather than segmentation. It might even enable students to learn 'more things', providing that our conceptions of the outcomes of learning can extend beyond the formal curriculum and recognise the wider benefits of learning.

However, higher education's diversity is not just a matter of differences *between* universities. A pro-vice-chancellor at one post-92 university coined the phrase 'parallel universities' to describe his own institution. One of the 'universities' followed the English residential tradition and comprised students who were recent school-leavers living away from home for the first time. The other took students who were mainly locally based, with a much wider age distribution and with all sorts of commitments outside the university. The latter students were in the clear majority. 'Part-time students on full-time courses' is another way this kind of student experience has been described. The pro-vice-chancellor who presided over the parallel universities refused to regard one as superior to the other. But the challenge of running the two side-by-side was considerable with implications for the way the university was organised and for the way courses were taught and assessed.

While much of this book has been about differences between universities and their academic programmes, it has also to be recognised that even within particular types of university and learning setting, there are likely to be students with many different kinds of orientation and engagement. Universities and their staff are themselves learning how to respond to these many diversities. To help them to do so, some shibboleths of UK higher education might need to be questioned, including the duration of study programmes and the distinction between full-time and part-time study.

Rethinking the role of the 'extra-curricular' and the nature of a 'liberal education'

This book has examined the experiences of students in a 'mass' system of higher education. The rationale for expansion, from both demand and supply perspectives, has been principally economic. Students want to get good jobs. Government wants a skilled workforce to meet the needs of a modern economy. Yet, a strong message from the hundreds of students who took part in the SOMUL project is that higher education is about more than academic study, more than preparation for a job.

A lot of today's higher education – and especially at the 'mass' ends – has been or is in the process of being 'vocationalised' with emphasis placed on the acquisition of work-related skills and competences and the achievement of an appropriate job at the end of it. And yet higher education in the UK has, in comparison with higher education in many other developed countries, always had a rather loose fit between the content of courses and the jobs entered by graduates. On the one hand, this may have been helpful to processes of 'elite reproduction' – so that 'where' one studied was more important than 'what' one studied – but arguably it was also important in terms of creating a workforce that would be flexible and adaptable in the longer term and citizens who could be expected to be critically engaged and civically responsible.

Thus, involvement in 'sports and societies' provided important entries on a student's CV, but they also provided new interests, new relationships and, quite often, new knowledge and skills. This 'non-academic' side of university life was much valued in elite universities and elite higher education systems. It might, therefore, be asked, whether a wider range of 'non-academic' experiences might also be valued and celebrated in today's expanded and differentiated higher education. In the same way as the research function of higher education has increasingly transcended the boundaries of the university, so perhaps should the teaching and learning function. Like their predecessors, today's students have interests, relationships, knowledge and skills acquired outside of the classroom walls. Initiatives such as 'personal development planning' attempt to give them recognition. To the extent that they do so successfully, they can enrich the learning experience for students in ways that may also be socially beneficial.

Thus, one of the several commonalities identified by the SOMUL project research is that the experience of higher education is more than its academic content. Recognising the value and importance of a much wider range of 'extra-curricular' activities will extend society's recognition of 'what is learned' as well as being socially equitable to a diverse student population.

'Improving' what is learned at university

What is learned is more than what is taught. The English tradition of a university education from Newman onwards has emphasised as much. But there is a danger that this truism may be forgotten in concerns about through-puts and short-cycle higher education. By international standards, especially in Europe, university students in the UK receive a shorter higher education. There is also some evidence to suggest that it is a less intense higher education, as part-time employment reduces the hours available for study. Students may still get their degrees and higher education may win plaudits for its efficiency, but learning outcomes may be limited and narrowed as a result. As students' engagement with their higher education takes increasingly different forms and as distinctions between full-time and part-time modes of study become increasingly blurred, a case can be made for a 'stretching' of higher education courses in order to recognise that fewer hours are available and that short courses and high completion rates in such circumstances may amount to an impoverishment of what is learned.

Contemporary higher education is an increasingly differentiated higher education but the differentiation of its forms and the diversity of its students should not disguise the continuation of important commonalities. These have been referred to at many points during this book and yet we find that many commentators, both inside and outside higher education, prefer to deny them. What has been called a 'vertical differentiation' remains a dominant way of perceiving higher education in the UK, with the emphasis on hierarchy and stratification of its institutions and participants. It may be that this is inevitable if education is to continue to play a differentiating role within the structure of society. While at one time access to any form of higher education bestowed (or legitimised) a range of social advantages, with increased enrolments internal differentiation within higher education is necessary in order for this elite function to be performed.

If higher education is, therefore, to be a mixture of commonality and differentiation, the question arises as to the amount and nature required of each. The obvious point to make here is that differentiation can take many forms and is not simply 'vertical' or hierarchical. And excellence in any or all of these forms need not be in limited supply. Many of the commonalities we have encountered relate to the values and 'ways of seeing' of particular academic subjects as transmitted by university teachers, to the approaches to learning and the relationships formed between learners, and to the kinds of changes perceived and valued among the learners. One person's achievements and 'excellence' need not be at the expense of someone else's. Yet the unreflexive ways in which increasing student achievements are cited as evidence of declining standards and 'dumbing down' implies the opposite and the consequent denial of commonality and a shared experience.

This book has been about many diversities, some of which are valued and some of which are not. Bourdieu's (1973) concept of the 'cultural arbitrary' comes to mind and with it the relationship between knowledge and power, including the power to define what is valid and valued knowledge. To some extent, the very notion of a 'higher' education cannot escape such a relationship. But at the same time, a widening of participation must involve a widening of the concept of higher education, of what might be included both within and beyond the curriculum. To do so in a democratic and egalitarian way, which at the same time retains rigour in learning and in conceptions of knowledge, represents one of the major challenges for higher education, not just for those who work and study in it, but for all in society – in particular the employers who use its graduates. This may require greater emphasis being placed upon 'ways of knowing' rather than 'what is known'. There are assessment implications in all this and also certification implications if both commonalities and diversities in the learning outcomes of higher education are to be fully recognised.

In considering the balance between commonality and diversity, it may be helpful to distinguish between aims, content and modes of delivery. The broad aims of a university education may share much in common across different fields of study and types of institution. However, when it comes to the content of courses, different subject-based 'tribes and territories' continue to dominate, although with considerable territorial changes bringing boundary implications both inside and outside the walls of academe. And the manner in which content is to be delivered (or constructed) will also be increasingly diverse if account is to be taken of the diverse aspirations, orientations and circumstances of the learners.

In considering the outcomes of learning, again both commonality and diversity are to be found. The mixture of both generic and subject-specific learning outcomes is emphasised in subject benchmarks and by academic staff but, most of all, by the students themselves. At the societal level, the economic and social outcomes of universities imply both positional advantage (differentiating) for the few and a larger public good, potentially to the benefit of all. And the outcomes of learning, whether for the individual or for the society, are essentially long-term. Students and graduates as active citizens are being prepared for futures largely unknown but futures that will be theirs to shape. Improving what is learned at university is about improving the future available to all!

Appendix
Methods used in the study

Introduction

The project adopted a case study methodology and concentrated on students and graduates in three contrasting academic subjects: biosciences, business studies and sociology. This combination of subjects allowed academic/vocational and science/non-science dimensions to be explored. For each subject, five study programmes from different universities were selected to represent the different social and organisational features in which the project was interested. Students from these programmes were investigated by means of questionnaires, focus groups and interviews at various stages during and after their undergraduate careers. There was a particular focus on their conceptions of learning and personal and professional identity, and on the factors that they saw as influencing these conceptions. There were also interviews with teachers at each of the 15 case study departments. During the final year of the project, a survey of students from a wider range of subjects at nine universities was undertaken to assess the general applicability of the case study findings.

As explained in Chapter 2, the three subjects were chosen to reflect variation in the hard/soft and pure/applied dimensions of Biglan's (1973) taxonomy of academic subjects. As explained in Chapter 3, the relevant departments or subject groups were chosen to exhibit variation in the structure of the undergraduate curriculum (closed versus open) and in the homogeneity or heterogeneity of the student population with regard to age, gender, ethnicity and social class. In most institutions, the undergraduate programme lasted for three years, but some of the business schools included an additional year (the third year) spent on work placement.

Questionnaire surveys

Over 1,600 questionnaires were completed from students at the 15 case study departments. In each department or subject group, questionnaires were administered to students in the first year (the 'entering' students) and the final year (the 'exiting' students) of the undergraduate programme. Similar questionnaires were given 2 years later (when the entering cohorts were in their third year of study and 12–18 months after the exiting students had graduated). This research design enabled a 'longitudinal' study of changes over 4–5 years to be carried out in just 2–3 years. It is analogous to Baltes' (1968) 'cross-sectional sequential' design and Schaie's (1965) 'cohort-sequential' design in research on human development.

In addition to this, over 600 students from a wider range of subjects at nine universities were investigated by means of a questionnaire administered in their final year of study. This wider survey consisted of the three original subjects (bioscience, business studies and sociology) but also included history, geography, mathematics, computing, engineering, film and media studies.

The five questionnaires differed slightly to take account of the different perspectives of students at different points in their academic careers. The questionnaire administered to the entering students in their first year is presented in A.1 (pp. 208–19) by way of example. There were ten sections, which are listed below together with the sources, where appropriate, from which they were adapted:

- Reasons for choice of institution and degree programme.
- Information about institution, degree programme and place of residence.
- Expectations of higher education (www.etl.tla.ed.ac.uk/question naires/LSQ.pdf).
- Mental models of learning (Vermetten *et al.*, 1999).
- Approaches to studying (www.etl.tla.ed.ac.uk/questionnaires/ ETLQ.pdf).
- Experience of being a student.
- Weekly activities.
- Personal and educational development (Lawless and Richardson, 2004).
- Personal change.
- Demographic information.

Wherever possible, the questionnaire was administered during normal classroom activities. Since many of the graduates were no longer engaged in formal education, their version of the questionnaire omitted the scales on conceptions of learning and approaches to studying, and it was administered by means of a postal survey.

Student interviews

Approximately 260 individual interviews were conducted with students at the case study institutions, coupled with focus groups and staff interviews. Groups of between six and eight students were recruited from the entering and exiting cohorts for individual interviews. Wherever possible, the same students were re-interviewed at the time

Table A.1 Student interviews by subject

Biosciences	Entering cohort 1	Entering cohort 2	Exiting cohort 1	Exiting cohort 2
Biosciences				
Fridaythorpe	5	5	5	3
Givendale	6	7	4	1
Langtoft	4	5	2	0
Ulleskelf	4	3	5	1
Warthill	8	6	7	1
Total	27	26	23	6
Business studies				
Bramham	7	5	7	2
Bugthorpe	5	7	9	3
Husthwaite	5	7	5	2
Weighton	6	7	6	2
Wistow	6	4	4	3
Total	29	30	31	12
Sociology				
Bilton	1	0	5	2
Fenton	7	5	3	2
Holme	10	4	6	2
Tockerington	6	4	4	3
Wilton	1	3	5	2
Total	25	16	23	11

of the relevant questionnaire surveys. To illustrate, an example of the schedule for the second set of interviews with the entering students can be found in A.2 (pp. 220–2). Interviews were recorded and transcripts of them were made. Initial coding of data was undertaken using NVivo. Table A.1 shows the numbers of students from each university interviewed ordered by subject and cohort.

Focus groups

Discussion groups (typically containing between six and eight students) were recruited from the entering and exiting cohorts. Normally these consisted of the students who had already taken part in individual interviews. As an opening exercise, they were asked to write down on pieces of card or paper their individual responses to the questions, 'What have you learnt here? How do you think you've changed?' They then shared their responses with the group. As an example, the schedule for the entering students is presented in A.3 (pp. 222–4). As with the individual interviews, the focus groups were recorded and transcribed.

Staff interviews

Finally, interviews were carried out with 56 members of staff from the participating departments or subject groups, including the head of department or other senior member of academic staff. To illustrate, the schedule for the staff interviews in sociology departments can be found in A.4 (pp. 224–6). The interviews were recorded but not transcribed with the interviewers writing up detailed notes soon after the interview, drawing both on the recording and on the notes made during the interview.

The figures in Table A.2 show the numbers of staff interviewed from the 15 cases.

The interview schedule for the members of academic staff began with the following notes:

Notes for interviewer

• The purpose of the staff interviews is to gather contextual information and opinions on departmental practice along with accounts of personal disciplinary perspectives/disciplinary cultures and policies on learning and teaching and research.

Table A.2 Staff interviews by subject

Subject	Institution	No. of staff interviews
Biosciences	Fridaythorpe	1
	Givendale	1
	Langtoft	1
	Ulleskelf	4
	Warthill	4
Total		11
Business studies	Bramham	2
	Bugthorpe	4
	Husthwaite	4
	Weighton	3
	Wistow	5
Total		18
Sociology	Bilton	5
	Fenton	6
	Holme	5
	Tockerington	4
	Wilton	7
Total		27

- Be prepared to provide interviewees with information that they should have received in advance but may not have read by highlighting the broad purposes of the research: the focus on students' learning, especially its organisational and social mediation.
- Give any assurances required that the research is not 'evaluative' of particular institutions but analytical, intended to contribute to general understanding and to policy and practice.
- Also give assurances regarding confidentiality, the protection of individual and institutional identities and institutions, unless agreed with institutions, e.g. for the purpose of informing practice.
- Remember that the interview will often be with highly experienced staff and knowledgeable 'peers'. Let the respondents define the terms of their own response where appropriate.
- Interviews are to be recorded but not transcribed. Interviewers may wish to keep brief notes on the Schedule as a supplement to later re-listening. Also after they may find it useful to write down aide-memoires, e.g. any general observations on the way the

interview went and ideas/interpretations for later consideration during the subsequent analysis.

- The interview schedule is a guide to the questions to be asked. It is not intended that the sequence should inhibit the free flow of discussion. Take the questions in a different order if necessary. Adapt for your subject. And probe where further questions might be interesting in relation to the general research objectives.

Data analysis

Data analysis proceeded using standard SPSS formats for quantitative data and NVivo coding for qualitative data. Interim reports were created on particular sets of data, e.g. staff interviews in particular case settings.

On the following pages are examples of the research instruments used in the project.

A.1 Example questionnaire

Questionnaire for first-year students

Please use a ballpoint pen to complete this questionnaire. Do not use fountain or felt pens, as the ink may be visible on the other side of the page. The questionnaire will be read with the help of a scanner, so please fill it in as described. Please put an 'X' in the appropriate box, keeping within the boundary of the box. For example: ☒. Do not spend too long on each item. If you make a mistake and cross the wrong box, please block out your answer and then cross the correct box.

For example: ■   ☐   ☐   ☒   ☐

Part A of this questionnaire is about your choice of institution and course. Please put a cross in the one box beside each of the following factors that indicates its importance to you in choosing your institution and course from 1 (of no importance) to 5 (of great importance'. If there was some other factor that influenced your choice, please include it at the end of the list.

Please put a cross in the box like this: ☒

		Of no importance				Of great importance
		1	2	3	4	5
A1.	It was in a subject that interested me................................	☐	☐	☐	☐	☐
A2.	It was in a subject that I had done well in previously	☐	☐	☐	☐	☐
A3.	The job prospects after graduation seemed good	☐	☐	☐	☐	☐
A4.	The reputation of the course or institution seemed high	☐	☐	☐	☐	☐
A5.	The geographical location suited me	☐	☐	☐	☐	☐
A6.	The social life seemed good	☐	☐	☐	☐	☐
A7.	Suitable accommodation was available	☐	☐	☐	☐	☐
A8.	I felt the standards expected would not be too high	☐	☐	☐	☐	☐
A9.	I already knew some people here	☐	☐	☐	☐	☐
A10.	It meant that I did not have to move house	☐	☐	☐	☐	☐
A11.	I could remain close to family and friends	☐	☐	☐	☐	☐
A12.	I could obtain paid work while studying	☐	☐	☐	☐	☐
A13.	Other factor (please specify)	☐	☐	☐	☐	☐

Now please look back over Part A to make sure you have answered each of the questions before continuing with Part B.

(Please continue overleaf ➡)

Part B of this questionnaire is about **being at university** and **your future plans**. Please write in the relevant information or put a cross in **one** box beside each question, making sure that you give a single clear answer.

*B1. What is the name of **your degree course**?*

_____

B2. Was the university you are attending

your first choice? ☐

your second or third choice? ☐

a lower choice? ☐

B3. Was the course on which you are enrolled

your first choice? ☐

your second or third choice? ☐

a lower choice? ☐

*B4. Please list the **modules/course units** that you are taking this year:*

_____   _____

_____   _____

_____   _____

_____   _____

_____   _____

_____   _____

*B5. Where are you living? (Please cross **one** box)*

In halls or other accommodation owned by the university ☐

Alone in private accommodation ☐

In private accommodation with friends or other students ☐

In private accommodation with your parents and/or other relatives ☐

In private accommodation with your partner and/or children ☐

	Yes	No
*B6. During your time at university, have you undertaken **regular paid employment** (excluding work placements) during term time?*	☐	☐

*B7. Have you decided **the kind of job** you would like to get after university?*

Yes (please specify) ☐ _____

No ☐

*B8. Do you intend to undertake **any further study** after graduation?*

Yes (please specify) ☐ _____

No ☐

Now please look back over Part B to make sure you have answered each of the questions before continuing with Part C.

Part C of this questionnaire is about **what you expected to get out of higher education**. Put a cross in the **one** box beside each statement that indicates how well it applied to your own expectations of higher education.

If you accidentally choose two boxes for any statement or leave a box blank, it will be difficult to use any of your responses, so please check that for each statement there is a single clear response. If there was something else that you expected to get out of higher education, please include it at the end of the list.

Please put a cross in the box like this: ☒

		Not at all	Not much	Fairly	A great deal
C1.	I wanted to develop knowledge and skills that I could use in a career	☐	☐	☐	☐
C2.	I hoped the things I learnt would help me to develop as a person and broaden my horizons	☐	☐	☐	☐
C3.	I was focused on the opportunities here for an active social life and/or sport	☐	☐	☐	☐
C4.	I hoped the whole experience here would make me more independent and self-confident	☐	☐	☐	☐
C5.	I mainly came here because it seemed the natural thing. I'd done well academically in the past	☐	☐	☐	☐
C6.	I wanted to learn things that might let me help people and/or make a difference in the world	☐	☐	☐	☐
C7.	I wanted to study the subject in depth by taking interesting and stimulating courses	☐	☐	☐	☐
C8.	I mainly needed the qualification to enable me to get a good job when I finish	☐	☐	☐	☐
C9.	I wanted an opportunity to prove to myself or to other people what I could do	☐	☐	☐	☐
C10.	When I look back, I sometimes wonder why I ever decided to come here	☐	☐	☐	☐
C11.	Other (please specify below)	☐	☐	☐	☐

Now please look back over Part C to make sure you have put a cross in one and only one box for each of the statements before continuing with Part D.

Part D of this questionnaire is about **your perceptions of learning**. Put a cross in the **one** box beside each of the following statements that indicates whether you agree or disagree with that statement.

1	means that you disagree entirely
2	means that you disagree for the most part
3	means that you are undecided or do not know
4	means that you agree for the most part
5	means that you agree entirely

If you accidentally choose two boxes for any item or leave a box blank, it will be difficult to use any of your responses, so please check that for each item there is a single clear response.

Please put a cross in the box like this: [X]

		Disagree entirely				Agree entirely
		1	2	3	4	5
D1.	The topics that I learn need to be useful for solving practical problems	☐	☐	☐	☐	☐
D2.	I like to be given precise instructions as to how to go about carrying out a task or doing an assignment	☐	☐	☐	☐	☐
D3.	For me, learning means trying to approach a problem from many different angles, including aspects that I hadn't previously thought of	☐	☐	☐	☐	☐
D4.	For me, learning is making sure that I can reproduce the facts presented in a course	☐	☐	☐	☐	☐
D5.	I should try to look for connections within the subject matter without having to be told to do so	☐	☐	☐	☐	☐
D6.	I should try to apply the theories dealt with in a course to practical situations	☐	☐	☐	☐	☐
D7.	If I have difficulty understanding a particular topic, I should consult other books without having to be told to do so	☐	☐	☐	☐	☐
D8.	Teachers should clearly explain what it is important for me to know and what is less important	☐	☐	☐	☐	☐
D9.	For me, learning means acquiring knowledge that I can use in everyday life	☐	☐	☐	☐	☐
D10.	I prefer teachers who tell me exactly what I need to know for an exam	☐	☐	☐	☐	☐
D11.	For me, learning means acquiring knowledge and skills that I can later put to practical use	☐	☐	☐	☐	☐
D12.	I should try to think of particular examples of points made in the study materials without having to be told to do so	☐	☐	☐	☐	☐

Now please look back over Part D to make sure you have put a cross in one and only one box for each of the statements. If you don't feel that the statement applies to you, please make sure you have put a cross under 3 ('Not sure') rather than just leaving it blank. Then continue with Part E.

Part E of this questionnaire is concerned with **how you <u>actually</u> go about learning and studying on your degree programme.** If you have not yet encountered the kind of situation described in a statement, try to imagine how you would react. As before, put a cross in the **one** box beside each of the following statements that indicates whether you agree or disagree with that statement.

1	means that you disagree entirely
2	means that you disagree for the most part
3	means that you are undecided or do not know
4	means that you agree for the most part
5	means that you agree entirely

Please put a cross in the box like this: X

		Disagree entirely				Agree entirely
		1	2	3	4	5
E1.	I often have trouble making sense of the things I have to learn	☐	☐	☐	☐	☐
E2.	I usually set out to understand for myself the meaning of what I have to learn	☐	☐	☐	☐	☐
E3.	Much of what I learn seems no more than lots of unrelated bits and pieces in my mind	☐	☐	☐	☐	☐
E4.	In making sense of new ideas, I often relate them to practical or real-life contexts	☐	☐	☐	☐	☐
E5.	Ideas I've come across in my academic reading often set me off on long chains of thought	☐	☐	☐	☐	☐
E6.	I look at evidence carefully to reach my own conclusion about what I'm studying	☐	☐	☐	☐	☐
E7.	It's important for me to follow the argument or to see the reasons behind things	☐	☐	☐	☐	☐
E8.	I tend to take what I've been taught at face value without questioning it much	☐	☐	☐	☐	☐
E9.	In reading course material, I try to find out for myself exactly what the author means	☐	☐	☐	☐	☐
E10.	I just go through the motions of studying without seeing where I'm going	☐	☐	☐	☐	☐
E11.	Working things through with other students is really useful	☐	☐	☐	☐	☐
E12.	I wish I'd had time to read more books	☐	☐	☐	☐	☐

Now please look back over Part E to make sure you have put a cross in one and only one box for each of the statements. If you don't feel that the statement applies to you, please make sure you have put a cross under 3 ('Not sure') rather than just leaving it blank. Then continue with Part F.

Part F of this questionnaire is about **your experience of being a student.** Put a cross in the **one** box beside each of the following statements that indicates whether you agree or disagree with that statement.

1	means that you disagree entirely
2	means that you disagree for the most part
3	means that you are undecided or do not know
4	means that you agree for the most part
5	means that you agree entirely

Please put a cross in the box like this: X

		Disagree entirely				Agree entirely
		1	2	3	4	5
F1	Being a student is a completely new way of life	☐	☐	☐	☐	☐
F2	I find I'm changing my attitude on all kinds of things	☐	☐	☐	☐	☐
F3	I've had problems over accommodation	☐	☐	☐	☐	☐
F4	I've made a lot of new friends	☐	☐	☐	☐	☐
F5	I don't seem to fit in here	☐	☐	☐	☐	☐
F6	I'm losing touch with my friends and family	☐	☐	☐	☐	☐
F7	The work is much _less_ demanding than I expected	☐	☐	☐	☐	☐
F8	The work is much _more_ demanding than I expected	☐	☐	☐	☐	☐
F9	Being a student gives me a sense of freedom and independence.	☐	☐	☐	☐	☐
F10	I'm thinking of dropping out of the course	☐	☐	☐	☐	☐
F11	I made the wrong choice of course	☐	☐	☐	☐	☐
F12	I made the wrong choice of university	☐	☐	☐	☐	☐
F13	It's hard to find out what is expected of me	☐	☐	☐	☐	☐
F14	I'd studied a lot of the material before I came here	☐	☐	☐	☐	☐
F15	I've encountered very different expectations of what learning is all about	☐	☐	☐	☐	☐
F16	I'm getting into too much debt	☐	☐	☐	☐	☐
F17	I can't find all the time I need for studying	☐	☐	☐	☐	☐
F18	I'm worried that there's not going to be a decent job for me at the end of the course	☐	☐	☐	☐	☐
F19	I'm starting to identify closely with the main subject(s) of my course	☐	☐	☐	☐	☐

Now please look back over Part F to make sure you have put a cross in one and only one box for each of the statements before continuing with Part G.

Part G of this questionnaire is about **how you spend your time during a typical week (including weekends).** Put a cross in the **one** box beside each activity to indicate how many hours you spend on that activity **during a typical week**. If there is some other activity that takes up a significant amount of your time, please include it at the end of the list.

Please put a cross in the box like this: X	Average number of hours per week					
	0	1-5	6-10	11-15	16-20	21+
G1. Attending lectures, labs, seminars or tutorials	☐	☐	☐	☐	☐	☐
G2. Studying or coursework	☐	☐	☐	☐	☐	☐
G3. Course-related work on the Internet	☐	☐	☐	☐	☐	☐
G4. Discussing course-related issues with other students	☐	☐	☐	☐	☐	☐
G5. Discussing with lecturers outside class .	☐	☐	☐	☐	☐	☐
G6. Wider reading relevant to the course	☐	☐	☐	☐	☐	☐
G7. Socialising with other students on your course	☐	☐	☐	☐	☐	☐
G8. Socialising with students taking other courses	☐	☐	☐	☐	☐	☐
G9. Socialising with non-university friends	☐	☐	☐	☐	☐	☐
G10. Other leisure activities (e.g. watching TV, reading for pleasure, prayer or meditation, phoning or text messaging)	☐	☐	☐	☐	☐	☐
G11. Interacting with members of your family .	☐	☐	☐	☐	☐	☐
G12. Participating in student clubs or societies	☐	☐	☐	☐	☐	☐
G13. Paid employment	☐	☐	☐	☐	☐	☐
G14. Community service or voluntary work	☐	☐	☐	☐	☐	☐
G15. Household tasks and/or childcare	☐	☐	☐	☐	☐	☐
G16. Travelling to university	☐	☐	☐	☐	☐	☐
G17. Other activities (please specify below) ...	☐	☐	☐	☐	☐	☐

Now please look back over Part G to make sure you have put a cross in one and only one box for each of the activities before continuing with Part H.

Part H of this questionnaire is concerned with **how much your degree programme is enabling you to develop different skills and abilities**. This time, put a cross in the **one** box beside each capability that indicates how much you feel you have developed as a result of your studies. If there are some other capabilities that your studies have helped you to develop, please include them.

Please put a cross in the box like this: [X]

		Not at all	Not much	Fairly	A great deal
H1.	*Ability to analyse numerical data*	☐	☐	☐	☐
H2.	*Ability to apply knowledge*	☐	☐	☐	☐
H3.	*Ability to use numerical data*	☐	☐	☐	☐
H4.	*Ability to work in teams*	☐	☐	☐	☐
H5.	*Computer literacy*	☐	☐	☐	☐
H6.	*Critical analysis*	☐	☐	☐	☐
H7.	*Evaluation skills*	☐	☐	☐	☐
H8.	*Interpersonal skills*	☐	☐	☐	☐
H9.	*Leadership skills*	☐	☐	☐	☐
H10.	*Oral presentation skills*	☐	☐	☐	☐
H11.	*Self-discipline*	☐	☐	☐	☐
H12.	*Self-reliance*	☐	☐	☐	☐
H13.	*Time management*	☐	☐	☐	☐
H14.	*Writing skills*	☐	☐	☐	☐
H15.	*A real expertise in my subject*	☐	☐	☐	☐
H16.	*Other capabilities (please specify)*	☐	☐	☐	☐

Now please look back over Part H to make sure you have put a cross in one and only one box for each of the capabilities before continuing with Part I.

Part I of this questionnaire is concerned with **the ways in which you feel you have changed** since coming to university. Put a cross in the **one** box beside each of the following statements that indicates whether you agree or disagree with that statement. If there is some other way in which you feel you have changed, please include it at the end of the list.

1	means that you disagree entirely
2	means that you disagree for the most part
3	means that you are undecided or do not know
4	means that you agree for the most part
5	means that you agree entirely

Please put a cross in the box like this: ☒

		Disagree entirely				Agree entirely
		1	2	3	4	5
I1.	I now have a much clearer view of what I want to do in the future	☐	☐	☐	☐	☐
I2.	I am a much more self-confident person than the person I was when I came here	☐	☐	☐	☐	☐
I3.	I feel that I no longer have much in common with my friends outside of university	☐	☐	☐	☐	☐
I4.	I am very committed to the subjects I've studied here and would like somehow to continue to read/study them in the future	☐	☐	☐	☐	☐
I5.	I can't imagine losing touch with some of the friends I've made here	☐	☐	☐	☐	☐
I6.	I would like to remain associated with the university in some way	☐	☐	☐	☐	☐
I7.	My time at university has really changed the way I see the world	☐	☐	☐	☐	☐
I8.	My life outside the university remains the most important to me	☐	☐	☐	☐	☐
I9.	I feel that I am now able to get on with a much wider range of people	☐	☐	☐	☐	☐
I10.	I don't really fit in here. I'll be quite glad to leave	☐	☐	☐	☐	☐
I11.	The qualification is the main thing. University has not changed me that much	☐	☐	☐	☐	☐
I12.	Other (please specify below)	☐	☐	☐	☐	☐

Now please look back over Part I to make sure you have put a cross in one and only one box for each of the statements before continuing with Part J.

Part J of this questionnaire is about **yourself**. Please give the following information by putting crosses or numbers in the relevant boxes or by writing your answers in the space provided. Make sure you give a single clear answer for every question.

J1. Your sex: Female ☐   Male ☐   *J2. Your age:* ☐☐ years

J3. What was your highest educational qualification before going to university?
(Please cross __one__ box only)

A levels	☐	*Grades achieved:* _____
Scottish Highers	☐	*Grades achieved:* _____
GNVQ/NVQ/SVQ Level 3/AVCEs	☐	
GCSEs/GCE O Levels	☐	
BTEC national diploma	☐	
Qualification from Access course	☐	
Other (please specify)	☐	_____

J4. What were you doing in the year before you came to university?
(Please cross __any__ that apply)

Studying at school or college ☐
In paid full-time work ☐
In paid part-time work ☐
Self-employed ☐
Retired ☐
Unwaged but seeking employment ☐
Unwaged with domestic responsibilities ☐

J5. Where were you living in the year before you came to university? (Give the nearest town)

_____

J6. What is your marital status?		*J7. Do you have any dependent relatives?*	
Single, never married	☐	Yes ☐	
Married or living with a partner	☐	No ☐	
Divorced, separated or widowed	☐		

J8. *To which one of the following ethnic groups do you consider that you belong?*
*(Please cross **one** box only)*

White British ☐	White Irish ☐	White Other ☐
Black African ☐	Black Caribbean ☐	Black Other ☐
Bangladeshi ☐	Indian ☐	Pakistani ☐
Chinese ☐	Mixed ethnic group ☐	Another ethnic group ☐

J9. *Have any members of your immediate family (your parents, brothers, sisters, partner, spouse or children) studied at university?*
*(Please include any family members who are currently at university. Please cross **one** box only in each row)*

	Yes	No	Not applicable
Father	☐	☐	☐
Mother	☐	☐	☐
Brothers or sisters	☐	☐	☐
Partner or spouse	☐	☐	☐
Sons or daughters	☐	☐	☐

J10. *Who is the main income earner in your family? (Please cross **one** box only)*

(By 'main income earner', we mean the person with the largest income, whether from employment, student support, pensions, state benefits, investment or any other source.)

Father or male guardian ☐
Mother or female guardian ☐
Brother or sister ☐
Partner or spouse ☐
Yourself ☐
Other (please specify) ☐ _____

J11. *If the main income earner is **working**, what is the name or title of the main earner's current job? If the main income earner has been **studying full-time, retired or unemployed** for less than 6 months, what was the name or title of the main income earner's most recent job?*

_____

Do you have any other comments about your time in higher education or about this questionnaire?

Data Protection Act

In accordance with the Data Protection Act, we have to ask you to sign the following declaration. We also need to know your name and institutional ID because we would like to send you another survey in about two years' time. You can be confident that the information we collect from you will be used only for the purposes of research, and that no student will be identified in any report of our findings. Your individual responses will be kept confidential to the research team; they will not be released to your University or to anyone else.

I agree that the data collected from me may be held and processed by the team for the purposes of research.

Sign

Print name   Date

Institutional ID

We would like to carry out interviews with a small number of students from your degree programme. If you would be willing to help us in this way, please let us have an e-mail address where you can be contacted in the near future. Your details will be treated confidentially by us and will not be passed on to anyone else.

Email address:

Many thanks for your help.

A.2 Interview schedule

The schedule for the second set of interviews with the entering students is as follows.

Introduction

We would like to look at the following three broad themes with you within the next 40 minutes or so. On all four issues, we would like you to reflect on how your attitude and views have changed since you entered the university and started this course.

Your interest in the course, and how you study it (engagement)

To start off: What programme are you doing? Is it the one you registered for in year 1? What final year dissertation topic are you thinking of? Still enjoying the course as much as you did when you started? Sub-questions: Why did you choose this course? Favourite options/modules so far? How do you make your choice of options/modules, projects, etc.? (*Prompts: degree of choice control over curriculum, influences.*)

Is it a demanding course in terms of workload? What difference is there between year 1 and year 3 in terms of workload (types of assignments, lectures/tutorials, use of facilities such as the library, use of textbook, web resources)?

What sort of training/skills are you getting here that you think will be the most important for your career?

How are you coping with exams and other types of assessment here? How important is the degree classification to you? Do you have particular targets, expectations? Do your grades affect your future plans (postgraduate course, job prospects)?

Have you noticed any differences in the way lecturers are now teaching you? In the way staff and students interact in and outside classes?

Your student life and identity

Can you describe where you are living at the moment and where you have been since you started at . . .? (*Prompts: university accommoda-*

tion, shared private, family home, etc.) Sub-questions: When you are not studying, what is your student life like? (*Prompts: contact with other students on campus, in town, involvement in student societies, volunteering.*)

Do you feel you are more connected to other students and to the university social life than before? Who are the students you hang out with the most (people from your course, those you share accommodation with, a wider circle of friends)? Do you socialise differently with students on your course and others?

How about your financial situation? Are you working part-time? (*Prompts: regular job, absolute necessity. How demanding is it? Do you think it is affecting your studies in any way? How did you get it?*) Has your financial situation changed in any significant way since you started here? What does cost you the most?

How often do you see your family (your parents) and 'old friends' (from college, neighbourhood, etc.)? Has this changed over the past couple of years (frequency of visits, nature of the relationship)? Do you feel that you are more dependent on or more independent from your parents than you were in year 1?

Overall, would you make a distinction between your student and your non-student life? Do you feel you are juggling with two worlds/identities? Or do you feel you are in a process of transition? Do you think you are getting more than a qualification here? (*Prompts: what it means to be a student, what it means to others – parents, friends, colleagues at work, etc.*). Is your student experience typical of the image you had of a student life before coming here?

Your short- and long-term plans

As far as you remember, did you have any career plans or aspirations when you started this course? Have your plans or ideas changed since then? (Elaborate on changes in career plans.)

Do you know what you will be doing next year yet? If gap year or few months' break, what projects (travelling, volunteering/travelling, temp jobs/travelling, others . . .)? If you stayed away from home while studying, are you envisaging the possibility of going back home and living with your parents while looking for jobs? If looking for a job or planning to do a postgraduate course, is it important to do something related to your field of study? Have you had guidance on this from the university/fellow students/lecturers?

Mature students with family commitments, what short or medium term changes do you expect (at home, at work, etc.)? If currently working as well as studying, have you changed job or been promoted while studying? Do you plan to stick with current job, or seek another one after graduation? Have you already got a job lined up once you graduate?

Will your financial situation influence your short term plans (perception of impact of level of debt on projects, etc.)? In the long term, do you expect the course you did and your experience as a student here to influence your career? (Elaborate on professional prospects, skills acquired in relation to possible jobs/placement, skills and knowledge acquired through involvement in student societies, necessity of extra training, etc.)

A.3 Focus group schedule

The following are the main headings used in the organisation of the focus groups.

Sociability (student and departmental cultures)

1   How well do you think people on your course have got to know each other?

- What sort of things do people tend to do together (course related or other)?
- When do they do it (i.e. 'university hours' or 'after hours')?
- Can you recognise or are you part of any groups that have formed on your course or in the university? Or, are you or anyone you can think of 'loners' or keep to yourselves?
- Have you made any friends on your course, or at university in general?

2   Apart from our courses, how involved are you and fellow students in the university?

- Sports, societies, student politics (Union).
- Eating and drinking, 'hanging out'.
- How do you think that student life may change you, or are you changing already?

3   Do students ever meet with staff socially? Do you think this is specific to your course/department/school?

Approaches to learning (departmental culture/expectations)

1 On the whole, do students do the minimum that is required of them by the course?

2 Do you think your lecturers are consistent in their expectations of you in terms of workload, preparation for classes/seminars, etc.? Do you think that this is the same on other courses?

3 How heavy is the workload on your course? Is this more or less than you expected? Can you compare it with any other courses?

4 How important is it for you to do well in your studies at this time? (Trying to get some sense of 'coasting' – degree classification schema – final year, aggregate second and third.)

Being a student beyond the campus gate (intensity of engagement)

1 What kinds of things do people do outside university?

- Paid employment (how many, how long and what type of work).
- Domestic responsibilities (how many students).
- Socialising, 'clubbing' and the Students Union (frequency, number and with whom – other students, existing friends).

2 What implications do the above have for the experience of being a student (academic work, making friends, wider aspects of university life)?

Disciplinary culture and networking (identity/loyalty)

1 Has the subject you are studying been as you expected in terms of content?

2 Do you think that your interest in the subject matter will continue after graduation. If so, in what ways (further study, job, just keep in touch)?

3 How far do you see yourselves as 'sociologists', 'biochemists' or 'businessmen/women'. (Doesn't really work for business does it? So what type of identity are business studies students likely to develop?) And do you classify other students upon their subject area?

4 Are there certain things that students on your course have in common (attitudes, values, beliefs, etc.)?

5   At this stage in your studies, do you think that you will still be in touch with any students from your course/university in five years' time?

Finally, just to bring the discussion to a close, is there anything you would like to add to what has already been said?

A.4 Staff interview schedule

As an example, the interview schedule for staff in sociology departments proceeded as follows.

Introduction

General question about current and previous academic position.

Academic and professional identity

(Please note: this relates especially to 'academic identities'.)

1   Are you a sociologist by training (referring to postgraduate and undergraduate training)?
2   What areas do you currently teach?
3   Can you say on average what proportion of your time is spent on teaching and preparing for teaching, on research and on administration?
4   How does your current teaching relate to your research interests?
5   Do you have any particular viewpoint on the prevailing definitions/ boundaries of your discipline, especially those relevant to teaching and learning? (Perhaps probe on issues of closed or openness, interdisciplinarity, performativity (Mode 2 vs. Mode 1 knowledge), post-empiricism/post-modernity.)

Institutional and departmental culture and personal commitments in relation to teaching and research and to course design

(Please note: this relates especially to 'organisational' and 'social' mediations.)

1   How would you summarise the importance the institution and the department attach to teaching relative to research – less or more important, or more evenly balanced?

2   How would you summarise your personal commitment to teaching – less or more important, or more evenly balanced?
3   What changes, if any, have occurred recently in approaches to course design within your department?
4   What, if any, has been the impact of recent national emphases on 'skills', 'outcomes'?
5   Have changes in the demand for degree programmes influenced the degree programmes currently offered by the department/ unit (e.g. new course titles/new focus/content)?
6   What has been the influence of subject benchmarks and QAA processes generally on programme specification and the overall design and the teaching and assessment of courses? (Probe regarding positive/negative influence, tokenism, not at all, etc. What general processes/negotiations are involved in curriculum design?)
7   Is your own teaching or teaching and learning within your department guided by particular educational theories (e.g. cognitive theories of learning, theories of personal development, evidence-based theories)?

Socio-economic relevance of subject

(Please note: this relates especially to 'academic identities'.)

1   How would you summarise the economic importance of your subject (including its vocational relevance, and the role of work-related and work-based learning)?
2   And how would you summarise your subject's wider social importance (e.g. in relation to student self-identity, critical thinking, etc.)?

(Please note: in this section it may be useful for interviewers to be familiar with the key outcomes seen for study of discipline, e.g. in national subject benchmarks and programme specifications for department awards, maybe using these as prompts. In the subsequent analysis, it may be relevant to seek to locate academic staff on a 'pragmatic'–'critical' continuum.)

Views on students

(Please note: this relates especially to student academic and personal identities, but also to organisational and social mediations.)

1   For the students you teach, would you describe their predominant orientation as broadly academic or more narrowly instrumental? Or if such an implied dichotomy is far too simple, how would you describe the balance of orientations?
2   It has been said that students are driven primarily by the requirements of assessment. Do you agree? And if so what are the implications of this?
3   Do you regard your students' levels of engagement with university life as having changed over the years (e.g. the implications of paid work)?
4   What do you see, if any, as the impact of widening participation, increasing student numbers and 'new kinds of students' on student commitment, pedagogy and disciplinary cultures?

Concluding section

1   Higher education has been subject to rapid change. Do you have personal ways of moving with the flow of (or just coping with) organisational change in higher education? (There may be opportunity here if it hasn't arisen to pick up views on managed change and the intensification of academic life.)
2   Do you have any further comments that you would see as relevant to our research?

References

Baltes, P.B. (1968) 'Longitudinal and cross-sectional sequences in the study of age and generation effects', *Human Development*, *11*, 145–71.

Lawless, C.J. and Richardson, J.T.E. (2004) 'Monitoring the experiences of graduates in distance education', *Studies in Higher Education*, *29*, 353–74.

Schaie, K.W. (1965) 'A general model for the study of developmental problems', *Psychological Bulletin*, *64*, 92–107.

Vermetten, Y.J., Vermunt, J.D. and Lodewijks, H.G. (1999) 'A longitudinal perspective on learning strategies in higher education: different viewpoints towards development', *British Journal of Educational Psychology*, *69*, 221–42.

Bibliography

Abbot, J. (1971) *Life in a Class Society*, Oxford: Pergamon Press.

Albrow, M. (1986) 'BSA Presidential Address 1986: the undergraduate curriculum in sociology – a core for humane education', *Sociology*, 20(3): 335–46.

Archer, L. (2007) 'Diversity, equality and higher education: a critical reflection on the ab/uses of equity discourse within widening participation', *Teaching in Higher Education*, 12(5–6): 635–53.

Archer, L. and Hutchings C. (2000) '"Bettering yourself": discourses of risk, cost and benefit in ethnically diverse, young working-class non-participants' constructions of higher education', *British Journal of Sociology of Education*, 21(4): 561–4.

Association of Graduate Recruiters (AGR) (1995) *Skills for Graduates in the 21st Century*, Cambridge: AGR.

Baker, S. and Brown, B. (2007) 'Images of excellence: construction of institutional prestige and reflections in the university choice process', *British Journal of Sociology of Education*, 28(3): 377–91.

Barnett, R. (1997) *Higher Education: A Critical Business*, Buckingham: SRHE/Open University Press.

Barnett, R. (1990) *The Idea of Higher Education*, Buckingham: SRHE/Open University Press.

Baxter Magolda, M.B. (1992) *Knowing and Reasoning in College: Gender-Related Patterns in Students' Intellectual Development*, San Francisco, CA: Jossey-Bass.

Baxter-Magolda, M.B. and King, P.M. (eds) (2004) *Learning Partnerships: Theory and Models of Practice to Educate for Self-Authorship*, Sterling, VA: Stylus Publishing.

Becher, T. (1989) *Academic Tribes and Territories: Intellectual Enquiry and the Cultures of Disciplines*, Buckingham: SRHE/Open University Press.

Becher, T. and Kogan, M. (1992) *Process and Structure in Higher Education* (2nd edn), London: Routledge.

Becher, T. and Trowler, P. (2001) *Academic Tribes and Territories: Intellectual Enquiry and the Cultures of Disciplines*, Buckingham: SRHE/Open University Press.

Becher, T. and Parry, S. (2005) 'The endurance of the disciplines', in I. Bleiklie and M. Henkel (eds), *Governing Knowledge. A Study of Continuity and Change in Higher Education – A Festschrift in Honour of Maurice Kogan*, Dordrecht: Springer.

Becker, H., Geer, B. and Hughes, E.C. (1968) *Making the Grade: The Academic Side of College Life*, New York: Wiley.

Becker, H., Geer, B., Hughes, E. and Strauss, A. (1961) *Boys in White: Student Culture in Medical School*, Chicago, IL: University of Chicago Press.

Bekhradnia, B.and Sastry, T. (2007) *The Academic Experience of Students in English Universities 2007 Report*, Oxford: Higher Education Policy Institute.

Bekhradnia, B., Whitnall, C. and Sastry, T. (2006) *The Academic Experiences of Students in English Universities*, Oxford: Higher Education Policy Institute.

Bekhradnia, B. (2009) *The Academic Experience of Students in English Universities 2009 Report*, Oxford: Higher Education Policy Institute.

Belenky, M.F., Clinchy, B.M., Goldberger, N.R. and Tarule, J.M. (1986) *Women's Ways of Knowing: The Development of Self, Voice and Mind*, New York: Basic Books.

Bernstein, B. (1975 and 1977) *Class, Codes and Control: Towards a Theory of Educational Transmissions*, Volume 3, London: Routledge.

Bernstein, B. (2000) *Pedagogy, Symbolic Control and Identity: Theory, Research, Critique* (revised edition), Lanham, MD: Rowman & Littlefield.

Biglan, A. (1973) 'The characteristics of subject matter in different academic areas relationships between subject matter sharacteristics and the structure and output of university departments', *Journal of Applied Pscychology* 57(3): 195–203.

Bourdieu, P. (1973) 'Cultural reproduction and social reproduction', in R. Brown (ed.), *Knowledge, Education and Cultural Change*, London: Tavistock.

Bourdieu, P. (1977) *Outline of a Theory of Practice*, Cambridge: Cambridge University Press.

Bourdieu, P. (1988) *Homo Academicus*, Cambridge: Polity.

Bourdieu, P. (1996) *The State Nobility: Elite Schools in the Field of Power*, Cambridge: Polity Press.

Bourdieu, P. (1998) *Practical Reason: On the Theory of Action*, Palo Alto, CA: Stanford University Press.

Bourdieu, P. and J.C. Passeron (1979) *The Inheritors: French Students and Their Relations to Culture*, Chicago, IL: University of Chicago Press.

Bourdieu, P. and Passeron, J.C. (1990) *Reproduction in Education, Society and Culture*, London: Sage.

Bourdieu, P. and Wacquart, L.J.D. (1992) *An Invitation to Reflexive Sociology*, Cambridge: Polity Press.

Bourgeois, E.D., C. Guyot, J-L. and Merrill, B. (1999) *The Adult University*, Buckingham: SRHE/Open University Press.

Bowl, M., Cooke, S. and Hockings, C. (2008) 'Home or away? Issues of choice', *Widening Participation and Lifelong Learning*, 10 (1), 4–13.

Brennan, J. (2008) 'It's not always what you know – why graduates get jobs', in B. Kehm (ed.), *Hochschule im Wandel. Die Universität als Forschungsgegenstan (Festschrift für Ulrich Teichler)*, Frankfurt: Campus Publisher.

Brennan, J. and Silver, H. (1988) *A Liberal Vocationalism*, London: Methuen.

Brennan, J. and McGeevor, P. (1988). *Graduates at Work: Degree Courses and the Labour Market*, London: Jessica Kingsley.

Brennan, J. and Shah, T. (2003) *Access to What? Converting Educational Opportunity into Employment Opportunity*, Milton Keynes: CHERI, Open University.

Brennan, J. and Patel, K. (2008) 'Student identities in mass higher education', in A. Amaral, I. Bleiklie, C. Musselin (eds), *From Governance to Identity. A Festschrift for Mary Henkel*, Dortmund: Springer, pp. 17–28.

Brennan, J. and Tang, W. (2008) *The Employment of UK Graduates: Comparisons with Europe*, Bristol: Higher Education Funding Council for England.

Brennan, J. and Singh, M. (2009 forthcoming) 'Playing the quality game – whose quality and whose higher education?', in C. Calhoun and D. Rhoten (eds), *The Public Mission of the Research University*, New York: Columbia University Press.

Brennan, J., Lyon, E. S., McGeevor, P. and Murray, K. (1993) *Students, Courses and Jobs: The Relationship Between Higher Education and the Labour Market*, London: Jessica Kingsley.

Brothers, J. and Hatch, S. (1971) *Residence and Student Life: A Sociological Inquiry into Residence in Higher Education*, London: Tavistock Publications.

Brown, P. and Hesketh, A.J. (2004) *The Mismanagement of Talent: Employability and Jobs in the Knowledge Economy*, Oxford: Oxford University Press.

Brown, P., Hesketh, A. and Williams, S. (2003) 'Employability in a Knowledge-Driven Economy', *Journal of Education and Work*, 16(2): 107–26.

Brown, P. and Scase, R. (1994) *Higher Education and Corporate Realities: Class, Culture and the Decline of Graduate Careers*, London: Routledge.

Castells, M. (2004) *The Network Society: A Cross-Cultural Perspective*, Cheltenham: Edward Elgar Publishing.

Chang, M.J., Denson, N., Sáenz, V. and Misa, K. (2006) 'The educational benefits of sustaining cross-racial interaction among undergraduates', *Journal of Higher Education*, 77: 430–55.

Chickering, W. (1969) *Education and Identity*, San Francisco, CA: Jossey-Bass.

Christie, H., Munro, M. and Wager, F. (2005) 'Day students' in HE: widening access students and successful transitions to university life', *International Studies in the Sociology of Education*, 15(1): 3–30.

Clark, B.R. (1983) *The Higher Education System: Academic Organization in Cross-National Perspective*, Berkeley, CA: University of California Press.

Clark, B.R., and Trow, M. (1966). 'The organizational context', in T.M. Newcomb and E.K. Wilson (eds), *College Peer Groups: Problems and Prospects for Research*, Chicago, IL: Aldine, pp. 17–70.

Coffield, F., Moseley, D., Hall, E. and Eccleston, K. (2004) *Should We Be Using Learning Styles? What Research Has to Say to Practice*, London: Learning and Skills Research Centre.

Cohen, J. (1988). *Statistical Power Analysis for the Behavioural Sciences* (2nd edn), Hillsdale, NJ: Erlbaum.

Crozier, G. and Reay, D. (2008) 'The sociocultural experiences of working class students in higher education', *Teaching and Learning Research Briefing* No. 44, TLRP/ESRC.

David, M. (ed.) (2009) *Improving Learning by Widening Participation in Higher Education*, London: Routledge.

Department for Education and Science (DES) (1978) *Special Courses in Preparation for Entry to Higher Education*, Letter to Chief Education Officers, 2 August 1978.

Dubet, F. (1994) 'Dimensions et figures de l'expérience étudiante dans l'université de masse' ('Student experience in mass higher education'), *Revue française de sociologie*, 35(4).

Edmunds, R. and Richardson, J.T.E. (2009) 'Conceptions of learning, approaches to studying, and personal development in UK higher education', *British Journal of Educational Psychology*, 79(2): 295–309.

Entwistle, N. and McCune, V. (2004) 'The conceptual bases of study strategy inventories', *Educational Psychology Review*, 16: 325–45.

Entwistle, N. and Hounsel, D. (2007) 'Learning and teaching at university – the influence of subjects and settings', *Teaching and Learning Research Briefing* No. 31, TLRP/ESRC.

EUA (European University Association) (2003) *Trends 2003 – Progress towards the European Higher Education Area*, Geneva: EUA.

Feldman, K. and Newcomb, T. (1969) *The Impact of College on Students*, San Francisco, CA: Jossey-Bass.

Geertz, C. (1983) *Local Knowledge: Further Essays in Interpretive Anthropology*, New York: Basic Books.

Gellert, C. (1998) *European Higher Education Systems*, London: Jessica Kingsley.

Gibbons, M., Limoges, H., Nowotny, H., Schwartzman, S., Scott, P. and Trow, M. (1994) *The New Production of Knowledge: The Dynamics of Science and Research in Contemporary Societies*, London: Sage.

Giddens, A. (1984) *The Constitution of Society: Outline of the Theory of Structuration*, Cambridge: Polity Press.

Giddens, A. (1991) *Modernity and Self-Identity: Self and Society in the Late Modern Age*, Cambridge: Polity.

Giddens, A. (1992) *The Transformation of Intimacy: Sexuality, Love and Eroticism in Modern Societies*, Cambridge: Polity Press.

Gill, J. (2008) 'Keep it stupid, simple', *Times Higher Education*, 23 October 2008.

Goffman, E. (1961) *Encounters: Two Studies in the Sociology of Interaction*, Indianapolis, IN: Bobbs-Merrill.

Goodsell, A. and Tinto, V. (1994) 'Freshman interest groups and the first year experience: constructing student communities in a large university', *Journal of the Freshman Year Experience*, 6(1): 7–28.

Gorard, S. (2008) 'Which students are missing higher education?', *Cambridge Journal of Education*, 38(3): 421–37.

Gorard, S., Smith, E., May, H., Thomas, L., Adnett, N. and Slack, K. (2006) *Review of Widening Participation Research: Addressing the Barriers to Participation in Higher education*, July 2006, HEFCE, RD 13/06, www.hefce. ac.uk/pubs/rdreports/2006/rd13_06/ (accessed 19 June 2008).

Gregory, D. (1994) *Geographical Imagination*, London: Blackwell.

Gurin, P., Dey, E.L., Hurtado, S. and Gurin, G. (2002) 'Diversity and higher education: theory and impact on educational outcomes', *Harvard Educational Review*, 72: 330–66.

Halsey, A.H. (1961) 'University expansion and the collegiate ideal', *University Quarterly*, 16(1).

Halsey, A.H. (2004) *A History of Sociology in Britain: Science, Literature and Sociology*, Oxford: Oxford University Press.

Halsey, A.H. and Trow, M. (1971) *The British Academics*, London: Faber & Faber.

Harré, R. (1983) *Personal Being*, Oxford: Blackwell.

Harvey, L. and Drew, S. with Smith, M. (2006) *The First Year Experience: Review of the Research Literature*, York: Higher Education Academy, www. heacademy.ac.uk/research/Harvey_Drew_Smith.pdf.

Higher Education Academy (HEA) (2009) *Reward and Recognition of Teaching in Higher Education: A Collaborative Investigation – Interim Report*, York: Higher Education Academy.

HEFCE (2004) *Widening Participation and Fair Access Research Strategy Consultation Document*, December 2003, www.hefce.ac.uk/pubs/hefce/ 2004/04_06/ (accessed 19 June 2008).

HEFCE (2005) *Young Participation in Higher Education*, Research Report, Bristol: HEFCE, January 2005/03, www.hefce.ac.uk/pubs/hefce/2005/05_ 03 (accessed 19 June 2008).

Henkel, M. (2000) *Academic Identities and Policy Change in Higher Education*, London: Jessica Kingsley.

Hockings, C., Cooke, S., Bowl, M., Yamashita, H., and McGinty, S. (2008) 'Learning and teaching for diversity and differences in higher education – towards more inclusive learning environments', *Teaching and Learning Research Briefing* No. 41, TLRP/ESRC.

Holdsworth, C. (2006) '"Don't you think you're missing out, living at home?" Student experiences and residential transitions', *Sociological Review*, 54(3): 495–519.

Holmes, L. (1994a) 'Is competence a "confidence trick"?', in Proceedings from 'What is Competence?', inaugural conference of the Competence Network, Centre for Labour Market Studies, University of Leicester, December 1994.

Holmes, L. (1994b) 'Competence, qualifications and transferability: beyond the limits of functional analysis', in D. Bridges (ed.), *Transferable Skills in Higher Education*, Norwich: University of East Anglia.

Holmes, L. (1995) 'Competence and capability: from "confidence trick" to the construction of the graduate identity', Paper presented at the Conference on 'Beyond Competence to Capability and the Learning Society', Higher Education for Capability, UMIST, November 1995.

Holmes, L. (2002) 'Higher education and the learning agenda: a degenerative programme?', Paper prepared for 'Students and Learning: What is Changing?', Annual Conference of the Society for Research into Higher Education, Glasgow, December 2002.

Houston, M. and Wood, E. (2005) *Biosciences: An Overview of Undergraduate Studies in the UK*, London: The Open University.

James, D. and Biesta, G.J.J. (2007) *Improving Learning* Cultures, London: Routledge.

Jary, D. and Brennan, J. (2005) *What is Learned at University?* SOMUL Project Working Paper 1, York: Higher Education Academy.

Jary, D., Gatley, D. and Broadbent, L. (1998) 'The US community college: a positive or a negative model for the UK', in D. Jary and M. Parker (eds), *The New Higher Education*, Stoke-on Trent: Staffordshire University Press, Chapter 5.

Jary, D. and Lebeau, Y. (2009) 'The student experience and subject engagement in UK sociology: a proposed typology', *British Journal of Sociology of Education*, 30(6): 697–712, November.

Kelsall, R.K., Poole, A. and Kuhn, A. (1972) *Graduates: The Sociology of an Elite.*, London: Methuen.

Kogan, M. (2000) 'Higher education communities and academic identity', in I. McNay (ed.), *Higher Education and its Communities*, Buckingham: Open University Press.

Laming, M. (2007) 'The place of university in the culture of young people', Paper presented at 'The Place of University in the Culture of Young People', First Year in Higher Education Conference, Brisbane, July 2007.

Latour, B. (1987) *Science in Action*, Cambridge, MA: Harvard University Press.

Lave, J. (1988) *Cognition in Practice: Mind, Mathematics and Culture in Everyday Life*, New York: Cambridge University Press.

Lave, J. and Wenger, E. (1991) *Situated Learning: Legitimate Peripheral Participation*, Cambridge: Cambridge University Press.

Lave, J. and Wenger, E. (1998) 'Communities of practice', retrieved from http://pubpages.unh.edu/~jds/CofPractice.htm.

Lawless, C.J. and Richardson, J.T.E. (2004) 'Monitoring the experiences of graduates in distance education', *Studies in Higher Education*, 29: 353–74.

Letherby, G. (2006) 'Between the evil and the deep blue sea: developing professional and academic skills and building an inclusive research culture in a climate of defensive evaluation', in D. Jary and R. Jones (eds), *Perspectives and Practice in Widening Participation in the Social Sciences*, Birmingham: C-SAP – the Higher Education Academy Network.

Maassen, P. (1996) *Governmental Steering and the Academic Culture: The Intangibility of the Human Factor in Dutch and German Universities*, Maarsen: De Tijdstroom.

Macfarlane, B. (1997) 'The business studies first degree: institutional trends and the pedagogic context', *Teaching and Higher Education*, 2(1): 45–57.

Marris, P. (1964) *The Experience of Higher Education*, New York: Routledge.

Martin, E. and Ramsden, P. (1987) 'Learning skills, or skill in learning?', in J.T.E. Richardson, M.W. Eysenck and D. Warren Piper (eds), *Student Learning: Research in Education and Cognitive Psychology*, Milton Keynes: SHRE/Open University Press, pp. 155–67.

Marton, F. (1976) 'What does it take to learn? Some implications of an alternative view of learning', in N. Entwistle (ed.), *Strategies for Research and Development in Higher Education*, Amsterdam: Swets & Zeitlinger, pp. 32–42.

Marton, F. (ed.) (1984) *The Experience of Learning*, Edinburgh: Scottish Academic Press.

Marton, F. (1986) 'Phenomenography: a research approach to investigating different understandings of reality', *Journal of Thought*, 21(3): 28–49.

Marton, F. (1994) 'Phenomenography', in T. Husén and T.N. Postlethwaite (eds), *The International Encyclopaedia of Education*, Volume 8 (2nd edn), Oxford: Pergamon Press, pp. 4424–9.

Marton, F. and Booth, S. (1997) *Learning and Awareness*, New Jersey: Lawrence Erlbaum Associates.

Massey, D. (1993) 'Power-geometry and a progressive sense of place', in J. Bird, B. Curtis, T. Putnam and L. Tickner (eds), *Mapping the Futures: Local Cultures, Global Change*, London: Routledge.

Mills, D., Jepson, A., Coxon, T., Easterby-Smith, M., Hawkins, P. and Spencer, J. (2006) *Demographic Review of the UK Social Sciences*, Swindon: Economic and Social Research Council.

Moore, R. (2004) *Education and Society: Issues and Explanations in the Sociology of Education*, Cambridge: Polity.

NAB/UGC (1984) *Higher Education and the Needs of Society*, London: National Advisory Board for Public Sector Higher Education/University Grants Council.

Nespor, J. (1994) *Knowledge in Motion: Space, Time and Curriculum* in *Undergraduate Physics and Management*, Philadelphia, PA: Falmer Press.

NUS/HSBC (2008) *Students Research*, London: GfK.

Osborne, M. (2005) 'Introduction', in J. Gallacher and M. Osborne (eds), *Diversity or Division? International Perspectives on the Contested Landscape of Mass Higher Education*, Leicester: National Institute for Adult and Continuing Education.

Parker, M. and Jary, D. (1995) 'The McUniversity: organization, management and academic subjectivity', *Organization*, 2(2): 319–38.

Pascarella, E.T. and Terenzini, P.T. (1991) *How College Affects Students: Findings and Insights from Twenty Years of Research*, San Francisco, CA: Jossey-Bass.

Pascarella, E.T. and Terenzini, P.T. (2005) *How College Affects Students*, Volume 2, San Francisco, CA: Jossey-Bass.

Patiniotis, J. and Holdsworth, C. (2005) '"Seize that chance!" Leaving home and transitions to higher education', *Journal of Youth Studies*, 8: 81–95.

Perry, W. (1970) *Forms of Intellectual and Ethical Development in the College Years*, New York: Holt, Rinehart & Winston.

Reay, D., David, M. and Ball, S. (2005) *Degrees of Choice, Social Class, Gender and Race in Higher Education*, Stoke-on-Trent: Trentham Books.

Reay, D., Ball, S.J., David, M. and Davies, J. (2001) 'Choices of degree or degrees of choice? Social class, race and the higher education choice process', *Sociology*, 35(4): 845–74.

Richardson, J.T.E. (1994) 'Mature students in higher education: I. A literature survey on approaches to studying', *Studies in Higher Education*, 19: 309–25.

Richardson, J.T.E. (2000) *Researching Students Learning. Approaches to Studying in Campus-Based and Distance Education*, Buckingham: SRHE/ Open University.

Richardson, J.T.E. (2007a) 'Mental models of learning in distance education', *British Journal of Educational Psychology*, 77: 253–70.

Richardson, J.T.E. (2007b) 'Variations in student learning and perceptions of academic quality', in N. Entwistle, P. Tomlinson and J. Dockrell (eds), *Student Learning and University Teaching* (*British Journal of Educational Psychology*, Monograph Series II, No. 4), Leicester: The British Psychological Society.

Richardson, J.T.E. and Edmunds, R. (2007) *A Cognitive-Developmental Model of University Learning* (SOMUL Working Paper No. 4), York: Higher Education Academy.

Ross, M. (1989) 'Relation of implicit theories to the construction of personal histories', *Psychological Review*, 96: 341–57.

Rustin, M. (1981) 'Integrated codes and professional education', *SIP Papers* 10.

Sadlo, G. and Richardson, J.T.E. (2003) 'Approaches to studying and perceptions of the academic environment in students following problem-based and subject-based curricula', *Higher Education Research and Development*, 22: 253–74.

Säljö, R. (1979) 'Learning about learning', *Higher Education*, 8: 443–51.

Schomburg, H. and U. Teichler (2006) *Higher Education and Graduate Employment in Europe*, Dordrecht: Springer.

Scott, J. (2005) 'Sociology and its others: reflections on disciplinary specialisation and fragmentation', *Sociological Research Online*, 10(1) (accessed online at www.socresonline.org.uk/10/1/scott.html).

Scott, P. (2004) *Hierarchy or Diversity? Dilemmas for 21st Century Higher Education*, Keynote, CHE Conference, April 2004, Berlin.

Sennett, R. (1998) *The Corrosion of Character: The Personal Consequences of Work in the New Capitalism*, New York: W.W. Norton.

Shapiro, N.S. and Levine, J.H. (1999) *Creating Learning Communities: A Practical Guide to Winning Support, Organizing for Change and Implementing Programs*, San Francisco, CA: Jossey-Bass.

Solomons, J. (2000) 'Bernstein interviewed', in B. Bernstein, *Pedagogy, Symbolic Control and Identity: Theory, Research, Critique* (revised edition), Lanham, MD: Rowman & Littlefield, Chapter 11.

Teichler, U. (2004) 'Changing views in Europe about diversification in higher education', in S. Neaman Institute (ed.), *Transition to Mass Higher Education Systems: International Comparisons and Perspectives*, Heifa: S. Neaman Press.

Teichler, U. (2007) *Higher Education Systems: Conceptual Frameworks, Comparative Perspectives, Empirical Findings*, Rotterdam and Taipei: Sense Publishers.

Terenzini, P., Springer, L., Yaeger, P.M., Pascarella, E.T. and Nora, A. (1996) 'First-generation college students: characteristics, experiences and cognitive development', *Research in Higher Education*, 37: 1–22.

Thomas, L., May, H., Harrop, H., Houston, M., Knox, H., Lee, M., Osborne, M., Pudner, H. and Trotman, C. (2005) *From the Margins to the Mainstream: Embedding Widening Participation in Higher Education*, London: UUK.

Trow, M. (1973) *Problems in the Transition from Elite to Mass Higher Education*, Berkeley, CA: Carnegie Commission on Higher Education.

Trow, M. (1974) 'Problems in the transition from elite to mass higher education', in *Policies for Higher Education*, from the general report on the Conference on Future Structures of Post-Secondary Education, Paris: OECD.

Trow, M. (2005) 'Reflections on the transition from elite to nass to universal access: forms and phases of higher education in modern societies since WWII', in P. Altbach (ed.), *International Handbook of Higher Education*, Dortrecht: Kluwer.

Trowler, P. (2008) *Cultures and Change in Higher Education*, London: Palgrave Macmillan.

Van Rossum, E.J. and Schenk, S.M. (1984) 'The relationship between learning conception, study strategy and learning outcome', *British Journal of Educational Psychology*, 54: 73–83.

Van Rossum, E. and Taylor, I.P. (1987) 'The relationship between conceptions of learning and good teaching: a scheme of cognitive development', Paper presented at the annual meeting of the American Educational Research Association, Washington, DC.

Vermetten, Y.J., Vermunt, J.D. and Lodewijks, H.G. (1999) 'A longitudinal perspective on learning strategies in higher education: different viewpoints towards development', *British Journal of Educational Psychology*, 69: 221–42.

Vermunt, J.D. (1998) 'The regulation of constructive learning processes', *British Journal of Educational Psychology*, 68: 149–71.

Vermunt, J.D.H.M. and van Rijswijk, F.A.W.M. (1988) 'Analysis and development of students' skills in self-regulated learning', *Higher Education*, 17: 647–82.

Watson, D. (1989) *Managing the Modular Course*, Buckingham: SRHE/Open University Press.

Wertsch, J.V. (1998) *Mind as Action*, New York: Oxford University Press. Cited in D. James and G.J.J. Biesta (2007) *Improving Learning Cultures*, London: Routledge.

Williams, M., Payne, G., Hodkinson, L. and Poade, D. (2008) 'Does British sociology count? Sociology students' attitudes towards quantitative methods', *Sociology*, 42(5): 1003–21.

Woolf, A. (2002) *Does Education Matter? Myths About Education and Economic Growth*, London: Penguin Press.

Index